Essential FrontPage 2002 for Web Professionals

ISBN 0-13-093254-X

9 790130 932548

9 0 0 0 0

The Prentice Hall Essential Web Professionals Series

Micah Brown, *Series Editor*

Essential FrontPage 2002
for Web Professionals

Tiffany K. Edmonds

Prentice Hall PTR
Upper Saddle River, NJ 07458
www.phptr.com

Library of Congress Cataloging-in-Publication Data

A CIP catalog record for this book can be obtained from the Library of Congress.

Editorial/Production Supervision: Patti Guerrieri
Acquisitions Editor: Karen McLean
Marketing Manager: Jim Keogh
Manufacturing Manager: Alexis Heydt-Long
Interior Design Director: Gail Cocker-Bogusz
Series Design: Patti Guerrieri

 © 2002 Prentice Hall PTR
A division of Pearson Education, Inc.
Upper Saddle River, NJ 07458

Prentice Hall books are widely used by corporations and government agencies for training, marketing, and resale.

The publisher offers discounts on this book when ordered in bulk quantities.
For more information, contact: Corporate Sales Department, Phone: 800-382-3419;
Fax: 201-236-7141; E-mail: corpsales@prenhall.com; or write: Prentice Hall PTR,
Corp. Sales Dept., One Lake Street, Upper Saddle River, NJ 07458.

Printed in the United States of America

10 9 8 7 6 5 4 3 2

ISBN 0-13-093254-X

Pearson Education LTD.
Pearson Education Australia PTY, Limited
Pearson Education Singapore, Pte. Ltd.
Pearson Education North Asia Ltd.
Pearson Education Canada, Ltd.
Pearson Educación de Mexico, S.A. de C.V.
Pearson Education—Japan
Pearson Education Malaysia, Pte. Ltd.

Contents

Introduction

It was my sister, Tricia, who sat me down in front of her computer and showed me around the Internet for the first time. I remember clearly the thrill and excitement I felt at all of the possibilities. To add to the excitement, she began showing me a software program that had the capability to help create Web pages and learn Web design—FrontPage! I quickly started working with the program and trying to learn it, as well as going out on the Internet in search of resources to help learn more about Web design and FrontPage. With a lot of help along the way and a lot of trial and error, it is a wonderful opportunity to play a part in writing a book that offers information and resources that I was not able to find anywhere else during my quest to master FrontPage.

With FrontPage 2002, you can build, manage, and maintain exciting and professional-looking Web sites without having to learn Hypertext Markup Language (HTML). Now, learn FrontPage 2002 from a professional Web designer and recognized FrontPage expert—through real-world projects you can view live on a companion Web site. Start with the basic tools of creating a Web site and work your way through to advanced skill-level features, such as adding discussion boards, working live on the server, and collaborating with teams on one project over the Internet. Best of all, the projects in this book are linked to the companion Web site, where you can see each step of the project Web site in each stage of completion. It's all the guidance you'll need—every step of the way!

You'll learn all this and much more!

- FrontPage 2002 basics
- Installing FrontPage 2002
- Creating your first Web site
- Inserting images and customizing your pages
- Adding forms and interactivity
- Inserting Dynamic HTML (DHTML) and other built-in FrontPage components
- Publishing your work to a server
- Database connectivity features using FrontPage 2002 and Microsoft Access

◆ How This Book Is Laid Out

This book is broken down into fairly logical sections and steps that can be used to create a Web site using Microsoft FrontPage 2002, from the introduction of what is new in FrontPage 2002 and installation of the software in Chapter 1 through the complete publishing process of your completed Web site and advanced features in the final chapters.

The first two chapters focus on becoming familiar with the software's interface and some of the tools used for planning and laying out a good foundation for your Web site. The next two chapters walk you through adding FrontPage components and functionality to your Web site, starting with some simple forms and working through examples and tasks to create advanced features, such as discussion webs and DHTML effects. In Chapter 5, we discuss and walk through the process of publishing your Web site pages to a remote server using the FrontPage publish feature, as well as using file transfer protocol (FTP) as an alternative method of publishing. The final chapters in this book cover the most advanced topics, such as collaborating on team projects, connecting to a remote copy of a Web site, database connectivity, and Personal Web Server (PWS).

Each chapter starts with a task, which addresses what we will be learning in the chapter, and ends with a set of advanced project steps to try. The book walks you through the creation and completion of the "Shelley Biotechnologies" Web site and has an accompanying Web site that includes additional files used in the book, images used in the examples throughout the book (which are available for download), and errata. This Web site address is *http://www.phptr.com/frontpage2002*.

◆ Acknowledgments

To my incredible husband, John: You are my best friend and have given me more support and patience than I can thank you for! I love you forever! To my beautiful kids, Taylor, Hunter, Seth, and baby Samantha: Thank you for hanging in there with me while I stayed so busy with work and writing, and for being so excited about this project with me!

I owe many thanks to my family for always believing in me and supporting me: to my sister, Tricia, for showing me the Internet and FrontPage for the first time; to my mother, for all of her encouragement and support in my education in this field; and to my father, for the Christmas gift of my first Web hosting account, so I could have a place to start my Web design work. I would also like to say a special thank you to my Aunt Fran, who gave me an enormous amount of help and feedback on the content of this book as I wrote it.

A huge thank you goes to both Karen McLean and Micah Brown for letting me join in this fantastic series and for giving me the opportunity to continue to help the FrontPage community of Web designers with this book. I can't thank you enough for your patience and all of the help along the way. This has been a great experience for me.

◆ About the Author

Tiffany K. Edmonds is the owner of Dynamite-it, which specializes in Web design and database development. She is a recognized Microsoft® FrontPage® expert. She is also the owner of the most active Microsoft FrontPage email forum in existence, *FPlist@yahoogroups.com*, which has more than 1,000 members. Additionally, she is the co-owner of the *AnyFrontPage Bytes* newsletter (*http://anyfrontpage.com/bytes*).

Tiffany designed and maintains the FrontPage tips and tutorials Web site (*http://www.at-frontpage.com*) and is the author of approximately 75 FrontPage tutorials. Her innovative Web site designs using FrontPage have won numerous awards, including two Netscape Rage of the Day awards.

Ms. Edmonds's extensive Internet experience includes co-teaching a three-part HTML course for Ziff-Davis™ University in 1998–1999, as well as providing HTML and FrontPage training for individuals.

1 Getting Started

IN THIS CHAPTER

- FrontPage Webs
- What's New in FrontPage 2002 at a Glance
- DBW versus PWS
- Installing FrontPage 2002
- Installing SharePoint™ Team Services and FrontPage Server Extensions
- FrontPage 2002 Interface
- FrontPage Editor
- Recap
- Advanced Project

FrontPage is a WYSIWYG (what you see is what you get) Web site editing tool. It is powerful enough to aid in the creation of very high-quality, professional-looking Web sites, yet user-friendly enough that any level of user may begin creating Web sites with the many templates and themes provided within the package. This book will help you learn how to use FrontPage 2002 to its full potential and answer many questions that you may have with using this program and all of its features.

In this book, we will focus primarily on FrontPage 2002. Microsoft did a wonderful job listening to the FrontPage users with this upgrade and addressed many of the most common complaints received from FrontPage 2000 users. If you have not yet upgraded to FrontPage 2002, now is an excellent time to do so. You will ask yourself why you didn't do it sooner.

◆ FrontPage Webs

One of the many features of FrontPage is its Web site management capability. The program allows you some visual aid in the management of your entire Web site, as well as having many features available for creating and editing individual pages within the Web site. We refer to a collection of files that make up a whole Web site, such as HTML (Hypertext Markup Language) pages, image files, and other documents as a FrontPage web. A FrontPage web, web, or Web site is virtually the same thing by slightly different names. We use the terms *web* and *FrontPage web* most often in describing a FrontPage-made Web site, or collection of files that make up your Web site, throughout this book.

◆ What's New in FrontPage 2002 at a Glance

• The FrontPage 2002 Interface—FrontPage 98 consisted of two programs: the FrontPage Explorer and the FrontPage Editor. FrontPage 2000 upgraded to run from one window, or program, that is closely related to other Office 2000 programs. It is both the Explorer and Editor in one package. This took some FrontPage 98 users a little getting used to, but nearly all of the hundreds of FrontPage users I have come in contact with have been very pleased with this upgrade. FrontPage 2002 has taken the new interface one step further and is even easier to use. The new interface gives the user easier access to menu items, the ability to search for help from the interface with a search box on the top of the screen, and a new pane of menu selections that opens on the right of the interface when you want to add a

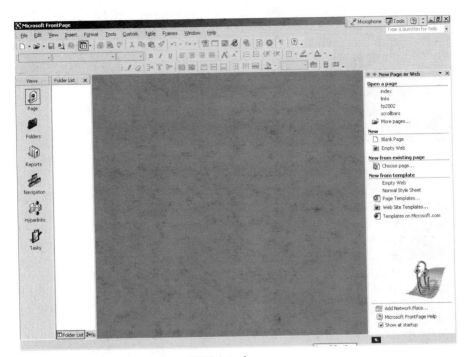

FIGURE 1–1 FrontPage 2002 interface.

new page or web. The new page or web pane on the right gives you quick and easy access to recently opened pages, FrontPage templates, and quick access to help files (see Figure 1–1).

- Hyperlink Dialog Box—Further integrated with Microsoft Office, the updated Insert Hyperlink dialog box has several enhancements. These include recent files, creating new documents, browsed pages, and email addresses. The email address addition also allows you to enter a subject line for the email hyperlink. Linking to a bookmark is simple now with the addition of the Bookmark button.
- Photo Gallery—This new feature enables the user quickly and easily to create a gallery to display photos or images. Images can be added to the Photo Gallery, and the user may select from several different customizable layouts, add

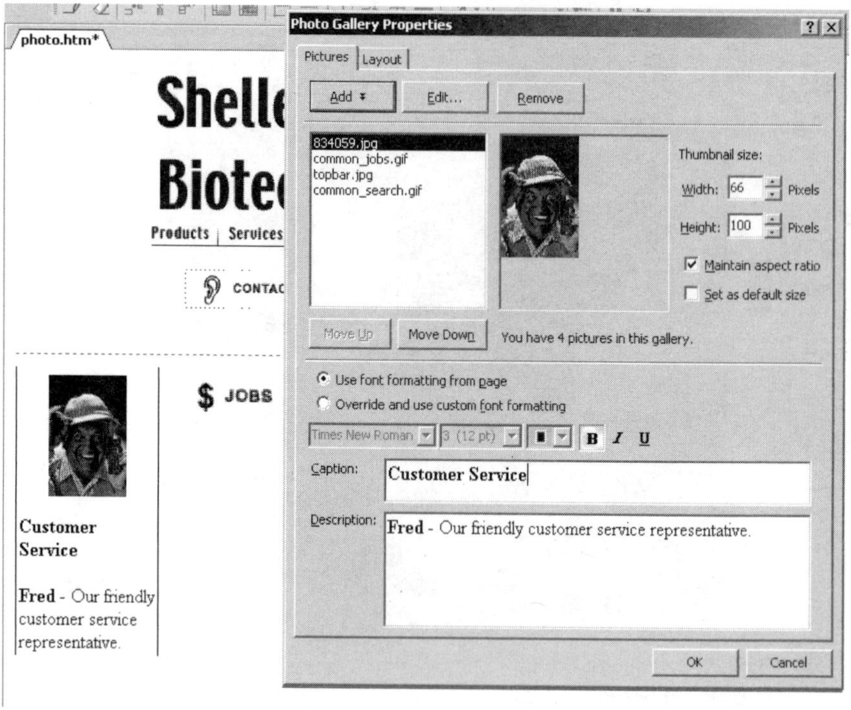

FIGURE 1-2 Photo Gallery.

captions and descriptions to images, rearrange images, change image sizes, and more (see Figure 1–2).

- Drawing Tools—FrontPage 2002 has implemented Power-Point®-like drawing tools into the program. Now you can create special effects text, auto shapes, drop shadows, and so much more from within the application. These tools are as easy to use with FrontPage now as they are in Word® or PowerPoint (see Figure 1–3).
- Page Tabs—FrontPage 2002 has added page tabs to the interface. This gives you quick and easy access to any page you have open when you have more than one page open at a time.
- Table Editing Tools—Table Auto Format, Table Fill, and Table Split are new table formatting tools. These tools offer preset formatting for tables and make creating exciting and professional-looking tables quick and simple.

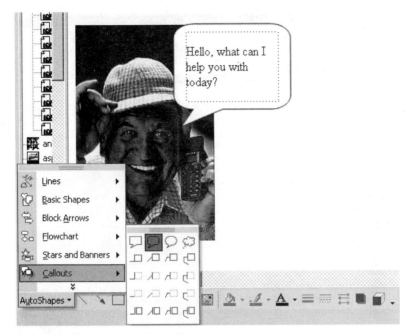

FIGURE 1–3 Drawing tools—Callouts.

- Navigation Pane—FrontPage 2002 now allows the navigation view to show in the main folder list pane so that you can continue to edit your pages and view your navigation view at the same time (see Figure 1–4).
- Automatic Web Content—This FrontPage 2002 feature enables you to add automatic web content to your Web site, such as MSNBC headlines and weather forecasts, MSN® search, Expedia maps, and bCentral™ small business tools. MSNBC content updates daily, so you can have fresh, new content on your Web site without having to manually update your site every day.
- Border Dropdown Tool—This allows you easily to add borders of any color or background color to text or graphics (see Figure 1–5).
- Hyperlink or CSS Formatting—This gives you the ability to add CSS formatting to any hyperlink or text you choose. Now you can choose whether to have underlines on your hyperlinks by simply using the Underline button, like you would with any text.

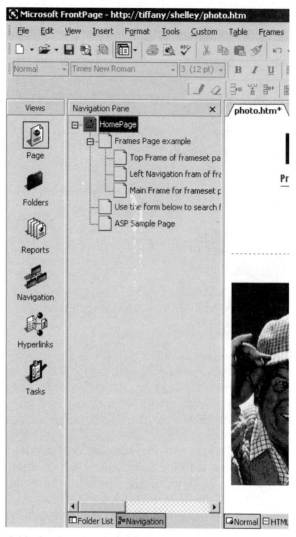

FIGURE 1–4 Navigation view in folders list pane.

FIGURE 1–5 Border Dropdown tool.

- Office® Clipboard—Now you can easily copy and paste from other Office programs and view the content of your Office Clipboard in the Task pane (Figure 1–6). You can choose to preserve the source code or paste only the text.

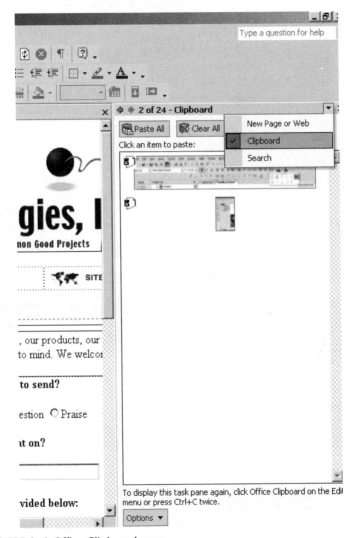

FIGURE 1–6 Office Clipboard pane.

- Custom Link Bars—With the new Custom Link bars, you can create navigation bars that link only to pages that you specify. This gives you the ability to manage your link bars across your entire Web site in one place without having to rely on the navigation structure, as you did with previous versions. You can modify your custom links in any custom bar you create. The Custom Link bars can be used with themes, so you can create the navigation structures you want and use the buttons in your theme.
- Web Components—The Web Components menu is new to FrontPage 2002. This is where you will find web components from previous versions of FrontPage, such as the Banner Ad Rotator, Scrolling Marquee, and Hover buttons. New to FrontPage 2002 are link bars, automatic web content, Photo Gallery, and SharePoint™ Team services (see Figure 1–7).
- Shared Borders—With the FrontPage 2002 shared borders feature, you can set the background color or image in a shared border, separate from the page background color or image.

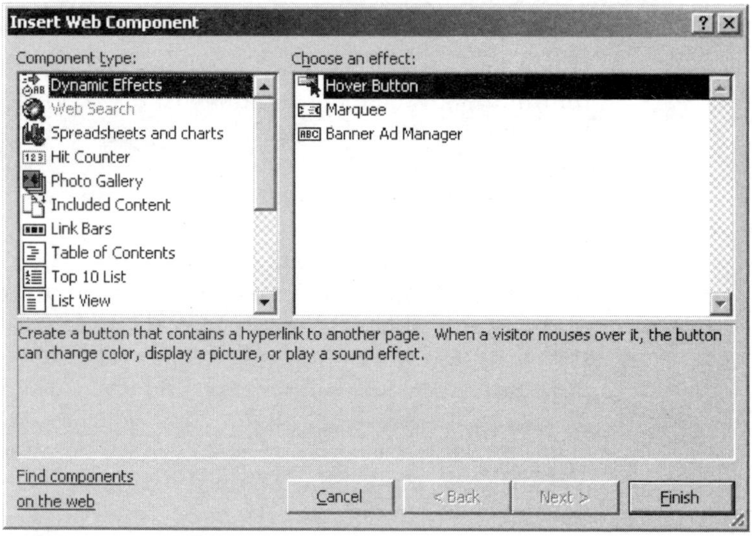

FIGURE 1–7 Web components dialog box.

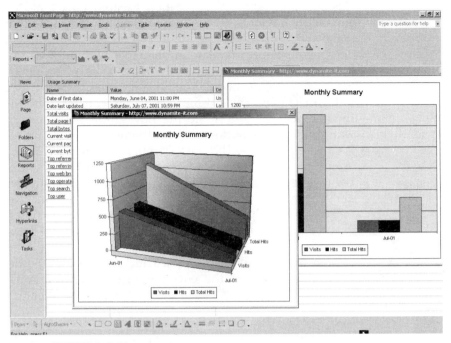

FIGURE 1–8 Usage reports.

- Usage Reports—Usage reports (Figure 1–8) show statistical information, such as how many visitors you receive to your Web site, where they came from, and how they are using your site. You can get information about your visitor's browsers, operating systems, and the color and display of their monitors.

- Reports—FrontPage 2002's reporting view has been improved and upgraded, now offering several more reports and custom reporting tools you can use to assign files for review and keep the flow of a project moving. You can use custom reports to view several different variants, such as choosing to view all .gif files in your Web site.

- Publish Features
  - Enhanced Publishing Dialog Box—FrontPage 2002's publishing dialog box is more innovative and user friendly. Now you see more of what is going on in the publishing process as FrontPage 2002 shows the content of the local web in the left pane and the content of the destination web in the right pane. Check marks

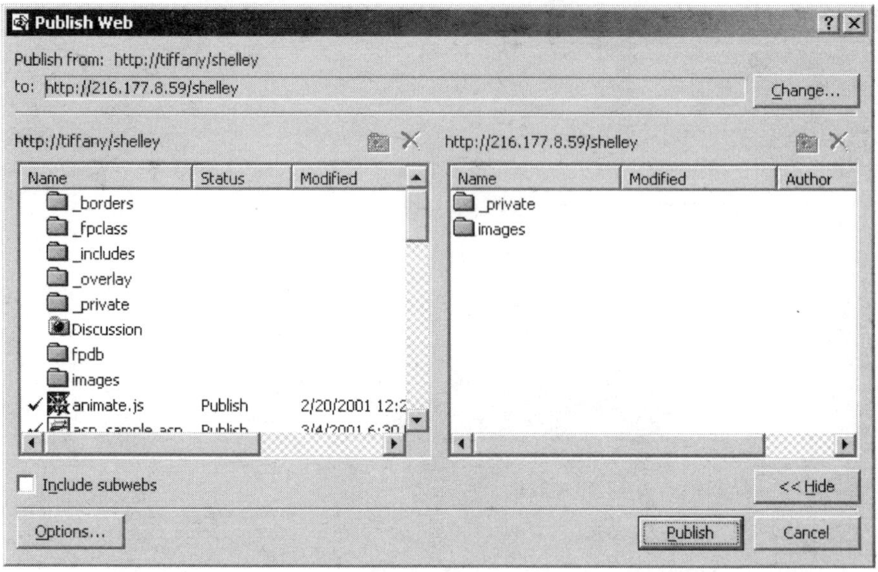

FIGURE 1–9 Publish Web dialog box.

are placed next to the content that has been changed and will be published when you click the Publish button (see Figure 1–9).

- Background Publishing—This feature allows you to continue working on the pages in your FrontPage web while Publish works in the background. You no longer have to stop working on your pages while FrontPage publishes your web.

- Single Page Publishing—This feature allows you to publish only the pages you want to publish with the ease of a right-clicking on the file in your web.

- Publishing Log Files—These log files help you keep clear and easy-to-read records of what was published and when.

- FTP Interface—FrontPage 2002 improved the FTP user interface to help make using the built-in FTP support easier to use for publishing your web to servers that do not have support for the FrontPage extensions (see Figure 1–10).

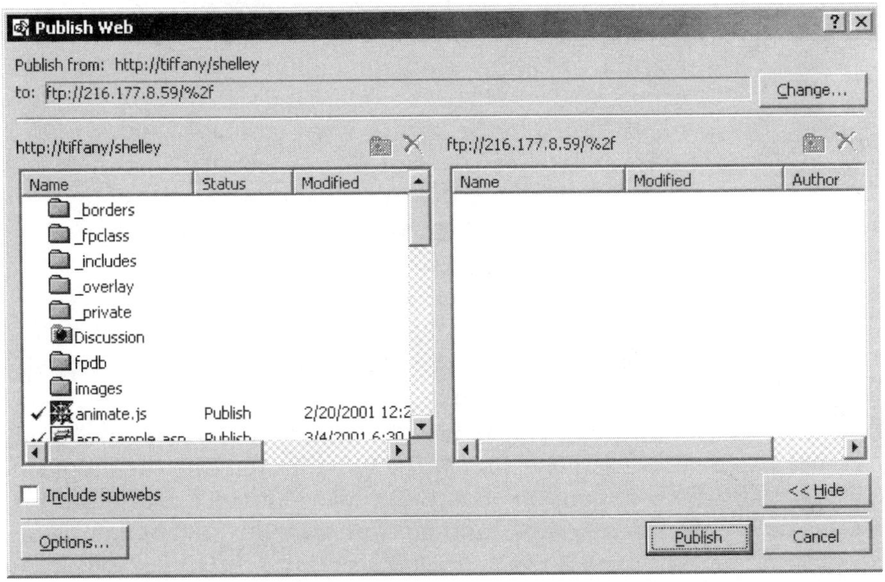

FIGURE 1–10 FTP Publish dialog box.

- SharePoint Team Services—This is a new Microsoft technology that enables you to quickly set up an elaborate team Web site for intranet or Internet users to store, find, and share information, documents, and Web pages. The following features depend on Windows® 2000 Server and the installation of the SharePoint Team Services extensions. SharePoint Team Services will not work on Win9x or UNIX servers. Check with your Web host provider or system administrator to find out whether you will have support for SharePoint Team Services. SharePoint Team Services include the following features:

  - Lists—These include lists of announcements, events, members, to-do items, contacts, and more. SharePoint comes with several preset lists that you can use as is or modify and customize. You can also create a custom list with your own data.

  - Discussions—Team members can use this threaded discussion board to post new comments and respond to existing posts. The user can also sign up to receive email notification when new posts are made.

- Surveys—Easily add polls to your team web to collect information from team members or site visitors.

- Document Libraries—Adding a library allows all users or specified users access to view, upload, and edit documents stored in the library. Users can add a new document based on a template you specify. Documents may be edited through the web browser. Lists of documents may also be sorted in the document libraries.

- Subscription features—Authorized users may ask SharePoint Team Services to notify them by email of any changes to lists, discussions, and document libraries. See Chapter 6 for more on Team webs and SharePoint Team Services

• E-Commerce Functionality—FrontPage 2002 comes with new e-commerce functionality built right into the program. These options include BCentral Commerce Manager. You can easily add e-commerce functionality to your FrontPage-based site with this feature. Through subscription service to the Microsoft bCentral Commerce Manager, simply insert Buy buttons and a shopping cart into your Web site. With an optional upgrade service, you may then take your products one step further by adding them to online auctions via the bCentral Commerce Manager add-in.

• New Form Fields—New to FrontPage 2002, form fields are File Upload, Group Box, and Advanced Buttons. These form fields are discussed in more detail in Chapter 3.

• Database Interface Wizard—Now you can easily create a Web page that displays the records of a database on the page. This interface allows you to set permissions for users to add, modify, and delete records in the database via the Web page it creates and makes sorting and finding data from the database quicker.

◆ DBW versus PWS

DBW and PWS are abbreviations commonly used in discussions about FrontPage webs. A DBW, or Disk-Based Web, refers to a FrontPage-created Web site that is stored locally on your computer's hard drive without the use of the PWS, or Personal Web Server. The path to a DBW would be like that of any other folder, directory, or file stored on your computer's hard drive, that is, *C:\MyWebs\shelleybiotechnology.*

PWS-based Web sites are those that are stored on your computer's hard drive, along with the PWS being installed on your computer. These webs are stored in the PWS's default directory and are treated as webs that have been published to a server with FrontPage extensions. The PWS imitates a Web server that has the FrontPage extensions installed and allows full testing of all FrontPage 2002 components on the user's local computer. The path to a PWS web will be something like: *http://localhost/shelley-biotechnology.* Depending on which version of the PWS is installed, the default directory is actually one of the following: *C:\WEBSHARE\WWWROOT* or *C:\Inetpub\wwwroot.* Refer to Chapter 7, "Personal Web Server," for more on the PWS, such as its installation.

◆ Installing FrontPage 2002

For Windows 2000 users, the Internet Information Server (IIS) components are on the Windows 2000 CD, which also includes the Personal Web Manager and FrontPage 2000 extensions. If you would like to install the FrontPage 2002 server extensions and the SharePoint Team Services, you will first need to ensure that you have installed the IIS. To install IIS:

- Open your Control Panel and double-click the Add/Remove Programs icon.
- Click the Add/Remove Windows Components button.
- In the Add/Remove Windows Components dialog box, check the box next to Internet Information Services.
- Make sure that you have your Windows 2000 CD in your CD-ROM drive and click the Next button to begin the installation.

The installation process for FrontPage 2002 is fairly simple.

- To start, place your FrontPage 2002 CD in your CD-ROM drive and let it auto-run. It should open right up to the installation window after detecting that you do not already have a copy of FrontPage 2002 installed on your hard drive (see Figure 1–11). Windows 98 users may begin with the Install Windows and Office Components Update screen, which tells you that the program needs to update system components (see Figure 1–12).
- Enter your name, optional initials and organization information, and CD key in this screen and click the Next button.

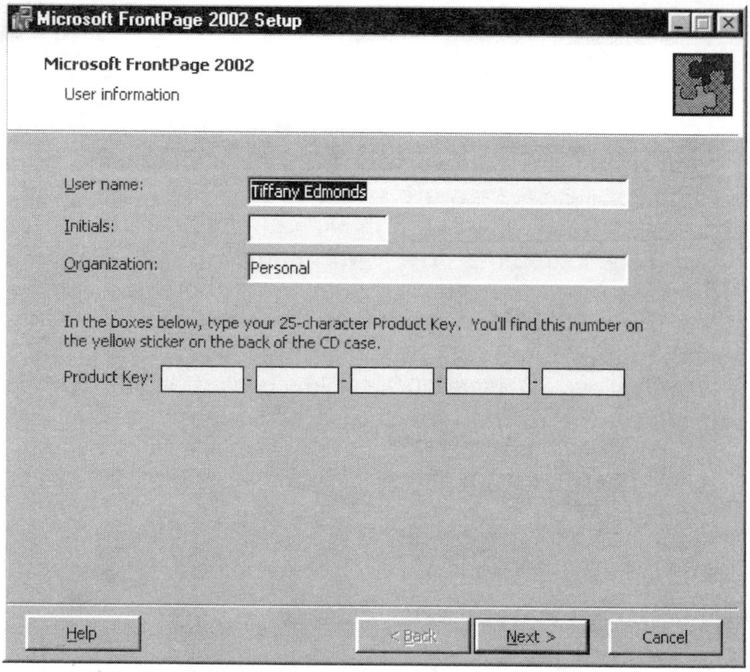

FIGURE 1–11 Installation startup.

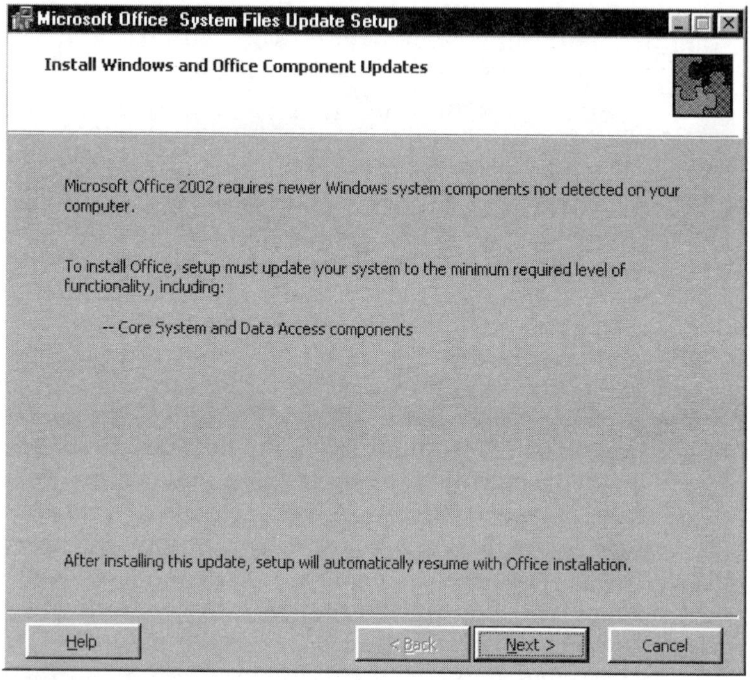

FIGURE 1–12 Install Windows and Office Components Updates.

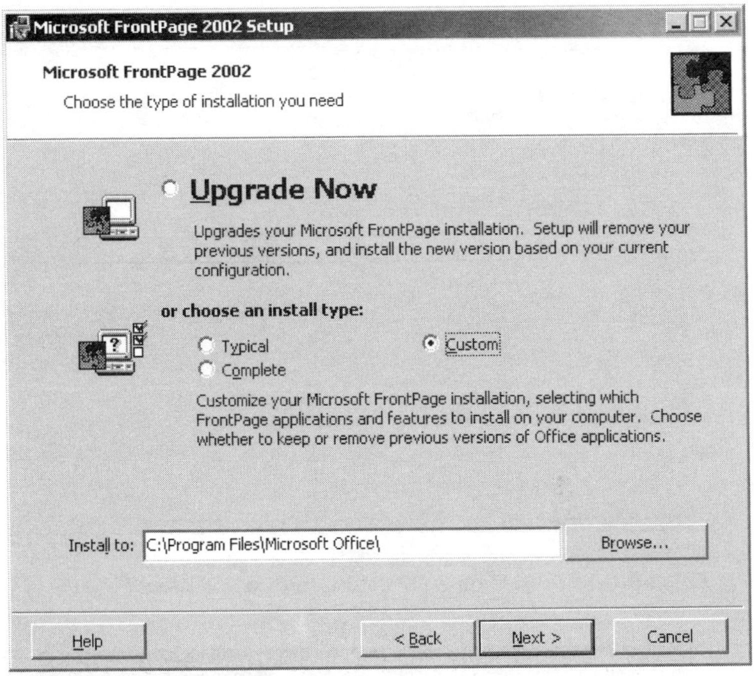

FIGURE 1–13 Installation screen.

- Once you agree to the end-user license agreement and click the Next button, you will see the installation screen (see Figure 1–13).
- Click the Install button, unless you are comfortable with the Customize option, which allows you to choose which components you would like to install and which you would not. If you intend to keep previous versions of FrontPage on your computer, you will need to do a custom install and opt to keep all previous versions (see Figure 1–14).
- Click the Next button once you have made your selection regarding any previous versions, or click Next on the installation screen to begin the installation. The installation progress bar will appear (see Figure 1–15).

After the installation appears to be complete, the Installation Wizard will alert you that you need to restart your computer. After your computer restarts, FrontPage will complete the installation process and update your Windows settings.

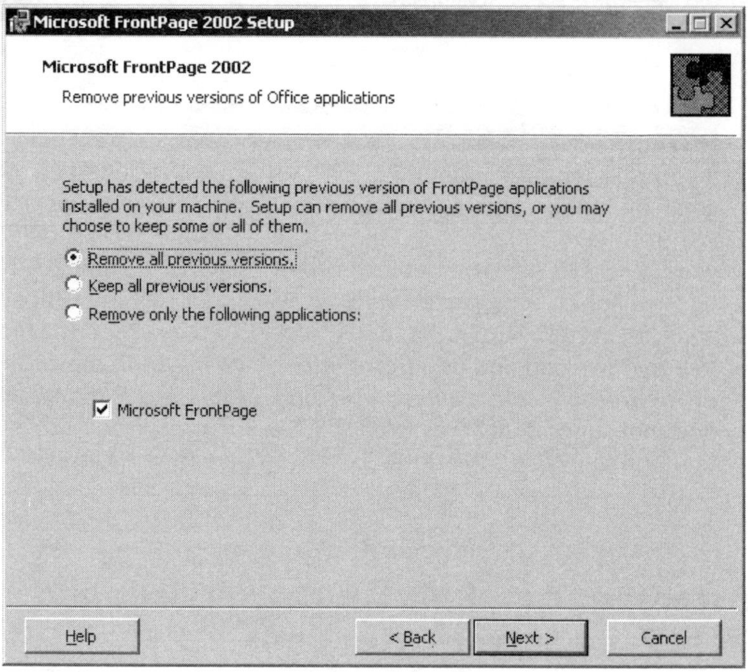

FIGURE 1–14 FrontPage 2002 Setup—previous versions.

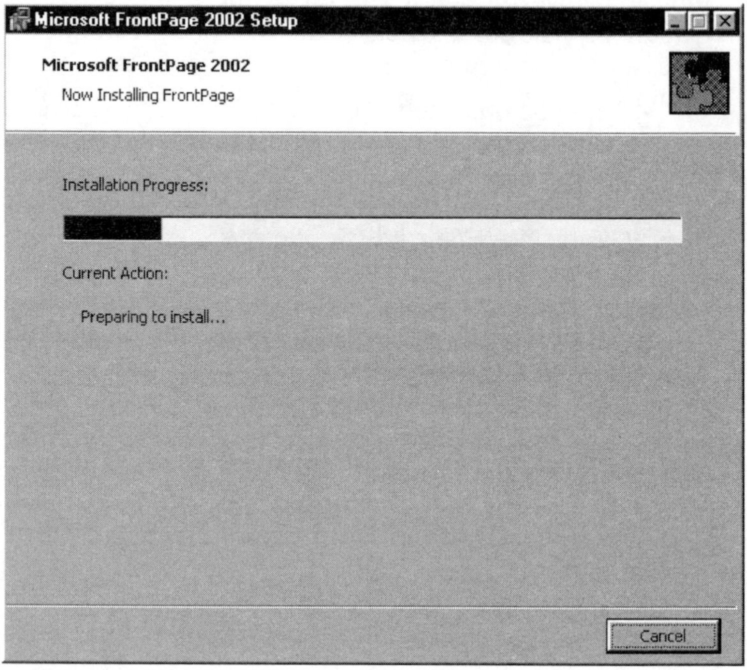

FIGURE 1–15 Installing Microsoft FrontPage 2002 screen.

NOTE:
If you are running Windows 98, PWS version 4 is included on the CD. It can be found in the *Add-ons* folder, *D:\add-ons\pws\setup.exe*, but the FrontPage 2002 server extensions cannot be run on the PWS. If you run the FrontPage 2000 extensions, some FrontPage 2002 features will not run properly. Windows 95 cannot run any Office XP applications. NT 4 users can download NT Option Pack 4, which is free to download and use, from: *http://www.microsoft.com/ntserver/ nts/downloads/recommended/NT4OptPk/default.asp*. Windows ME does not support any available PWS. See Chapter 7 for more information on the PWS for Windows 9x version operating systems.

◆ Installing SharePoint Team Services and FrontPage Server Extensions

To install the SharePoint Team Services and FrontPage 2002 server extensions on your IIS server, you will first want to be sure that you have the latest version of the FrontPage 2002 server extensions. The latest version can be obtained from Microsoft's Web site at *http://www.microsoft.com/frontpage/fpse*. The version included on the FrontPage 2002 CD is 5.0.2.2623.

Install from the FrontPage 2002 as part of the SharePoint Team Services:

- Insert the FrontPage 2002 CD in your CD-ROM and navigate to the *SharePT* folder.
- Double-click the *setupse.exe*.
- Follow the on-screen wizard

Install the FrontPage 2002 extensions from the download:

- Navigate your browser to the Microsoft Web site *http:// www.microsoft.com/frontpage/fpse*.
- Click the link to download the server extensions file and select the Save the file to disk option to run the installation later from your hard drive or the Run this program from its current location option to begin the installation immediately.
- If you chose to Save the file to disk option, you will need to double-click the file to begin the installation process.

• Follow the steps in the Installation wizard to complete the installation process.

If you installed the SharePoint Team Services, you can administrate your extensions from the Microsoft SharePoint Administrator, located in the Administration tools in your Control Panel. Opening this administrator launches a Web page with easy-to-manage tools.

Activating FrontPage 2002

Each time you start FrontPage 2002, you will see an activation screen come up. FrontPage 2002 will run approximately 50 times before you have to activate the product. To get rid of the nag screen, simply follow the on-screen steps to activate your product. You can use the wizard and activate the product online, or you can phone in your activation request.

◆ FrontPage 2002 Interface

Before we get started with building our first Web site, let's briefly examine the FrontPage 2002 interface and its basic menus and toolbars. We will start with the basic menu features you will need to get started and look at all of the menu features specifically throughout the book.

By default, FrontPage will begin in Page view (see Figure 1–16). Under the horizontal menus at the top of the window are four vertical frames: Views, Folder List, Editor window, and Task Pane. The Views frame, Folder List frame, and Task pane can be toggled on and off to allow more room in the Page view. To toggle these frames on and off, click the View menu at the top of the page and select Views Bar, Folder List, or Task Pane to toggle between them (see Figure 1–17).

Each button in the Views bar will show you different FrontPage views of your web:

• Folders view—shows the Folder List in the left pane and the contents of the selected folder in the right pane. Highlight a folder in the Folder List, and the contents of that folder will display in the right pane. You may drag and drop files and/or whole folders from the right pane to a folder in the left pane or Folder List.

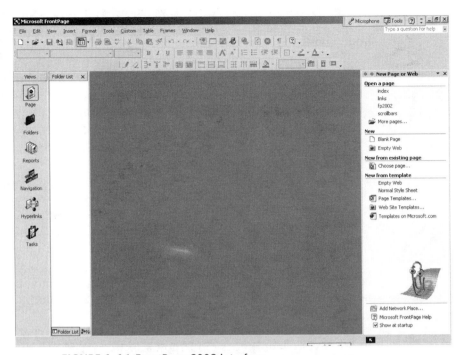

FIGURE 1–16 FrontPage 2002 interface.

FIGURE 1–17 FrontPage's View menu.

- Reports view—shows an array of valuable reports that can be run against your web from within FrontPage. The available reports that can be run are:
- Site Summary
  - Files: All Files, Recently Added Files, Recently Changed Files, Older Files
  - Problems: Unlinked Files, Slow Pages, Broken Hyperlinks, Component Errors
  - Work Flow: Assigned To, Review Status, Categories, Publish Status, Checkout Status
  - Usage: Usage Summary, Monthly Summary, Weekly Summary, Daily Summary, Monthly Page Hits, Weekly Page Hits, Daily Page Hits, Visiting Users, Operating Systems, Browsers, Referring Domains, Referring URLs, Search Strings
- Navigation view—a great visual aid to discern the structure of your Web site. If used correctly, this view can benefit you not only as a visual aid, but in automatically updating your FrontPage navigation bars, as well.
- Hyperlinks view—offers a visual representation of all hyperlinks in your Web pages. You may select any page in the Folder List to be the starting point for the Hyperlinks view, which will show all pages that are hyperlinked to and from the selected page.
- Tasks View—shows all tasks that have been assigned in a web. Tasks may be assigned for collaboration on a project web with other users and marked as completed or cleared from the Tasks view. Tasks that have been hyperlinked to a particular page within the web can be started by double-clicking the tasks from the Tasks view.

◆ FrontPage Editor

The FrontPage Editor is the mainframe, or pane, of the FrontPage window. Double-clicking a file in the Folder List will launch that page in the Editor for you to edit. The FrontPage Editor has three main "views" of its own: Normal view (which is the default view; Figure 1–18), HTML view, and Preview view.

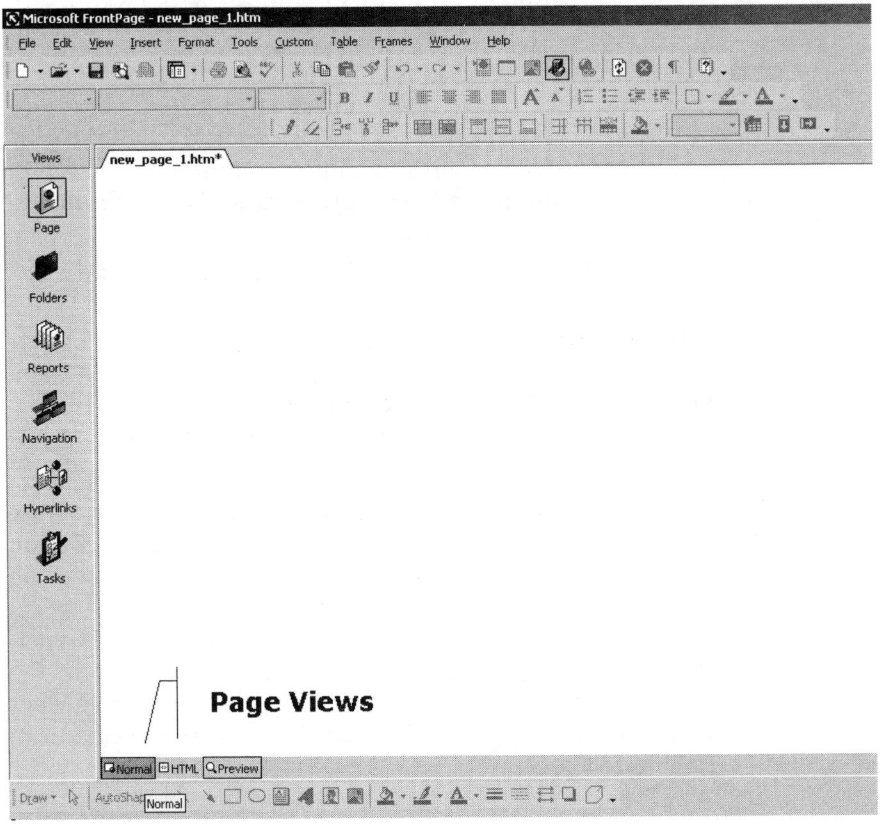

FIGURE 1–18 Page view—normal view new page.

Normal view is where you do all of your WYSIWYG editing using the tools and menu functions. HTML view shows you the HTML code behind-the-scenes and allows you the opportunity to edit the HTML code. This view can be very helpful for those who know HTML. It also allows for easy pasting of HTML code and JavaScript into the HTML view, if desired. Preview view gives a general idea of what a page will look like when viewed in a browser. This is a general idea and should not be considered absolute. Often, the page looks a little different in the browser than it does in Preview view. It is a quick way to view a page without the lines and borders shown in Normal view to outline tables and forms.

◆ Recap

In this chapter, we learned many of the basic features necessary to install FrontPage 2002. We looked at what is new with FrontPage and discussed some of the basic tools and views of the FrontPage 2002 interface. With this information, you are well on your way to learning to use FrontPage 2002 to create an exciting Web site for personal or business use.

◆ Advanced Project

Install FrontPage 2002 on your computer.

chapter

2 Create a Web

IN THIS CHAPTER

- Creating a Web
- Frames Pages
- Importing Whole Webs into FrontPage
- Working with Your Webs
- Images in FrontPage Webs
- Tables
- Recap
- Advanced Project

Now that you have installed FrontPage 2002 and become familiar with the basic layout of the program, you are ready to begin the task of creating a Web site. The primary task for this chapter is creating your FrontPage web and beginning to learn to work with the web and pages within it. Let's begin by creating a web on your computer.

◆ Creating a Web

- In FrontPage 2002, select the File menu. From the menu, select New then Page or Web (see Figure 2–1).

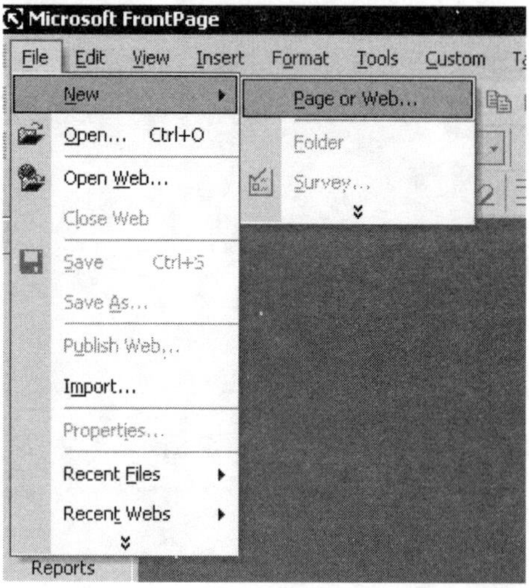

FIGURE 2–1 File menu.

- This will launch the Task pane on the right of the screen. Under the section New from template, click the link to Web site templates to launch the New web dialog box.
- In the New web dialog box, select a location for your new web. The location will be entered to the right of the New web dialog box (see Figure 2–2).
- If you are working on a system that has the Personal Web Server (PWS) (see Chapter 7, "Personal Web Server," for more on the PWS) or Internet Information Server (IIS) installed, you will want to name and store your web in the server default directory by naming the web *http://localhost/ Shelley*. If you are working on a system that does not have the PWS or IIS installed, you will need to name your web with a path to where you will store your FrontPage webs (for example, *C:\My Documents\My Webs\shelley*).

Once you have specified the location for your new web, along with a name (*shelley*), you will select a template for your web.

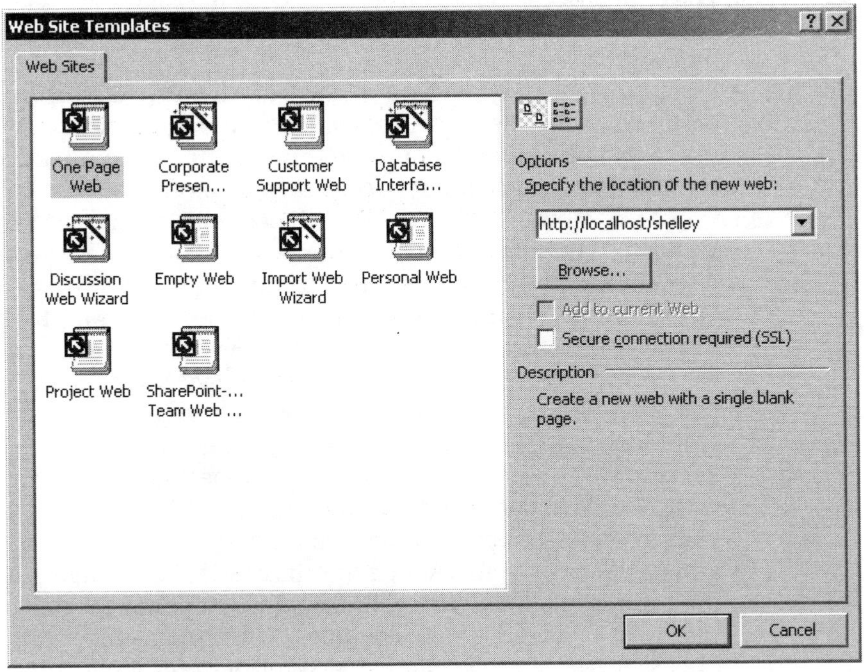

FIGURE 2–2 New web dialog box.

Choosing a Web Template

As you can see in the New web dialog box, there are several template webs from which to choose. Highlighting any of the template web icons will give a description of that template on the right side of the New web dialog box (see Figure 2–2).

- One Page Web—a new web with a single blank page.
- Corporate Presence Wizard—a complex set of template pages already linked together, named, and grouped for you to modify and convert into a web presence for your corporation. If selected, the FrontPage wizard will ask a series of questions that pertain to your corporation to include on all pages of this web template.
- Customer Support Web—a web template designed to improve your customer support services; this selection is geared particularly to software companies.
- Database Interface Wizard—a wizard that steps you through creating a web that will connect to a database.

This web will create a front-end administration to add, modify, and delete records in your database through a browser.

- Discussion Web Wizard—a wizard to create a discussion group with threads, a table of contents, and full-text searching. This web can be included within a current web already created, but it is recommended that you create a discussion web as a subweb if it is to be included within an existing Web site. The final product of this wizard is an interactive discussion web that makes use of frames for the layout.
- Empty Web—a FrontPage web with no pages or files in it.
- Import Web Wizard—a wizard that allows you to import a web from your computer or a remote file system. This gives you the ability to bring a set of files created outside FrontPage into FrontPage.
- Personal Web—a template to create a personal Web site with template pages already set up for you to modify for your interests, hobbies, photos, and more.
- Project Web—a web created specifically for managing a project of some kind. This web contains templates for creating a list of members, a schedule, status, an archive, and discussions. Choose a One-Page Web for your Shelley Biotechnologies web. Throughout this book, we will build on this web, starting with creating a home page.
- SharePoint-based Team Web Site (Wizard)—use this template if you have SharePoint Team Services installed and would like to create a team web with features such as surveys, lists, document libraries, threaded discussions, and more.

Creating a Home Page

The file name for your homepage is very important. It must be named according to the operating system requirements of the server that will host your web. On Windows 9x with the PWS or Windows 2000 with IIS, the default page will need to be named *default.htm*. This is true on an NT server, as well. On a UNIX server, the primary default page must be *index.html*, and the secondary default page must be *index.htm*. On a UNIX server, the browser will first look for *index.html*, and if a file by this name is not found, it will look for *index.htm*. This is how the home page is found when simply entering a URL such as *www.microsoft.com*

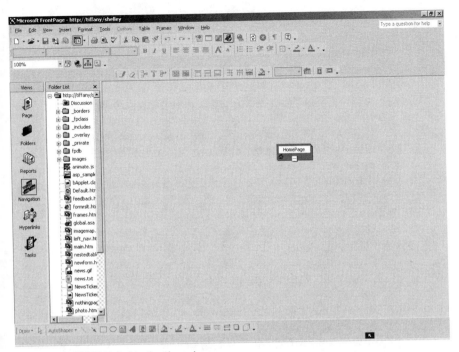

FIGURE 2-3 Navigation view.

without including a file name and file extension, such as
www.microsoft.com/index.htm.

If you click the Navigation view button, you will see your
default page with a house icon on it in the view on the right (see
Figure 2–3). The house icon symbolizes that this is the home
page.

Adding Pages to Your Web

Much like creating a new web, FrontPage offers a quick and easy
way to create a new Web page within your web, along with a fantastic array of template pages from which to choose. In the File
menu, choose New then Page or Web to open the New Task pane.
Click the Page Templates link under the New from template section of the New Task pane (see Figure 2–4).

By default, the New page dialog box opens in the General tab
screen (Figure 2–5). There are many template pages from which
to choose to help you create a quick and easy layout for your new
page. Several of the templates include forms, such as the Feed-

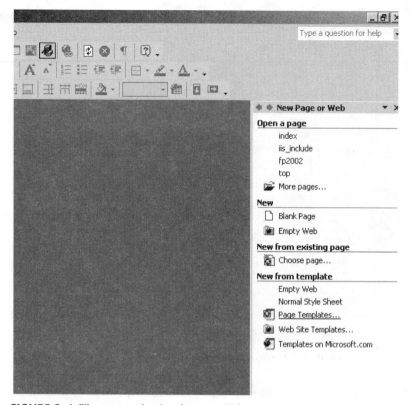

FIGURE 2–4 File menu selection for new Web page.

back Form and Confirmation Form, which require little customizing on your part to use. All of the templates are designed in such a way that you can spend as much or as little time customizing the template items, along with inserting your own information into the template layout, as you choose.

Choosing Normal Page opens a plain blank page, without any tables or columns as some of the template pages have, for you to work on.

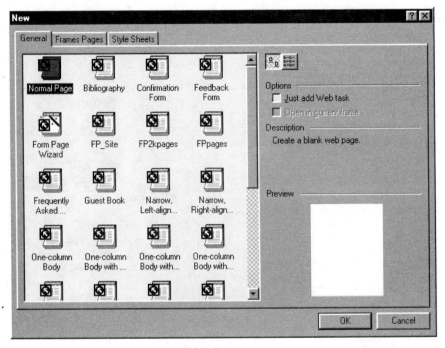

FIGURE 2–5 New page dialog box.

◆ Frames Pages

Clicking the Frames Pages tab at the top of the New page dialog box (Figure 2–6) offers several variations of frames layouts from which to choose.

Figure 2–6 shows the more common type of frames page layout, the Banner and Contents page, or frameset, as it is most often called.

This layout is called a *frameset* because it is actually a page coded to pull in three individual pages into one browser window. There are many pros and cons to using framesets. Some of these are listed below.

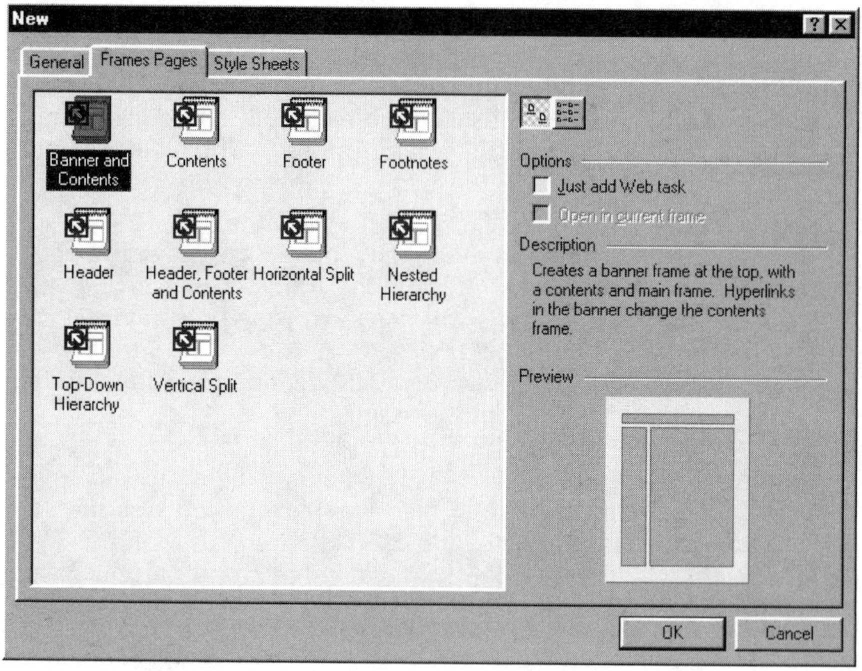

FIGURE 2–6 New page dialog box—Frames Pages tab.

Pros:

- Framesets allow for common features on each page, such as a set of navigational links and a logo banner on the tops of all pages, to remain in one place while the user browses the rest of the pages in the Web site without having to refresh these items on each new page. They can make page load time faster in some cases because only the main frame will be reloading with new content.

Cons:

- Many search engines do not index framesets.
- It is not possible for users to bookmark any particular page within a frameset Web site because all of the pages are loaded within the frameset and not by individual pages in the browser. Bookmarking (adding pages to your Favorites list) any page within a frameset will only return you to the main set of default pages within the frameset, which is usually the home page of the site.

- It is very difficult to optimize a web for search engines when pages are within frames. For instance, a search engine may index a single page within your web. If this is a page that is intended to be viewed within a frameset, one that has a navigation frame instead of navigation links on each individual page, then the person finding your page linked in a search engine will have no way to navigate to the other pages within your web.

There are JavaScripts that can be placed on individual pages to force a page to open only in the frameset in which it was intended to open, but this will depend on the user having JavaScript enabled in his or her browser.

A good frameset resource is found at *http://www.at-frontpage.com/framestips.htm*.

My opinion is that the cons outweigh the pros for using frames for an entire site; however, I have found many good uses for frames within a standard Web site. Sections of a Web site that feature images are a great use for a frames page within a web. For example, thumbnail images can all be placed in the top left frame, with hyperlinks targeting the larger versions of the images in the main frame.

Once you have chosen the format for your frameset from the New page dialog box (see Figure 2–6), you can begin either creating new initial pages or setting the initial page for each frame in the frameset (see Figure 2–7). The initial page will be the first set of pages that appears when the frameset page is called from the browser. For example, if you name your frameset *frame.htm*, when you load *frame.htm* in the browser, the initial pages are the pages that are called into the frames first.

To set the initial page using an existing page in your web, click the Set Initial Page button in the appropriate frame. To create a new page for any or all frames in the frameset, click the New Page button. Clicking the New Page button will load a new, blank page in that frame. You will need to save this page when you save the frameset. We will assume for this book that we are creating new pages for this frameset and will explain the saving process in FrontPage 2002.

Saving Frames Pages in FrontPage

Saving a frameset for the first time in FrontPage 2002 can be a little confusing. The process is fairly logical, but the highlighted

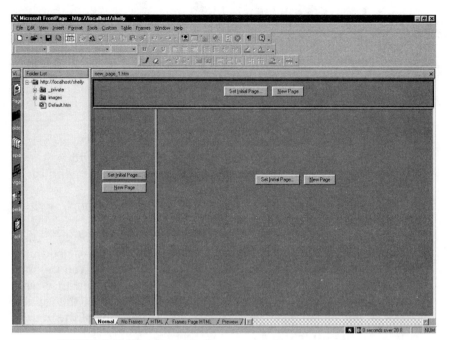

FIGURE 2–7 New frameset.

page being saved can be missed if you don't know what FrontPage is doing during the save process.

First, FrontPage will save the whole frameset page. You can see that FrontPage is doing this by the blue outline that surrounds the entire frameset in the Save As dialog box (see Figure 2–8 and notice the dark shading in this image example). Select a name for the frameset and a page title, then click the Save button.

FrontPage will next begin saving the pages within each frameset. These pages must be saved individually within your "web" for the browser to be able to call the pages into the proper frames, once your web is published (see Chapter 5, "Publishing Webs," for more on publishing your Web site) to the Internet.

In Figure 2–9, notice how FrontPage has shaded the top frame. This is the page that FrontPage will be saving next. Give this page a name and a page title, and click the Save button again. FrontPage will repeat this process until all frames within the frameset have been saved.

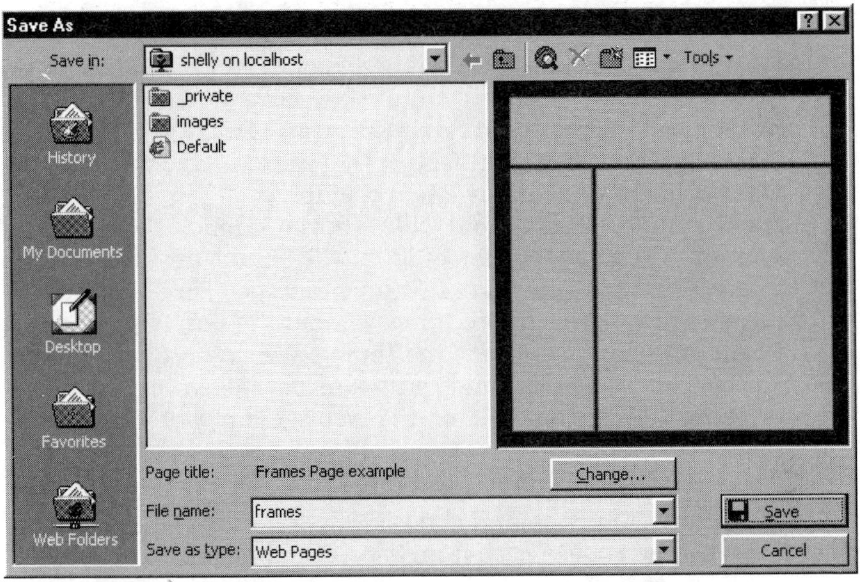

FIGURE 2–8 Saving a frameset.

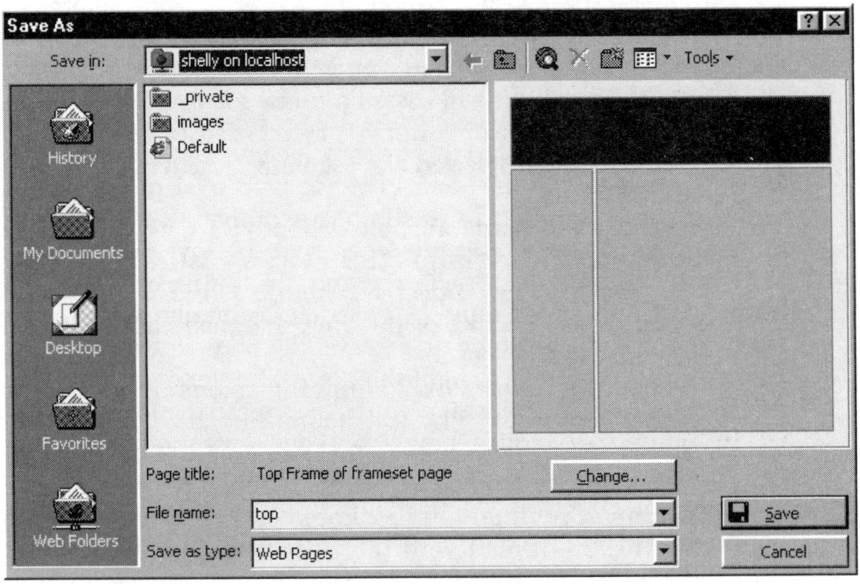

FIGURE 2–9 Saving a frameset.

◆ Importing Whole Webs into FrontPage

What if you have been given the assignment of working on an existing Web site? Perhaps you already have a Web site that you would like to continue working with using FrontPage. FrontPage 2002 has a built-in import feature that makes gathering all of the files within a non-FrontPage web a snap.

The Import Web Wizard will walk you through the process of importing a web. FrontPage 2002 will import any web on the Internet; however, it will not be able to import any files that are in password-protected directories without the password to do so. During the import process, the Import Web Wizard will prompt you for a username and password if hidden or password-protected files are detected on the Web site that you are trying to import.

To import a web from the World Wide Web:

- Start FrontPage and choose New from the File menu, then choose Page or Web from the New submenu.
- So far, this process is similar to creating a new page or a new web, but after choosing Web from the New submenu, you must select the Import Web Wizard icon. Make sure that you specify the location of the new web box before you click the OK button. This is an important factor that is often overlooked. If you do not enter the location to which to import, FrontPage will assign a name for your web for you, and it may not be one that you recognize (see Figure 2–10).
- Once you have selected the location for saving this web, click OK.
- FrontPage will create the new web for you, then you will see the Import Web Wizard. This process is step-by-step and very easy to follow. Select the From a World Wide Website option; enter the URL of the Web site, then click Next (see Figure 2–11).
- The next step allows you to limit the amount of space and/ or files you would like to import from the location you selected. Once you answer these questions and click the Next button; FrontPage will begin to import the web for you.
- The import routine simply automates the process of saving each file associated with any Web page on the Internet, which involves manually viewing the source code and saving that code as an .htm file, then saving each image that is shown on that page on your computer.

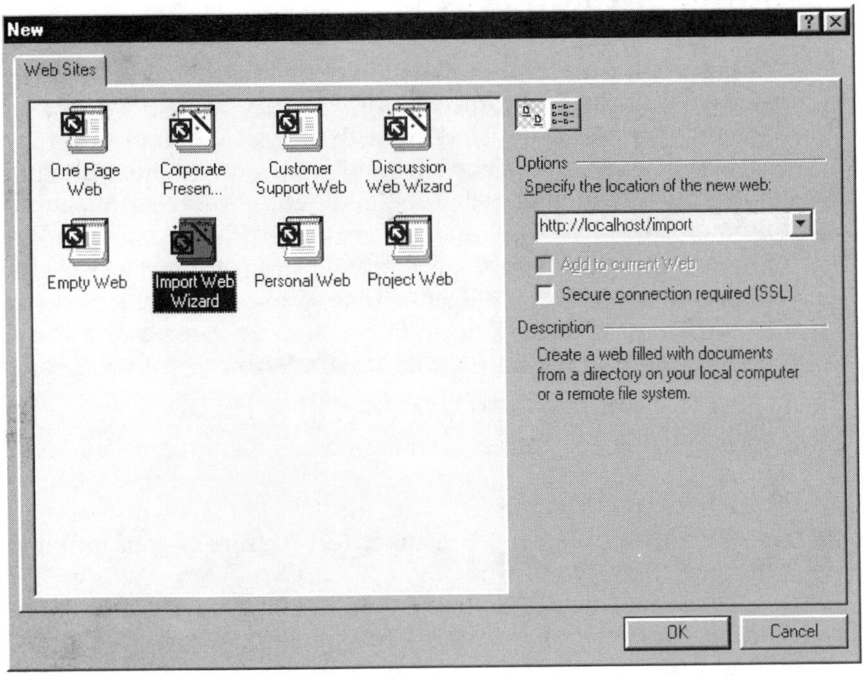

FIGURE 2–10 New web dialog box.

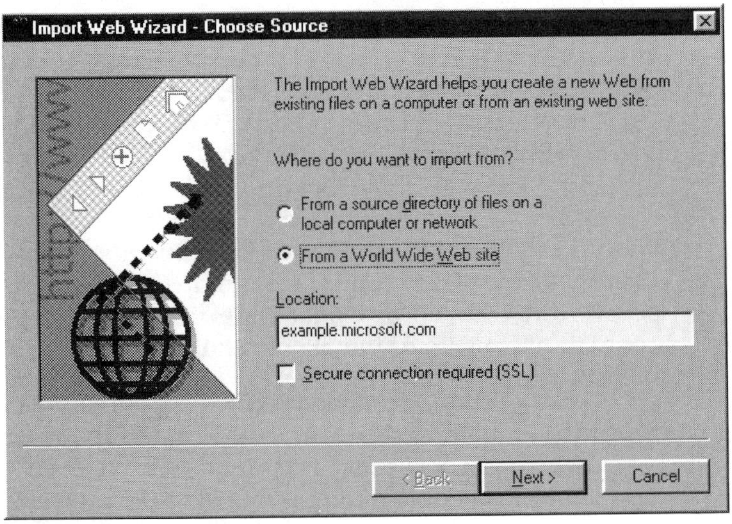

FIGURE 2–11 Import Web Wizard dialog box.

◆ Working with Your Webs

Working with the files that make up a Web site can be difficult to manage and keep organized. With FrontPage, this important aspect of managing and working with the files that make up your web is much less daunting. The ability to clearly see the file and folder structure of your web, set global settings and editing capabilities, format FrontPage to create and edit HTML code in a format that you set up, and open HTML files within your web for easy editing is all built in to FrontPage 2002.

File Structure and Management Strategies

One of the main benefits of FrontPage is the superior way in which it helps you manage your webs. The FrontPage interface shows you all of the files and folders that you have grouped together to create your web. Using the different views discussed in the previous chapter, you can easily sort the files of your web and arrange them as you like.

Good file structure is always helpful in organizing and maintaining your work. For instance, all image files are often stored within an *images* folder. In some cases, when numerous images are used in a web for several different areas of a web, different *images* folders can be used, such as */productimages*, */servicesimages*, and */staffimages*.

Pages that you do not want to be seen in search results or indexed by search engines should be stored in a *_private* folder or another folder that you create, beginning with an underscore. This prevents it from being pulled into the search results of a local web search or a search engine index.

FrontPage hides some files and folders from the user initially. It is assumed that a new user may not want the clutter of seeing files and folders that will not be edited regularly, including the *_borders* folder, which contains the shared border files. These can be edited directly on any page that uses shared borders, but on occasion, it is necessary to open a shared border file individually to edit some piece of it. To see pages in the hidden directories and files, select Tools then Web Settings. Next, click the Advanced tab. Under the Options section, check the Show documents in hidden directories option (see Figure 2–12).

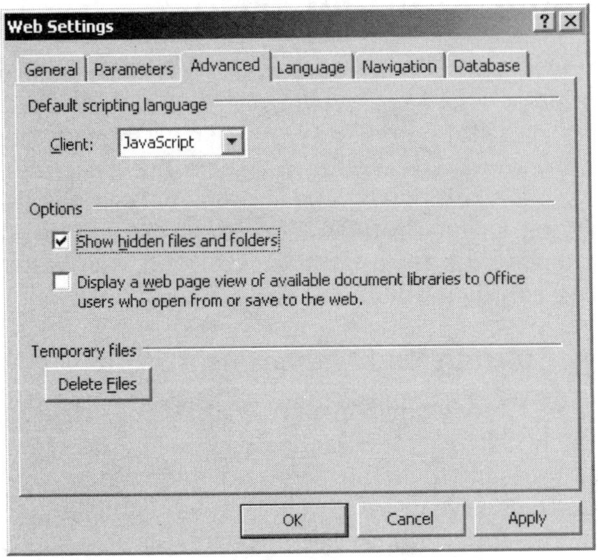

FIGURE 2–12 Web Settings dialog box.

Compatibility Options and Settings

Browser compatibility issues are a big factor when designing Web pages. It is important to know your audience so that you can design pages that will work to their full potential. There are many differences in how the various browsers interpret your code. If your web is aimed at a wide audience, you should consider that those users might consist of Microsoft Internet Explorer® (IE) and Netscape® Navigator® (NN) users. Among those, many may still be using generation 3 browsers with much less capability than generation 4 and newer browsers.

It is possible that your Web site may be just for an intranet and that all of your audience is made up of IE 4 and newer browsers. IE version 4 and newer browsers will recognize items such as cascading style sheets and DHTML without any adverse effects, like you might experience with an older browser or with NN.

FrontPage 2002 makes it easy to ensure that you design your pages with features and tools that apply to your expected audience if you set your compatibility options correctly (see Figure 2–13). To do this, select Page Options from the Tools menu, then click the Compatibility tab.

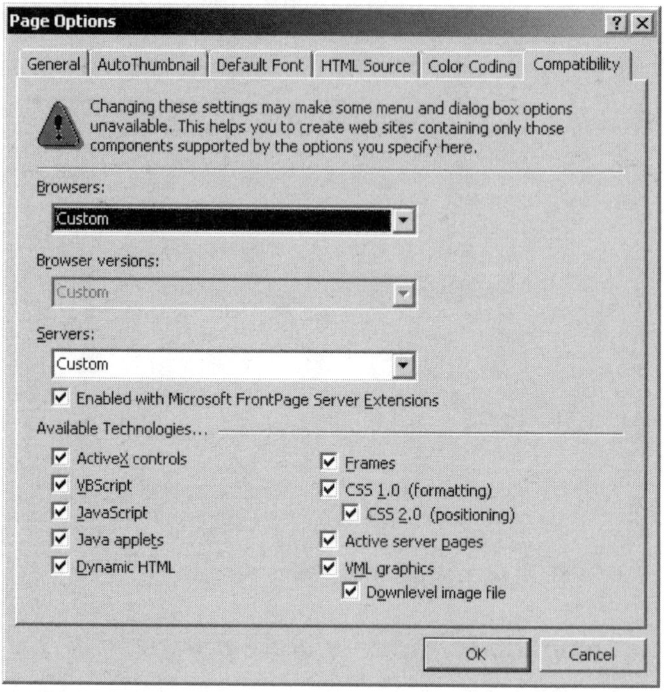

FIGURE 2–13 Page Options dialog box—compatibility settings.

The compatibility settings allow you to tell FrontPage who your audience is and what features and technologies to incorporate into your Web pages, as well as force FrontPage to make advanced technologies unavailable on pages within a web that has its settings programmed for older or NN-only browsers (see Figure 2–14).

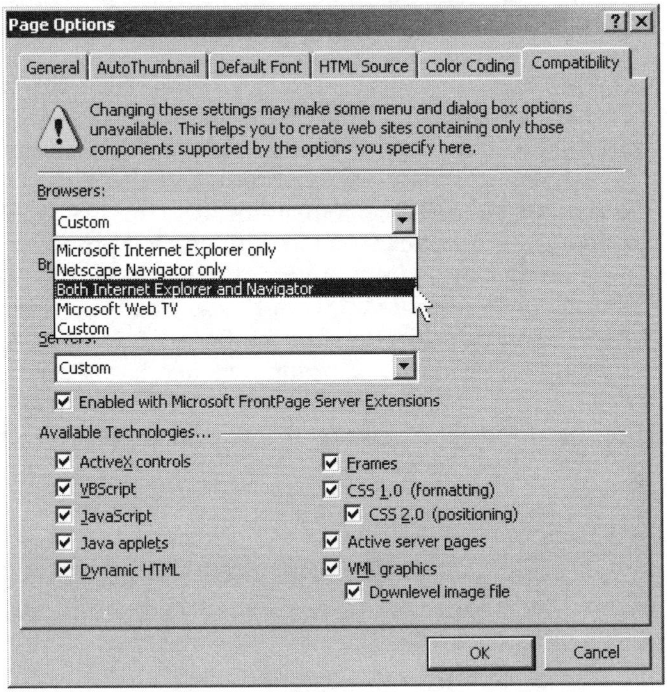

FIGURE 2–14 Page Options dialog box—compatibility settings.

MYTH:
Microsoft FrontPage codes pages that work only in IE browsers.

FACT:
Microsoft FrontPage has a tool that allows you to take advantage of the many advanced technologies supported by IE. The FrontPage user is responsible for learning about browser compatibility and choosing the features that will be best received by his or her audience. FrontPage 2002 makes it easy for users, new and advanced, to set the audience requirements and limit the features available via the compatibility settings.

Training FrontPage to Use Custom Formatting or Preserve HTML Source Code

A big complaint of FrontPage 98 concerned the way in which FrontPage alters HTML code inserted in the HTML view. FrontPage 2002 has overcome this annoyance with a Preserve HTML option. This setting is found in the Page Options dialog box, under the HTML Source tab. It is the first option under the General section, near the top of the dialog box.

Another nice feature in FrontPage 2002 is the option to teach FrontPage to format your HTML code. You may set rules for HTML code using preset options in the Page Options dialog box, under the HTML Source tab, or you may teach FrontPage to format your code, based on an example page (see Figure 2–15).

In Figure 2–15, notice the several preset rules that you can select and configure.

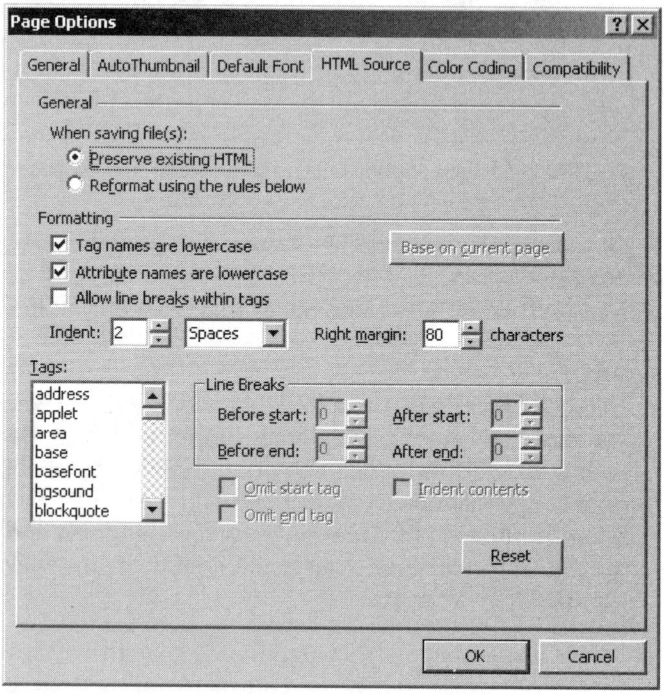

FIGURE 2–15 Page Options dialog box—HTML Source tab.

If you have a page that you would like for FrontPage to use as an example of the formatting rules that you want set for your HTML code, open that page in FrontPage and select the HTML View tab. Then, in the Tools menu, choose Page Options and click the HTML Source tab. Select the Reformat using the rules below option and click the Base on current page button. FrontPage will set the formatting rules for all of the pages within the web, based on that example page.

Adding and Formatting Text on Your Pages

If you have ever worked with Microsoft Word or even Corel Word-Perfect, you have a good idea of what it is like to add and format your text in FrontPage. Let's get started by simply adding some text to a blank page.

Open a new or existing page in your web and place your cursor on the page in the editor. Now just type in a line of text, something such as "Let's practice adding and formatting some text today." Simply typing this line of text in will cause FrontPage to use default settings for this text because we didn't set any formatting options before we started typing. Once we have some text on the page, we can use the formatting tools to add some specific formatting options.

By default, FrontPage loads the text formatting tools at the top of the editor. These tools include:

- Text dropdown—This first dropdown menu lets you select the type of text you are working with. The default is Normal, but you can choose from Heading text, Bulleted list, Numbered list, Directory list, Defined term, and more.
- Font dropdown—Use this dropdown to select the font you want to use. FrontPage will load all of the fonts that you have on your system in this dropdown, but be advised that not all fonts are standard fonts. If you use a font other than a standard one, visitors to your Web site may not be able to view your Web pages the way you intend them to look.
- Font size—Use this dropdown box to select the font size. Standard or default is size 3 (10 pt). Size 2 (8 pt) is a popular font size, as well.
- Font style attributes—The next three buttons give you one-click ability to change your text to Bold, Italics, or Underlined.
- Alignment attributes—Set your text alignment with the next four buttons, Left, Center, Right, or Justify.

- Increase and Decrease font size buttons—These buttons give you one-click access to make a specified font one size bigger or one size smaller. These buttons were excluded from FrontPage 2000, and in FrontPage 98, clicking these buttons produced a `<big>` or a `<small>` tag. However, in FrontPage 2002, these buttons actually produce a `<font size=x>` tag instead.
- List buttons—Numbered list and bulleted list, the two most commonly used types of lists, are included on the formatting bar for one-click access.
- Indent buttons—Both Increase and Decrease indent buttons give you the ability to add a `<blockquote>` in your code quickly and the appearance of indented text. When used in a bulleted or numbered list, the Increase button creates a nested bulleted or numbered list.
- Border dropdown menu—This is a new feature in FrontPage 2002. This menu gives you several different types of borders that you can apply to your text or images. This feature makes use of inline styles, so be sure that your target audience will be able to view the page as you intend.
- Highlight Color menu—Again, this is a feature that makes use of inline style tags and creates a highlight or background color on your selected text. Generally, the features that use inline styles are geared for an IE 4 or newer browser, although some do work with other browsers or are gracefully ignored.
- Font Color menu—Use this menu to select the font color. Choose a standard color or select from more colors.

Now you can use your cursor to highlight the text you have on your page and use any of these formatting tools to format the text the way you want it to appear on your page. Later in the chapters, we review many other ways to arrange and lay out your pages using tables, web components, and even automatic content.

Adding Elements—Global and Local

When you use FrontPage to manage your web, you have the ability to add global elements to your FrontPage Web, such as themes, shared borders, and navigation bars. Each of these components can be added to all pages within the web, a selected few pages, or individually.

THEMES

Themes are applied to webs in FrontPage 2002 with the Theme Editor, accessed by selecting Themes from the Format menu. The list of available themes is shown in a list box in the Theme Editor; at the right is a preview of the highlighted theme (see Figure 2–16). Microsoft supplies approximately 67 different themes with the current release of FrontPage 2002, but only 13 are installed by default. To install the remainder, select the Install additional themes option that appears at the top of the theme list (with the FrontPage 2002 CD in the CD-ROM drive). Any themes that have been modified or created by the user and saved in the standard way under a new theme name should also appear in this list.

New themes can be created easily by clicking the Modify button on the Theme Editor window and saving the modified theme under a new name using the Save As option. (Using just the Save option may overwrite the existing theme!)

A theme may be applied to individual pages within a web by first opening the web in Folders view and selecting the pages in which you would like to apply a particular theme. Next, open the

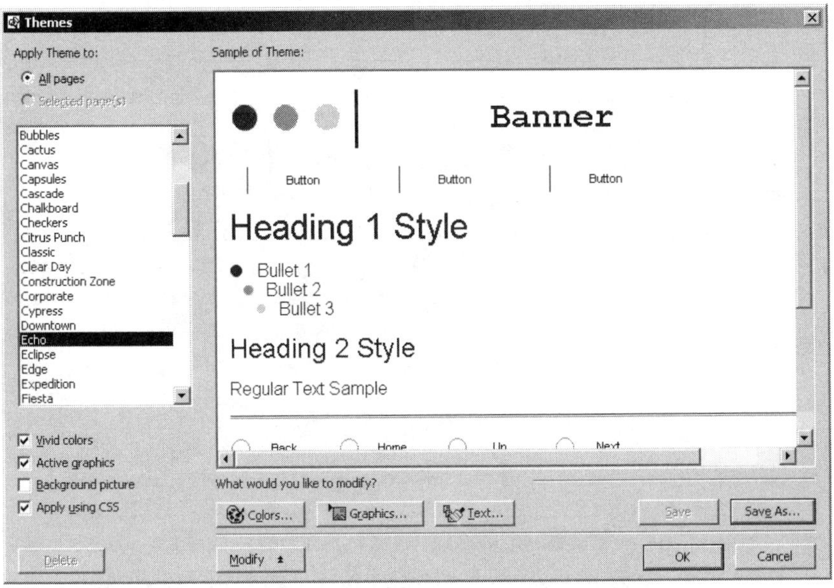

FIGURE 2–16 Theme Editor.

Theme Editor and choose Selected page(s) under the Apply theme to options at the top left of the Theme Editor window. You may also apply your theme choice to all pages within your web.

For more on FrontPage themes, see the supplemental information provided at *http://www.at-frontpage.com.*

SHARED BORDERS

Shared borders are another FrontPage element that make maintaining your web easier, as well as lend a consistent look across all pages of your web. They can be applied to all pages within a web or they can be limited to specific pages. These files are stored in the hidden *_borders* directory and named *top.htm, left.htm,* and *bottom.htm.* They may be edited from any page in which they are applied, and those edits will be applied to the shared border on all pages of the web that share that border.

To insert shared borders in an entire web:

- Select Shared Borders from the Format menu.
- In the Shared Borders dialog box, check the borders that you would like to apply to your pages and make sure that the option for All pages is selected at the top of the Shared Borders dialog box (see Figure 2–17).
- Click OK, and FrontPage will apply the selected borders to all of the pages in your web.

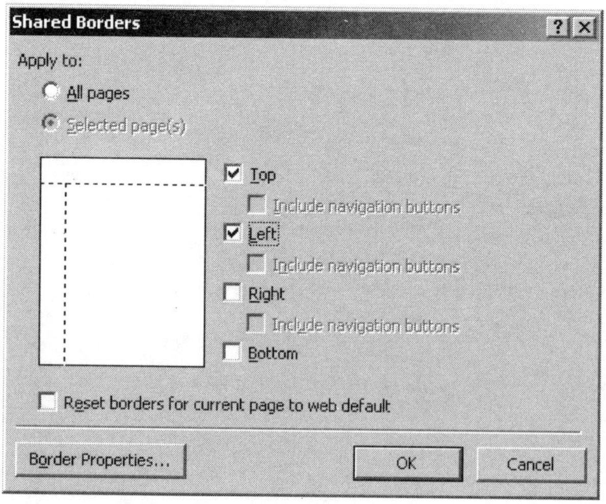

FIGURE 2–17 Shared Borders dialog box.

New to FrontPage 2002 is the Border Properties button in the Shared Borders dialog box. Previous versions of FrontPage did not allow any background color or picture properties to be set in a shared border different from that of the page in which it resides. FrontPage 2002 Border Properties allow you to set the background color and/or a background image for the shared border alone, separate from the page properties.

To set the border properties:

- Open the Shared Borders properties dialog box from the Format menu.
- Click the Border Properties button on the bottom left of the screen (see Figure 2–17).
- In the dropdown menu at the top of the Border Properties dialog box, choose the border you want to set the properties (see Figure 2–18).
- Select the color or the background image that you want to use for this border and click the OK button.

To apply a shared border to only one page in your web:

- Open the page on which you want the border and right-click anywhere on the page.
- Select Shared Borders from the menu to access the Shared Borders dialog box (see Figure 2–17).
- Check the Selected page(s) option, then check the border you would like to apply.
- Lastly, click OK, and FrontPage will apply that border to your page.

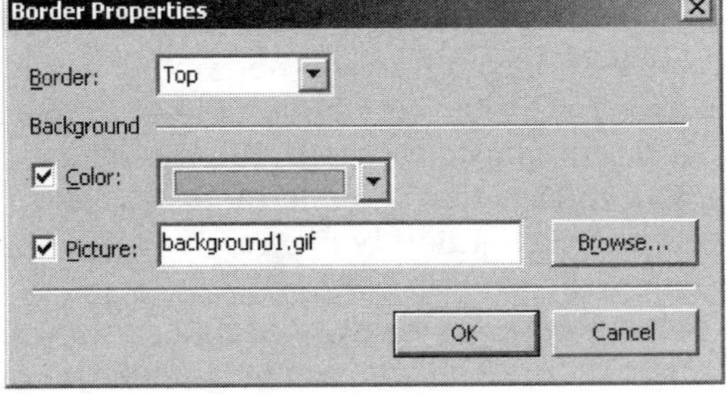

FIGURE 2–18 Border Properties dialog box.

To add shared border(s) to more than one page but not all pages within a web:

- Choose the Folders view and highlight the pages you would like to add the shared border(s) to by holding the <Ctrl> button and clicking on the pages you want to select.
- Access the Shared Borders dialog box from the Format menu in FrontPage (see Figure 2–17) and select the Selected page(s) option.
- Check the borders that you would like to apply to the pages at the right and click OK.

NOTE:

The HTML view will not show you the HTML code of a shared border. To work with the HTML code of a shared border, you must view the code in the _/borders/ border file directly. (See the "File Structure and Management Strategies" section in this chapter for information on making hidden files and directories visible.)

NAVIGATION BARS

FrontPage 2002 Navigation bars are a component of FrontPage. The Navigation bars display links to other pages in your web relative to the page placement in the Navigation view. The Navigation Bar Properties dialog box allows you to set which level links to display for any particular bar, as well as the option to include links to the home page. You may also set the Navigation bar properties to display Next and Back links, which would create links back and forth between pages that you have established on the same level in the Navigation view. If you created a web from a wizard and are starting with a template such as the Corporate Web, you will see that a navigation structure was already started for you and navigation bars already inserted on the pages of the template web.

When you insert a navigation bar into a shared border from the Insert then Web Components menu and choose a bar based on navigation structure, FrontPage will automatically create links to the pages on the level that you select in the Navigation Bar Properties dialog box, according to the page that it is displayed on *and* according to its place in the navigation structure (see Fig-

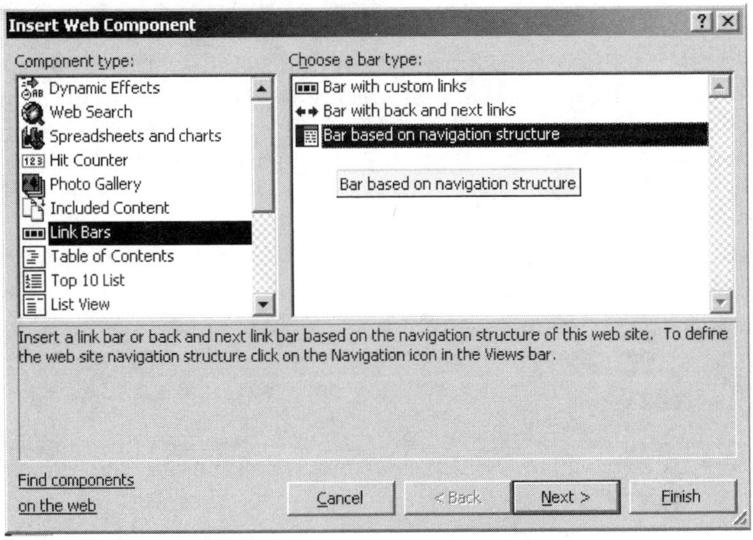

FIGURE 2–19 Insert Web Component—Navigation bar.

ure 2–19). If a page has not been placed in the navigation structure, no links will show on that page. For instance, if you have a
navigation bar in a top shared border, and all of the pages in
your web share that border, the links on each page will not neces-
sarily be the same on each page. In the Navigation Bar Properties
dialog box, you must select the option for the navigation bar to
show "child"-level pages; then, the links that will show on each
page will be at the child level, relative to that page and its place
within the navigation structure in the Navigation view.

There are several ways to create a navigation structure in
your Navigation view:

1. Drag and drop pages into the Navigation view (see Figure
   2–20).
2. Create new pages right from the Navigation view.

You can build on an existing structure or start from scratch. If
you already have pages in your web that you would like added to
the Navigation view structure or want to rearrange the structure,
you can drag and drop the pages in place. The titles of the pages
as you see them in the Navigation view are the titles you will see
in the Navigation bar, once it is inserted onto a page.

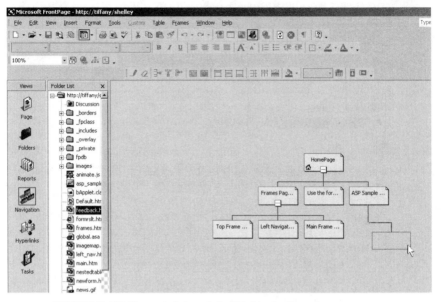

FIGURE 2–20 Drag and drop into the Navigation view.

TIP:

If you have multiple levels of pages in your navigation structure and would like to keep the appearance of every page having the same links in a shared border, you can accomplish this. In the shared border, simply add more than one Navigation bar. For instance, if you have a Navigation bar on your home page and would like for it to show links to all the child-level pages, set the Navigation Bar Properties dialog box option to show the child level. Then, on the child-level pages, there will appear to be no links in the shared border because those are the child-level pages. Next, add a second Navigation bar and set its properties to show the same level and a link home. Now, all child-level pages will have a Navigation bar that displays the same links as the Navigation bar that appears on the home page. On the home page, the same level Navigation bar will not appear.

To insert and configure a Navigation bar based on the navigation structure:

- Select Navigation from the Insert menu to launch the Web Components dialog box. The Link Bar option on the left will already be selected by default. On the right pane, choose a bar based on navigation structure and click the OK button (see Figure 2–19).
- In the Insert Web Component dialog box, select the type of button or link you would like to use as your navigation bar. FrontPage 2002 provides a nice selection of theme buttons, as well as text links. Click the Next button (see Figure 2–21).
- Choose the orientation of the links; either vertical or horizontal, and click the Finish button.
- The Link Bar Properties dialog box will open, and you can choose which level links you would like to display on this bar, as well as include a link to the home page, Back and Next links, and parent page (see Figure 2–22).
- Click the OK button, and FrontPage will insert your Navigation bar on your page.

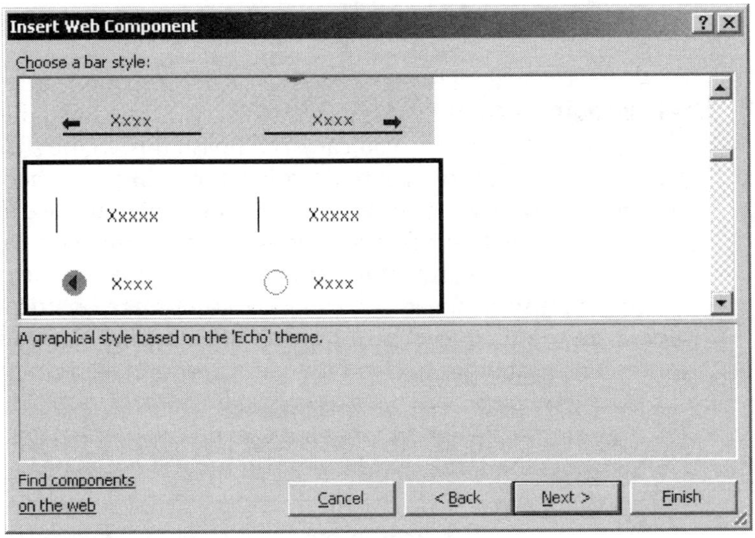

FIGURE 2–21 Insert Component dialog box.

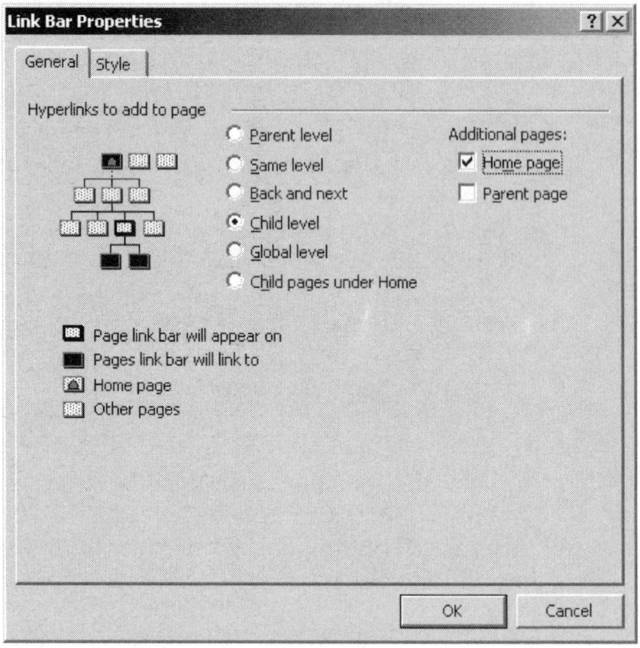

FIGURE 2–22 Link Bar Properties dialog box.

◆ Images in FrontPage Webs

This is the method recommended for bringing images into a FrontPage web when it is in use with the Web server, either PWS or IIS. This method preserves the integrity of the FrontPage extensions by not accessing the default directory with a graphics program. To import an image or several images at one time:

- Highlight the folder in the Folder List into which you want to import the files.
- Select Import from the File menu.
- Click the Add File button and navigate to the files that you would like to import.
- Click Open.
- Repeat the process until you have selected all of the files you would like to import.
- Click OK.

Another option for importing is simply to drag and drop the files directly into a folder in your FrontPage web from their current location on your hard drive.

Once you have your images saved within your web, you may insert the images on any of the pages within your web. Simply open any page, place your cursor where you would like an image placed, and select Picture from the Insert menu. Then, select From File from the Picture menu. In the Insert Image window, navigate to the folder in which you have your image stored (we will assume that it is the /images folder). Highlight the image you wish to insert and click OK. You may also drag an image from the Folder List on the left and drop it onto a page.

FrontPage allows some manipulation of images within the application. Some of the image features within FrontPage include:

- Auto thumbnail
- Image mapping
- Beveled edges
- Selecting a transparent color for a .gif image
- Resampling
- Positioning and rotating
- Adjusting brightness and contrast levels
- Cropping
- Converting to black and white

Most of these features are best suited for .gif images because of the lossy format (a "lossy" format loses quality, or degrades, each time it is edited and saved) of .jpg images. FrontPage, by default, will save changes to a .jpg image at 75% image compression. This often distorts an image because FrontPage assumes that the user has not yet saved the .jpg in a compressed format. All of these features are accessible via the Image Formatting toolbar that appears as a floating menu in the FrontPage Editor when an image is highlighted (see Figure 2–23).

Another format that is becoming popular for images is the Portable Network Graphics (.png) format. This file format is a loss-

FIGURE 2–23 Pictures formatting toolbar.

less format that supports up to 48-bit true color and 16-bit gray-scale. The *.png* format was designed to replace the older and simpler format of the *.gif* image to some extent, although it does not replace the animation ability of the *.gif* format. Browser support for the *.png* format is fairly limited still, but most major Web browsers support the basic *.png* image format. An advantage to using the *.png* format is the 32-bit transparency, which allows special effects, such as drop shadow and antialiasing, to be applied to an image against any background. However, many of the major Web browsers do not yet support 32-bit transparency. Microsoft IE 5.x still supports only paletted transparency, such as *.gif*-style transparency. NN 6.0 has much better transparency support for the *.png* file format. More information on the *.png* file format can be found on the *.png* Web site at *http://www.photodex.com/png/*.

Using the Auto Thumbnail feature will create a very small version of your image in FrontPage, and you will be prompted to save that small version within the web when you save the page you were working on. This will not affect your original image at all. It simply creates a new, smaller version of the image (or thumbnail) and automatically hyperlinks to the larger version of that image. By default, FrontPage will save that image to a specified width and height and create a beveled edge on the thumbnail version. You have control over these settings within the Page Options dialog box. Click the tab for Auto Thumbnail and make your changes within this window (see Figure 2–24).

Within the Auto Thumbnail screen, you have options to set:

• Width
• Height
• Shortest side
• Longest side

FrontPage will keep the aspect ratio of the thumbnail image (see Figure 2–25).

To apply the Auto Thumbnail feature to an image, select the image in the FrontPage Editor and use the Auto Thumbnail icon on the Image Formatting toolbar at the bottom of the screen (see Figure 2–26) or simply highlight the image in the FrontPage Editor and hold the <Ctrl> button while pressing the <T> key on your keyboard.

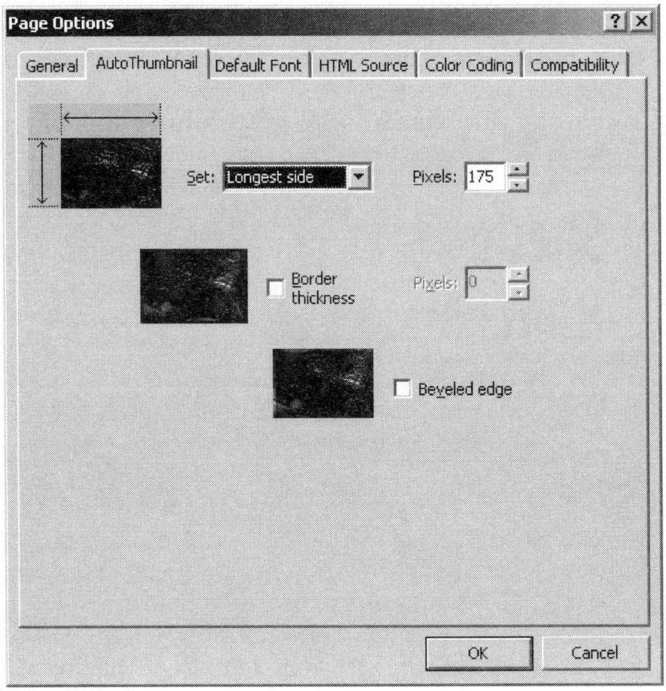

FIGURE 2–24 Page Options dialog box—Auto Thumbnail tab.

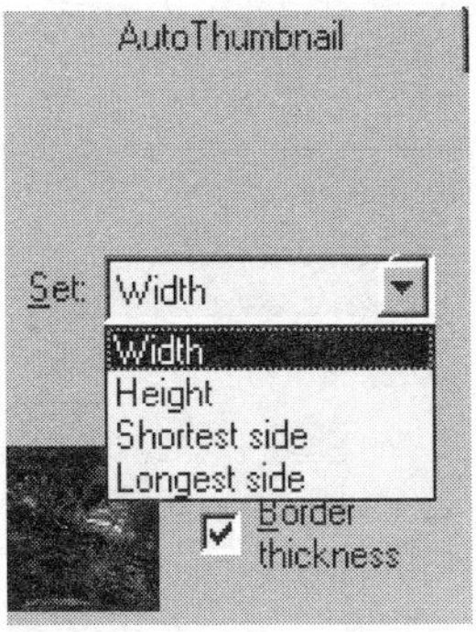

FIGURE 2–25 Auto Thumbnail configurations.

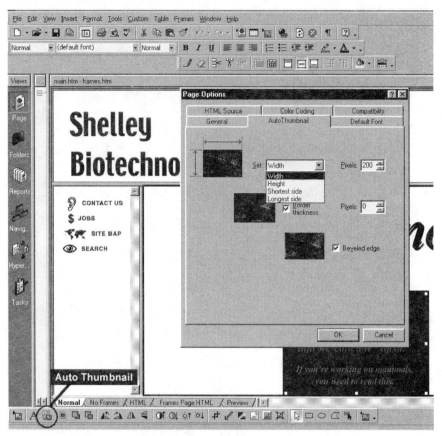

FIGURE 2–26 Image Formatting toolbar—Auto Thumbnail icon.

◆ Tables

Creating tables in FrontPage is easy, even easier in FrontPage 2002. You can create plain tables, borderless tables to aid in layout, tables with exciting borders and backgrounds, nested tables, and so on. FrontPage helps take the complicated coding out of creating tables. There are some things to consider when getting creative with tables; for instance, one thing to consider is browser compatibility. I will point out other known issues in each section.

First, let's set up our Table toolbar in the FrontPage Editor. To do this, select Toolbars then Tables from the View menu at the top of the FrontPage Editor (see Figure 2–27).

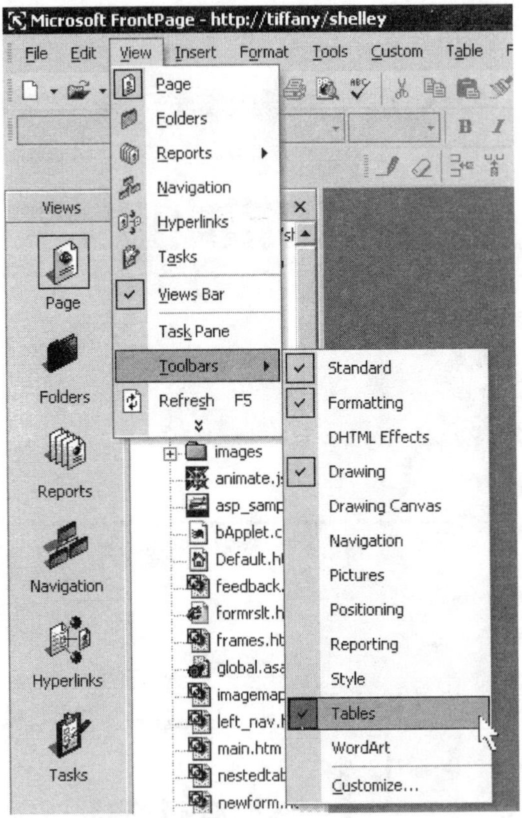

FIGURE 2–27 Tables selection of Toolbars menu.

Selecting the Tables toolbar will create a floating toolbar in FrontPage. You may use it like this and close it after you are finished with it, or you can drag it into your standard toolbars on the top of your screen for a more permanent location if you intend to use the table tools often, which I do (see Figures 2–28 and 2–29).

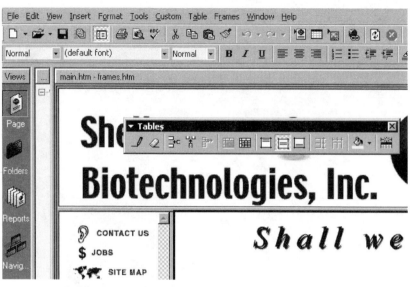

FIGURE 2–28 Floating Tables toolbar.

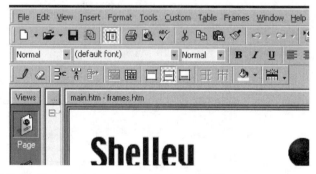

FIGURE 2–29 Drag and drop toolbar to top of Editor.

To insert a table on your Web page:

- From the Table menu, select Insert then Table. The Insert Table dialog box offers just a few initial configuration options for your new table, such as width, alignment, cell spacing, cell padding, number of cells, number of rows, and border width (see Figure 2–30).

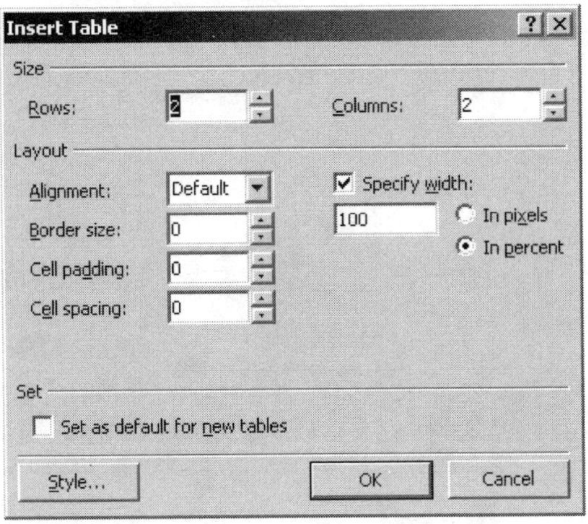

FIGURE 2–30 Insert Table dialog box.

- These options can be further enhanced in the Table Properties dialog box. Place your cursor within a cell in your new table and right-click. Select Table Properties from the menu.
- The Table Properties dialog box allows you to set many options for your table, such as border colors, background colors, and even a background image. Setting the Float option will allow you to set up a small table that allows text to wrap or flow around it to the right or left. Once your table is inserted, you can further customize the table using the draw and erase tools and setting properties specifically for each cell (see Figure 2–31).

If you create a table in FrontPage that is coded to 0 borders, meaning you do not have visible table borders in Normal view, FrontPage will show you the table with a dashed line. If you start with the default settings of 2 rows and 2 columns, then realize that you need more cells, rows, or columns, grab your Draw tool from your Tables toolbar and get to work (see Figure 2–32).

- To create a cell that spans some or all of the rows of a table, the Erase tool can be extremely handy and quick to handle the task. Click the Erase icon on the Tables toolbar, and left-click and hold the mouse as you move over the line you wish to remove. When the border you want erased turns

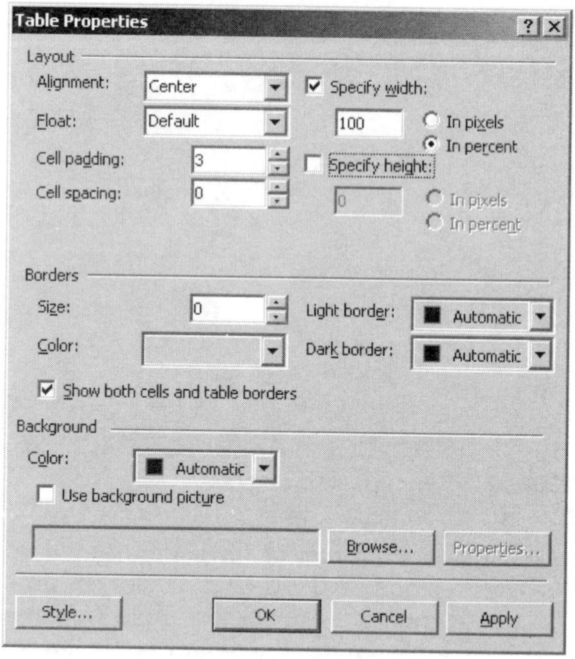

FIGURE 2–31 Table Properties dialog box.

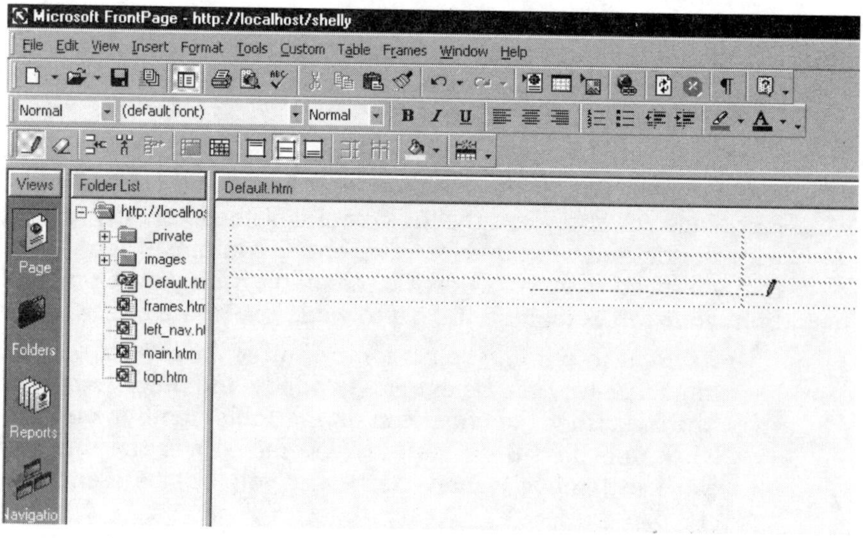

FIGURE 2–32 Draw tool—Tables toolbar.

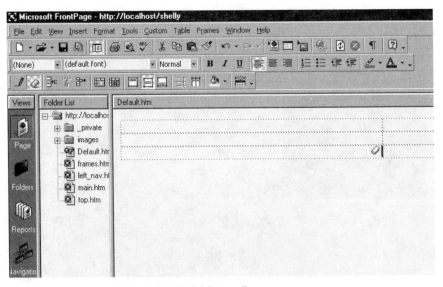

FIGURE 2–33 Erase tool—Tables toolbar.

red, let go of the mouse button, and that line/border will be removed (see Figure 2–33). If more is erased than you intended, fear not! FrontPage has a very handy Undo command in the Edit menu. It will undo everything you have done since you last saved your work, too.

• Now let's add some color and customize a cell in this table, as well as use some of the align options. First, insert an image in the bottom cell (see the "Images in FrontPage Webs" section in this chapter).

• Next, right-click inside this cell and select Cell Properties from the menu.

• In the Cell Properties dialog box, set the following options (also see Figure 2–34):
  – Set Horizontal alignment to Center.
  – Specify width should remain on the default setting, 100, and In percent should be checked.
  – Change the Background Color to black in the drop-down menu.
  – Click OK.

• Your image should now be centered in the cell, and the entire cell should be black in color.

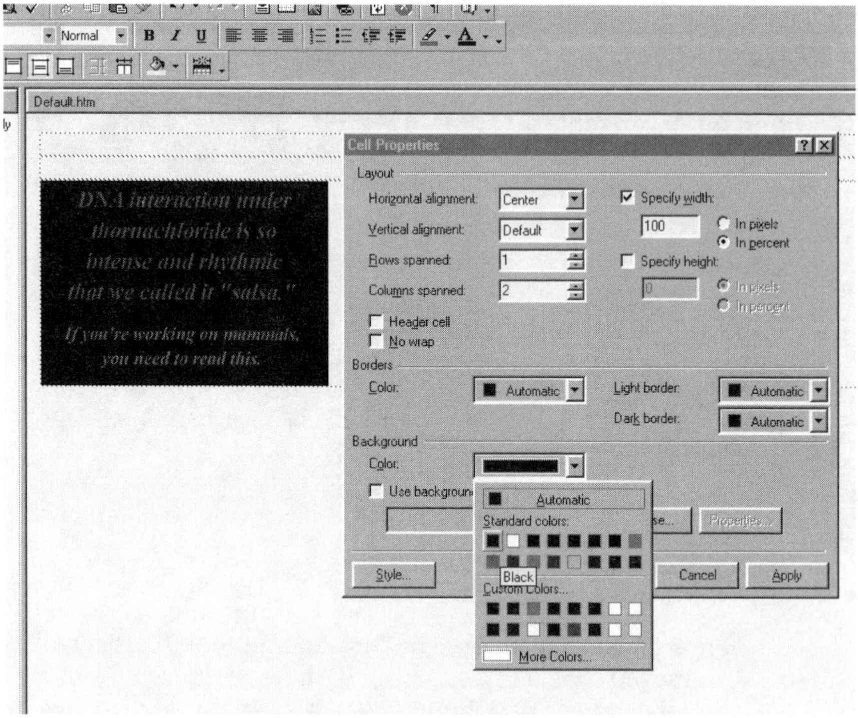

FIGURE 2–34 Cell Properties dialog box.

Nested Tables

There are many uses for nested tables. Many designers use a table to contain all of the content of a Web page and control the width of a page. Using pixel widths for the table size, the contents can be controlled to remain at a width that will accommodate viewers using an 800x600 resolution browser window or even smaller. Using percentage widths for the table properties, a designer can create a page that will expand or contract according to the viewer's monitor or browser's window size. The percentage widths depend on the contents not exceeding a fixed pixel width; for example, if you set a table to 100% and place two images in any particular cell of the table side by side, and those two images' widths equal 850 pixels, the table will contract to a width of only 850 pixels, rather than contracting to 640 or less when viewed by a user who has a 640x480 screen resolution.

Nested tables can be used within a main page table to create the appearance of "boxes" with highlighted information or to create a set of columns on a page. In this section, we will create a page that uses a table for the contents, then we will nest tables within this main table.

We will start with a new page in our Shelley Biotechnologies web. First, we will insert the main table on the page:

- Select Insert then Table from the Table menu.
- In the Insert Table dialog box (see Figure 2–30), set the width to 100%. Leave the default Columns and Rows set at 2 each, and add a Cell padding of 3.
- We will draw and erase cells that we need and don't need, respectively. To start, erase the cell divider in the top row, making the top row one wide cell that spans the width of the two columns below it.
- Right-click inside this cell and select Cell Properties from the menu. In the Cell Properties dialog box, select Center for the Horizontal alignment of the cell (see Figure 2–35).

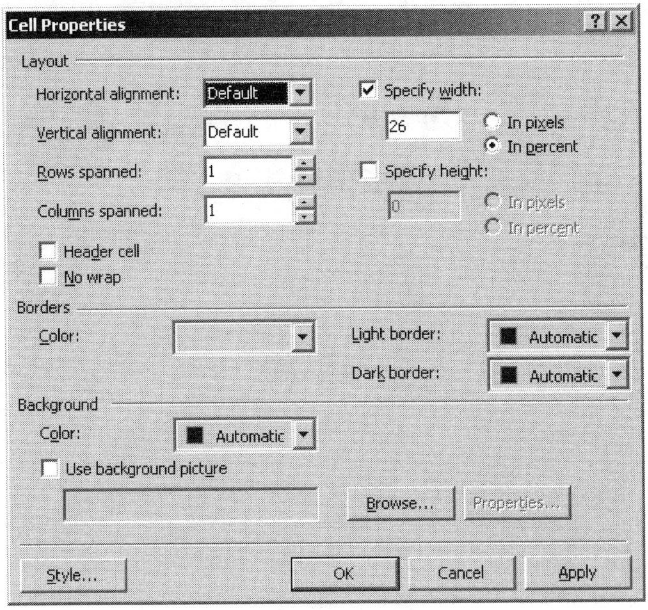

FIGURE 2–35 Cell Properties dialog box.

- Now, insert an image in the top cell. This image will be centered in the cell and appear centered on the page at any browser width because the table is set to 100% width.
- Using the Draw tool, draw a cell to create another cell just under the top cell that spans the width of the two columns below it (see Figure 2–36).
- In the new cell just below the top cell with the centered image, we will nest a table. This nested table will hold our navigation buttons in cells of their own so that they appear to be side by side. We use a nested table so that we can set the width of the nested table to the total width of the buttons, rather than having spaces between the buttons as they try to expand the to 100% width of the main table. We have four navigation buttons we want to use at the top of the page. Using a nested table, we can center the table in the cell and have the buttons appear to be side by side.

FIGURE 2–36 Drawing a new top cell.

Place your cursor in the cell just under the top cell with the image. Select Insert then Table from the Table menu.

- In the Insert Table dialog box, set the Rows to 1 and the Columns to 4. This will create a one-row table with four cells, one cell for each button.
- Set the Alignment to Center.
- Uncheck the Specify width option. When we insert the button graphics into the cells, FrontPage will automatically set the total width of the nested table.
- Set the following options to 0:
  - Borders
  - Cell padding
  - Cell spacing
- Place your cursor in each cell and insert one button graphic in each of the four cells in your nested table (see Figure 2–37).

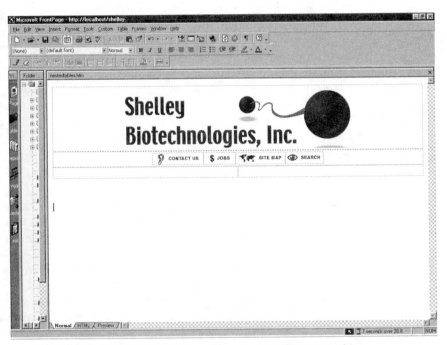

FIGURE 2–37 Nested table with navigation button graphics.

NOTE:
Remember, the graphics used in this book may be downloaded and used at the Web site that accompanies this book, *www.phptr.com/ essential/frontpage2002.*

- Lastly, you may want to add items in the same cell as the nested table outside of the nested table; for example, you may add a horizontal line under the nested table. The easiest way to do this is to place your cursor at the far right cell of the nested table. This will highlight the button graphic in that last cell. With that graphic highlighted, use your right arrow key to get the cursor flashing next to the button. Hold the <Ctrl> key on your keyboard and press the <Enter> key one time. This will force the cursor out of the nested table and place it below the nested table in the cell. Now you may insert a horizontal bar from the Insert menu.

Another example of using nested tables is to give the appearance of text wrapping around an image. For this example, we will nest a table in the left column of the main table, just under the top two cells in which we centered an image and a nested table with navigation buttons.

- Place your cursor in the left cell of the main table.
- Select Insert then Table from the Table menu.
- In the Insert Table dialog box, set the Rows to 3 and the Columns to 2.
- Set the Cell padding to 3—this will give a little padding between the image we will insert and the text that will appear to wrap around the image. Leave the Cell spacing and Borders set to 0.
- Set the width of the nested table to 80%. This will allow the table to fill 80% of the cell in which it is nested.
- Erase the divider between the top two cells in the top row, allowing the top row to span the width of the two columns below it. Remove the bottom cell divider, as well, so that we have only two cells in the center row of the table. The top and bottom rows of the table will be only one cell each.
- In the top cell, add the text "Meet the President" (do not type the quotation marks).

- In the center left cell, right-click and select Cell Properties. Set the Horizontal alignment to Center and insert the photograph image.
- In the right center cell, right-click and select Cell Properties. Set the Vertical alignment to Top (see Figure 2–38). This will allow the text added to this cell to begin at the top of the cell, rather than at the default, which is the middle of the cell.
- Now enter enough text in the cell to the right of the photograph to fill the cell to nearly the bottom of the photograph. The rest of the text will be added to the cell below the center two cells, creating the appearance of the text wrapping the image (see Figure 2–39).

Nested tables can also be nested inside each other to create even more effects. For example, we will create a "box" appearance around a nested table. Nesting a main table with a border in the right cell of the page we have been working with, then nesting a table within that will create this effect.

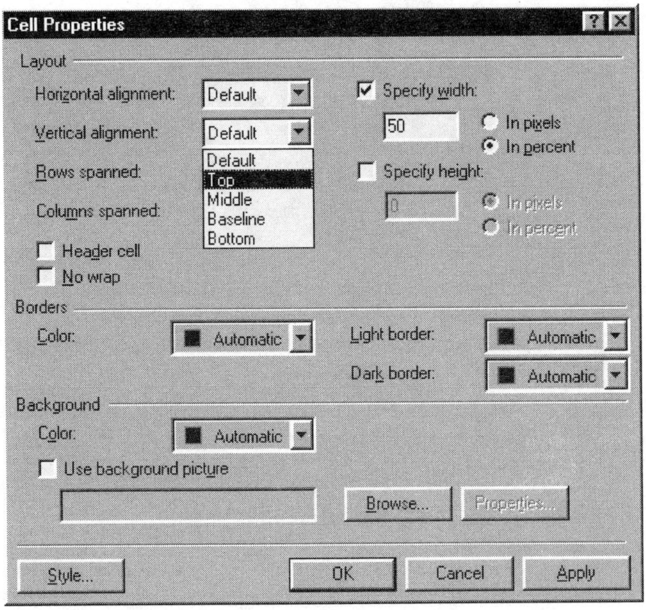

FIGURE 2–38 Cell Properties dialog box—Vertical alignment.

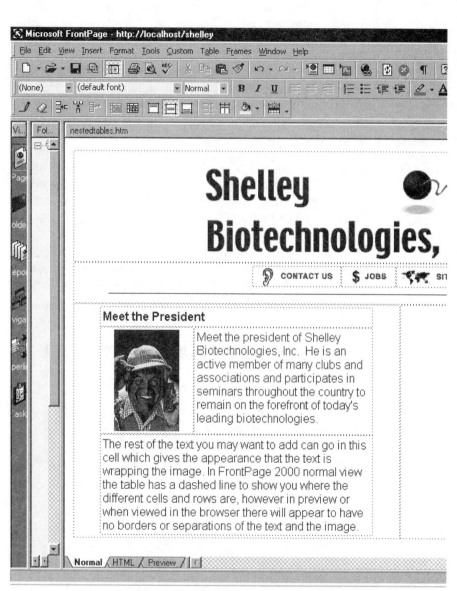

FIGURE 2–39a Nested table in Normal view.

- Place your cursor in the right main cell of the main table on the page.
- Right-click inside this cell and select Cell Properties.
- Click the dropdown menu next to Vertical alignment and choose Top from this menu. Click OK.

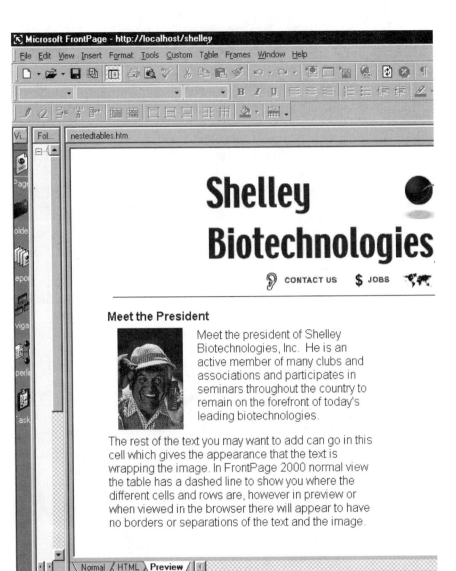

FIGURE 2–39b Nested table in Preview view.

- Select Insert, then Table from the Table menu.
- In the Insert Table dialog box, enter 1 for both the Rows and Columns options.
- Select Center as the Alignment.
- Enter 1 in the Borders properties.

- Enter 5 in the Cell padding—this will create a 5-pixel padding around the table that we will nest inside this table.
- Make sure there is a 0 in the Cell spacing property.
- Select 80% in the Specify width option.
- Click OK.
- This will create a one-cell table nested in the right cell of the main page table. This table will have the default border color, which is gray.
- Right-click inside this nested table and select Table Properties from the menu.
- Next to the Borders settings in the Table Properties dialog box, click the arrow next to Color to select Black as the border color (see Figure 2–40).
- Next, select the color for the background of the table by clicking the arrow next to Color in the Background section (see Figure 2–41).
- Click OK.
- With the cursor inside the one-cell table we just added, select Insert. then Table from the Table menu again.
- Allow the default, 2 Columns and 2 Rows.
- Set a Specify width option of 100%.

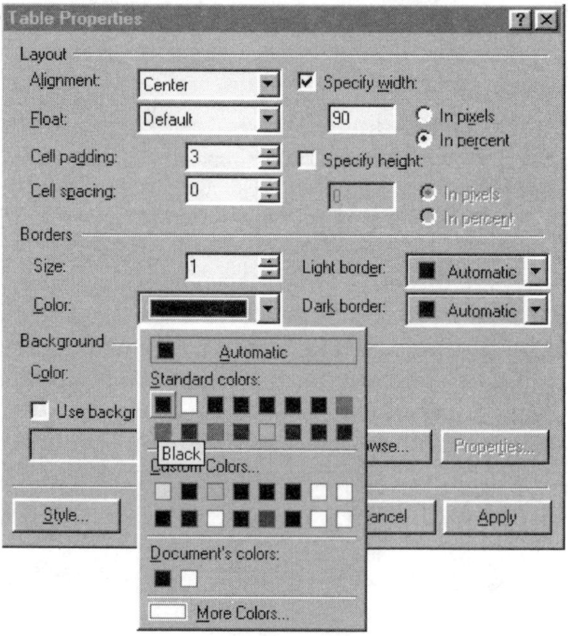

FIGURE 2–40 Table Properties dialog box—Border Color.

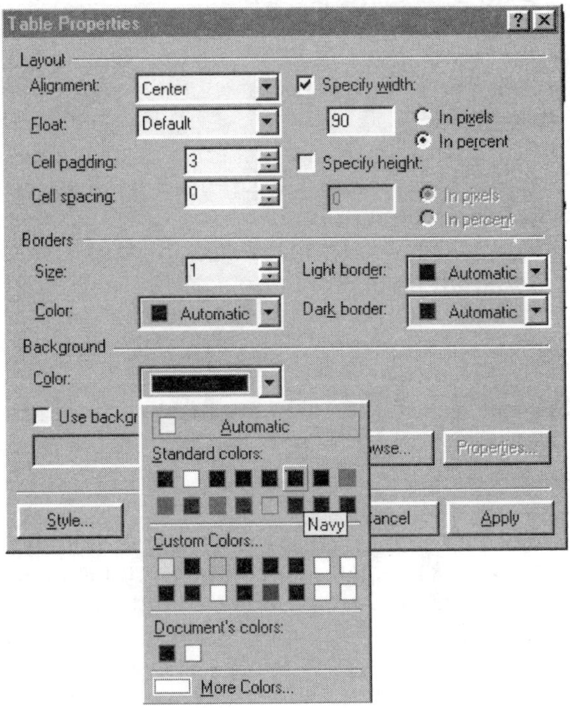

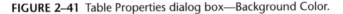

FIGURE 2–41 Table Properties dialog box—Background Color.

- Set Borders to 0.
- Set Cell padding to 5.
- Leave Cell spacing at 0.
- Click OK.
- Right-click inside this nested table and select Table Properties.
- Select White from the Background Color option (see Figure 2–35) to create a white background color for this nested table.
- Add a bold heading in the top left cell, such as "Genetic News," and a bold heading to the top right cell, such as "Latest Products."
- In each of the cells below these headings, right-click and select Cell Properties from the menu.
- Select Top for the Vertical alignment of each cell.
- Add to each cell any text or information that you want highlighted on the site; for example, see Figure 2–42.

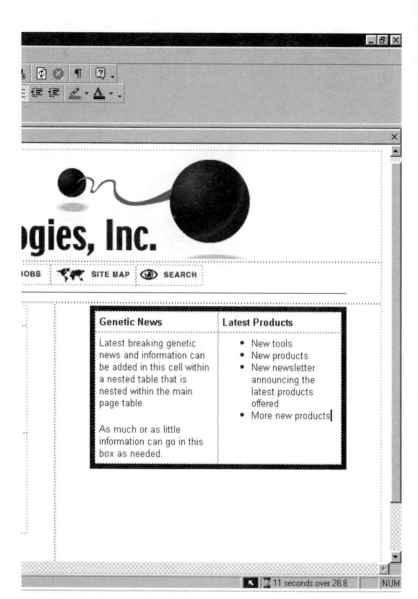

FIGURE 2–42a Nested tables in Normal view.

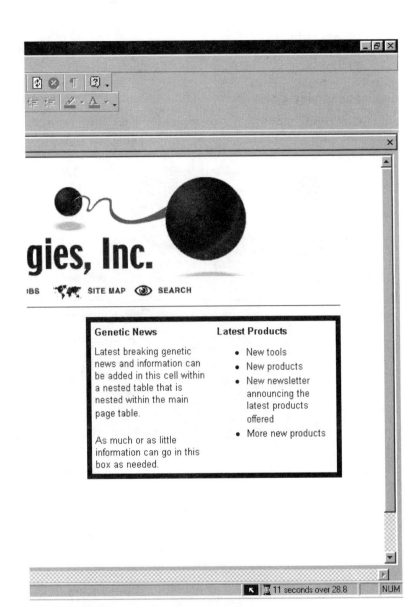

FIGURE 2–42b Nested tables in Preview view.

Experiment with different widths of nested tables, different cell padding and cell spacing options, and different border colors and sizes.

Background Images in Tables

Background images are supported in both IE versions 3 and 4 and NN version 4 browsers. They are not supported in NN version 3, however. The way the browsers handle them is another story. IE tiles the image throughout the table (Figure 2–43a), whereas NN places the image separately in each cell (Figure 2–43b).

FIGURE 2–43a IE background image in table.

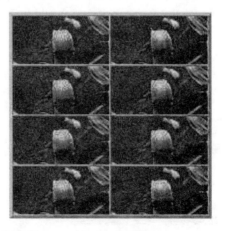

FIGURE 2–43b NN background image in table.

FIGURE 2–44 Background image in each cell in NN.

Guess what? There is no known cure for Netscape. Testing an idea of creating a table that was one cell only, then nesting another table within that one-celled table and creating several cells without a border, Netscape *still* managed to create the same look as above by placing the background image in each individual cell (see Figure 2–44).

If you use a background image in the table, then specify a background color in the Cell Properties dialog box, the results will be as follows:

- IE 3 and 4—the cell shows the BGCOLOR, not the background image.
- NN 4—the cell shows the background image. If you want Netscape to show the BGCOLOR in a cell, you must manually add the word *background* in the HTML view in the <TD> tag preceding the cell that uses the bgcolor attribute. That sounds complicated, but is easily done:
  - Place your cursor in the cell in which you want the color, rather than the image, to show and click once.
  - Click the HTML View tab at the bottom of the screen in the FrontPage Editor (doing this will enable you to see the part of the code you need to edit as soon as you click the HTML tab, rather than having to search through code that you may not understand). The HTML tag that codes the table cells looks like this:

```
<TD> or <td bgcolor="#FFFFFF">
```
- Add the word *background* to the cell that shows the `bgcolor` attribute, changing it simply to:

```
<td background bgcolor="#FFFFFF">
```
- Select File then Save. The background color for that cell will now display correctly in NN 4 browsers, as well as in IE.

NN 4, IE 3, and IE 4 all support a background image in a cell.

New FrontPage 2002 Table Features

FrontPage 2002 has built in several new and exciting table features. These features enable you to create exciting and professional-looking tables in just a couple of clicks of your mouse. These features include:

- Table Auto Format
- Table Fill
- Table Split

TABLE AUTO FORMAT

The Table Auto Format tool is located on the Table toolbar and becomes available after you have inserted a table on your page. When clicked, this tool gives you several present format options to choose from that you can apply to your table, making formatting cells, colors, and table borders an effortless task. To use the tool:

- Insert a table on your Web page.
- Click the Table Auto Format button on the Table toolbar to launch the Table Auto Format dialog box (see Figure 2–45).
- Under Formats, you have many preset formats to choose from. Highlight one of them to see the preview in the preview pane on the right.
- In the Formats to apply, choose the items that you want to include in your table format. Add and remove check marks in these boxes and view the preview of the effect.
- Under Apply special formats, there are several options to choose. Again, add and remove check marks in these boxes to achieve the desired format for your table and see a preview of the effects in the preview window.

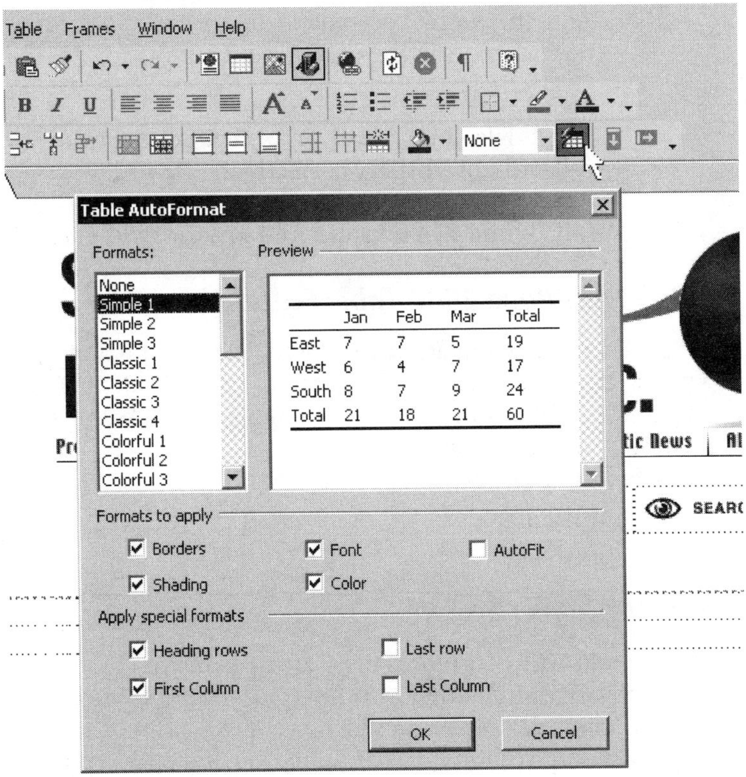

FIGURE 2–45 Table Auto Format dialog box.

• Click OK when you have made your selections, and the formatting will be applied to your table. You can further customize your table using the Table, Draw, and Erase tools.

Another way to use Table Auto Format is with the Quick Toolbar dropdown menu. This option allows you to add a format selection quickly without going through the Auto Format Properties dialog box.

• With your cursor placed in any cell of your table that you want to format quickly, click the Table Auto Format dropdown menu and select one of the preset formats available (see Figure 2–46).

FrontPage 2002 will apply those changes immediately to your table.

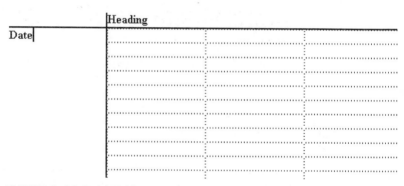

FIGURE 2–46 Quick Table Auto Format dropdown menu.

TABLE AUTO FILL

When you have content in one cell that you need in many cells of your table, instead of having to copy and paste into each individual cell, you can use the Auto Fill tools to copy automatically into the cells next to the content or in the same column.

For example, let's assume that you have a table set up that has 5 columns and 12 rows. In each column, you need a date entered, and each heading at the top of the columns is the same. We will type in some text to use for the heading and the word *Date* in the cells and use Auto Fill to copy the text automatically into the other cells we need (see Figure 2–47).

By placing the cursor into the cell with the word Heading in it and clicking and dragging across the table cells on the top, you can highlight the top four cells. Then click the Auto Fill right button, and FrontPage 2002 will copy *Heading* into each of the cells (see Figure 2–48).

The same can be done to copy the word *Date* into each of the left cells below it or to copy images from one cell to several more cells, either to the right or below.

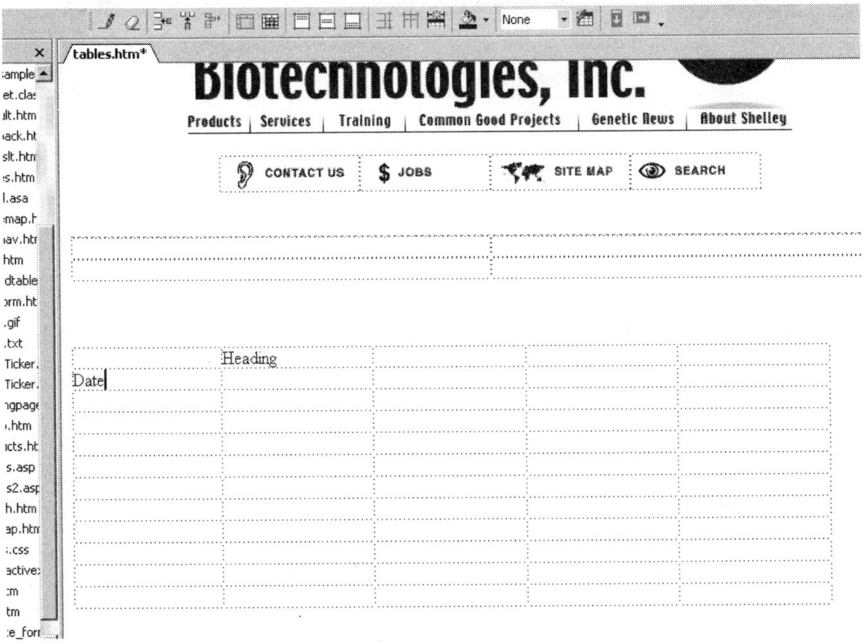

FIGURE 2–47 Auto Fill tool.

FIGURE 2–48 Auto Fill right.

TABLE SPLIT

Another new Table tool in FrontPage 2002 is the Table Split tool. If you ever create a large table with several columns and rows and realize that you need to split the table into two or more different tables, the Table Split feature makes quick work of it. Rather then having to create a whole new table with new formatting and cell formatting, you can simply split the table. To split a table:

- Place your cursor in the middle of the table where you want the table split.
- Select Table Split from the Table menu (see Figure 2–49).

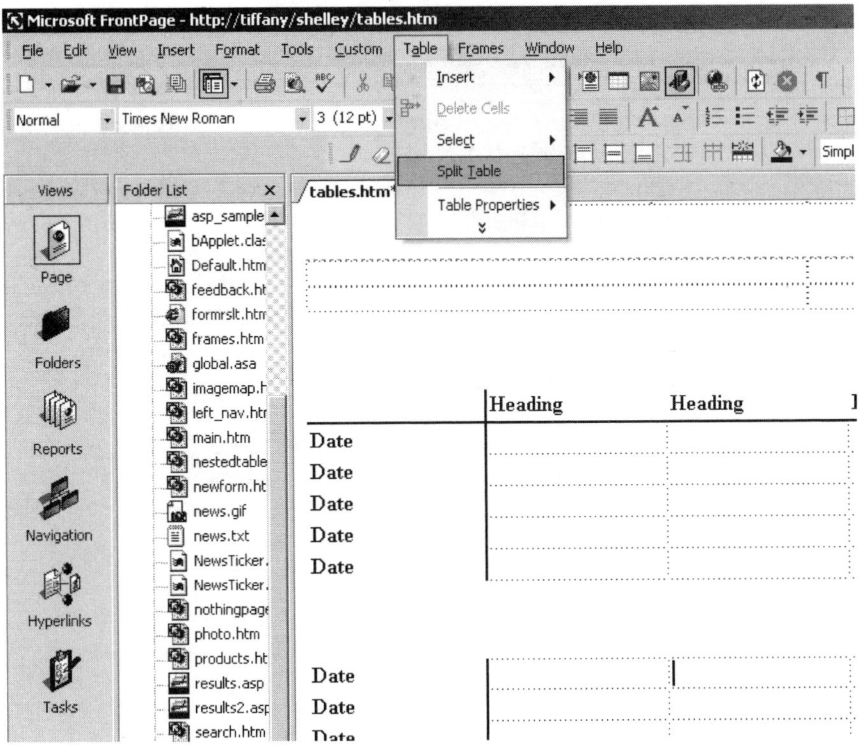

FIGURE 2–49 Table Split.

◆ Recap

In this chapter, you learned some key points in preparing to create a solid Web site using FrontPage 2002. Overall, we covered opening the program, creating a web, good file structure, and browser compatibility issues. We also discussed some of the basic tools to begin working with and building your web.

◆ Advanced Project

Create the Shelley Biotechnologies Web site using the skills you have learned in this chapter.

1. Start by creating a one-page web, making sure to save it to a location you will easily recall.
2. Create and set up your global settings before starting on the Web page. Remember to define your audience and set the compatibility options.
3. Explore the different views in FrontPage and the different reports available.
4. Import your images into your *images* folder
5. Open the *Default.htm* page and create a table on the page. Use the formatting tools we reviewed in this chapter to create a calendar.
6. Close the web and FrontPage.

3 Adding and Using FrontPage Components and Features

IN THIS CHAPTER

- Which Components Require FrontPage Extensions?
- Editing Web Pages
- Forms, Discussion Webs, Hit Counters, and More
- Photo Gallery
- Interactive Content
- Global Site Editing
- Recap
- Advanced Project

◆ Which Components Require FrontPage Extensions?

FrontPage comes with built-in features and components that, when published to a server that has FrontPage server extensions installed, work without additional programming or script installations. Features such as forms, hit counters and search features are FrontPage components that can be added and configured to your FrontPage Web, but require that the server the files are published to is also running the FrontPage server extensions.

If you are publishing to a server that does not have the FrontPage server extensions installed, you will need to know what components require the extensions on the server so that you can avoid using them.

If you are publishing to a server that has an older version of the FrontPage server extensions installed, it is helpful to know which FrontPage 2002 features won't work as well.

Features that Require at Least FrontPage 98 Server Extensions

The following components will run fine with either FrontPage 2002 or FrontPage 98 extensions:

- Confirmation Field
- Discussion Form Handler
- FrontPage-Created Server-Side Image Maps
- Hit Counter
- Registration Form Handler
- Save Results Form Handler
- Search Form

Features that Require at Least FrontPage 2000 Server Extensions

These features will not work with anything less than or older than FrontPage 2000 extensions:

- Database Results Wizard
- Send to Database Form Handler
- Nested Subwebs
- Lightweight Source Control (document check-in/check-out without VSS)
- Categories Component
- Style Sheet Links to Multiple Files or ASP Files

Features that Require FrontPage 2002 Server Extensions

The following features are new to FrontPage 2002 and will work only with FrontPage 2002 server extensions

- File Upload
- Custom Link Bars
- Shared Border Background Properties
- Usage Analysis Reports

- Top Ten List Web Components
- New Security Features (User Roles)

Features that Require FrontPage 2002 Server Extensions and SharePoint Team Services

- Document Library
- List
- Survey
- Team Discussion Board (this is not the same feature as the Discussion Web Wizard)
- List and Document Library Views
- List Forms
- SharePoint Team Web Site Wizard

◆ Editing Web Pages

To edit your Web pages, you must first open your FrontPage web. If you have the Personal Web Server (PWS) or Internet Information Server (IIS) installed on your computer, you will be able to open your web via the server by typing in the URL in the Folder name box of the Open Web dialog box.

To open your *shelley* web that you created in the last chapter, if it was created against your PWS or IIS on *localhost*:

- Open FrontPage.
  - In the File menu, select Open Web, and the Open Web dialog box will open (see Figure 3–1).
  - In the Folder name box at the bottom of Open Web dialog box, type in *http://localhost/shelley* (that is, if you named the web we created in the previous chapter *shelley*). Figure 3–1 shows the Open Web dialog box.
  - The next time you open the Open Web dialog box, you will see a shortcut to *shelley on localhost* Under My Network Places
  - If you do not have the PWS installed and you stored your web on your hard drive, use the Look in drop-down menu at the top of the Open Web dialog box (see Figure 3–1) to navigate to the web's location on your hard drive.

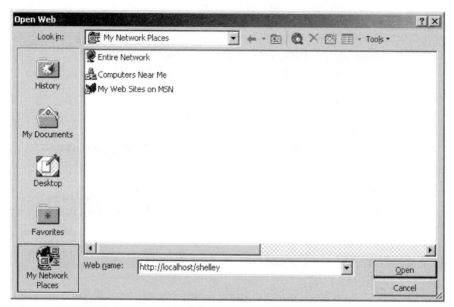

FIGURE 3–1 Open Web dialog box—Web Folders.

Hyperlinks

Adding a hyperlink in FrontPage is very simple. You may hyperlink text or images in much the same way. To add a hyperlink to a block of text, select the text you want to hyperlink by left-clicking on your mouse at the beginning of the word, text, or sentence, drag the mouse to the end of that block of text, and let go. The text you want to hyperlink should now be highlighted for you. Now, right-click on your mouse and choose Hyperlink from the menu, or click the Hyperlink icon (see Figure 3–2) from the toolbar at the top of the FrontPage Editor.

In the Insert Hyperlink dialog box, you may enter a full URL to a page outside of your web, or you can choose a file or page from within your web in the window just under the Look in drop-down menu (see Figure 3–3).

The Insert Hyperlink dialog box includes the Target frame selection. By clicking the Target Frame button on the right of the dialog box, you can choose a target for your hyperlink in the Target dialog box. Selections in this dialog box include:

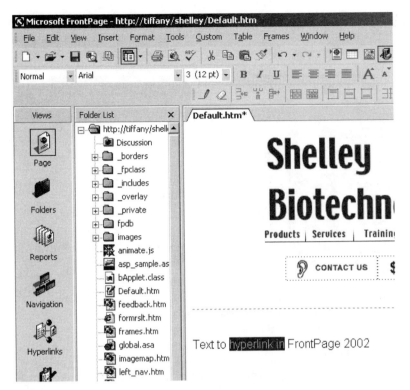

FIGURE 3–2 Adding a hyperlink to text.

- Page Default—This is the default target chosen, which is no target selected.
- Same Frame—Used in framesets, this targets a hyperlink to open in the same frame.
- Whole Page—This forces a target to open in the full browser; useful in frames if you want a target to open in a whole browser window, rather than in the frameset.
- New Window—This opens the target link in a new browser window.
- Parent Frame—This is also used in frames; it loads the document into the immediate frameset parent of the current frame. This value is equivalent to _self if the current frame has no parent.

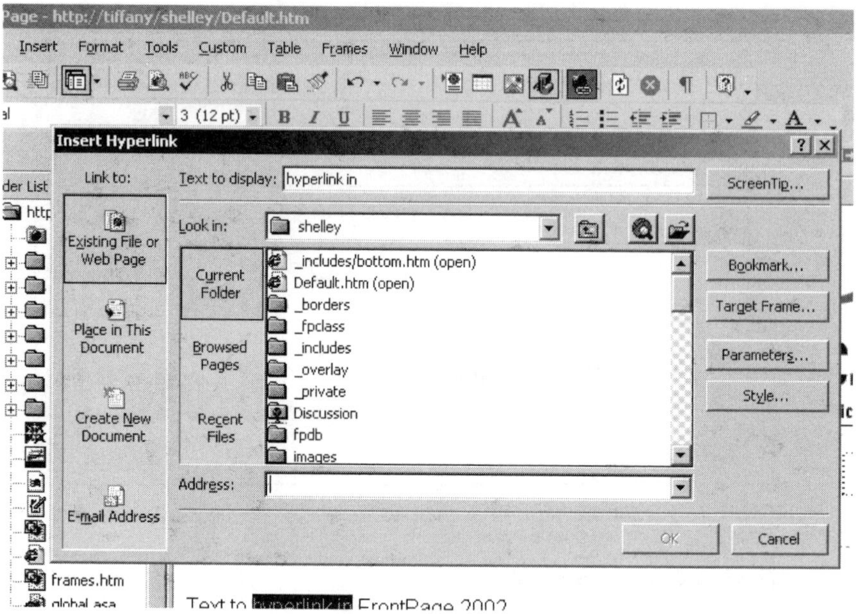

FIGURE 3–3 Create Hyperlink dialog box.

MAILTO HYPERLINKS

Click the E-mail Address button on the bottom left of the Insert Hyperlink dialog. This screen is where you create a hyperlink that will launch the visitors email software and send an email from the site. Enter the email address that you want linked or select an email address from the recently added email addresses box on the bottom (if applicable). You may also enter a line in this screen for the subject line of the email address. Click the OK button to complete this task (see Figure 3–4).

Note about Mailto hyperlinks with subject lines

Some email clients will not add anything past the first space into the subject line of an email message. To keep the entire message intact, add underscores in the subject line instead of spaces, for example:

mailto:test@shelleybio.com?subject="Shelley_Biotechnologies_email_request"

To have a Mailto hyperlink sent to more than one email address using the CC field, add the following to the Mailto line in the Create Hyperlink dialog box:

mailto:id@company.com?Cc=id2@company.com?Subject="Subject_test"

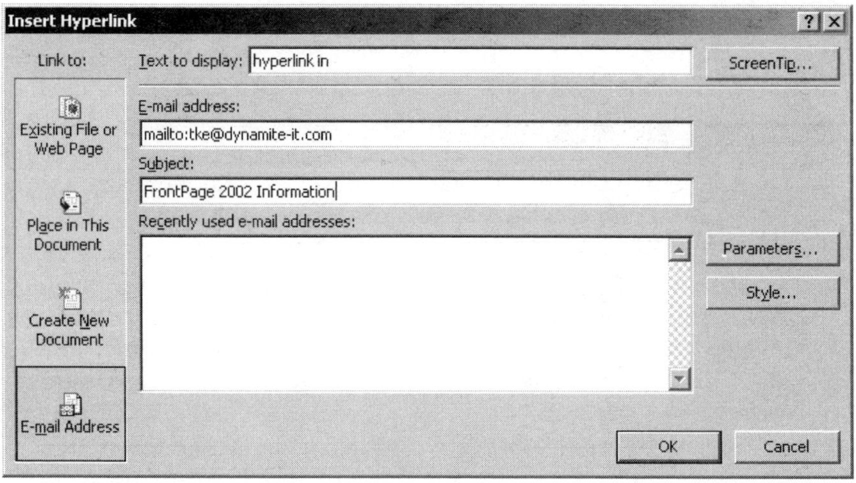

FIGURE 3-4 Insert Hyperlink—E-mail Address.

BOOKMARK HYPERLINKS

Bookmarks are hyperlinks that link to a "spot" on a page. One of the more popular uses of the bookmark hyperlink is the Top of Page links that, when clicked, take the visitor back to the top of the page. To create a bookmark link, you must insert the bookmark onto the page where you want visitors taken when they click on the bookmark link.

Let's create a bookmark on a page for the Top of Page link, then create the Top of Page hyperlink.

- Place your cursor at the highest point on the top of your Web page that you can.
- Select Bookmark from the Insert menu, or press and hold the <Ctrl> key on your keyboard and press the <G> key at the same time to open the Insert Bookmark dialog box.
- Type in *top* for the bookmark name and click the OK button. Your bookmark is marked in normal view only as a blue flag. FrontPage does this to let you know at a glance that you have a bookmark in place, but this flag will not show in preview or in the browser.
- Now place your cursor on your page where you would like to create a Top of Page hyperlink, usually at the bottom of the page, and type the text *Top of Page*.
- Highlight the *Top of Page* text and either:

- Click the Hyperlink button or
- Right-click and select Hyperlink from the popout menu to launch the Insert Hyperlink dialog box.
- Click the Bookmark button on the right and highlight the *top* bookmark that is threaded under the Bookmarks menu (see Figure 3–5).
- This hyperlink will take the viewer to a bookmarked place on the page, which in this example is the top of the page. You can create several bookmarks on a page.

Another common use for the bookmark is a directory listing. When you have numerous members in a directory and you want to give your site visitors a way to view members by last name, state, or some other variable, you can use the bookmark feature for this.

To link to a bookmark on another page, in the Insert Hyperlink dialog box, highlight the page to which you want to link. Then click the Bookmark button. This enables FrontPage to load the bookmarks from the highlighted page into the Select Place in the Document dialog box.

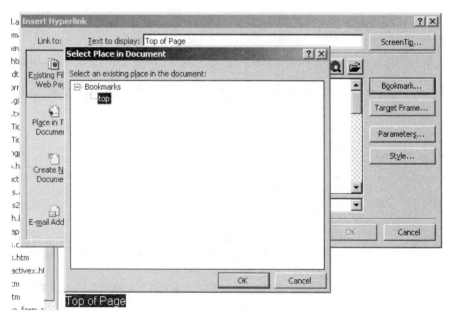

FIGURE 3–5 Select Place in Document dialog box—Insert a Bookmark.

◆ Forms, Discussion Webs, Hit Counters, and More

FrontPage 2002 is loaded with dynamic and interactive features that are easily configured, edited, and maintained in FrontPage. These are features that would otherwise need to be configured on the server by installing scripts to handle results, interactivity, and other dynamic features. These features do require that the Web server hosting the web have FrontPage server extensions installed correctly. We will discuss this in more detail later in the book, along with publishing your finished web and resources for hosting companies that provide FrontPage server extensions.

If you find that you must have your web hosted on a server that does not have FrontPage extensions, you can use outside scripts to handle features such as forms and CGI-based discussion boards. It is usually a matter of installing the scripts on the server in the cgi-bin, then adding the proper code in the HTML view in the FrontPage Editor in forms or on the page as needed.

Forms

Among the many valuable and helpful templates available in the New Page dialog box are the Form Page wizard and several premade forms ready for you to configure and use with your own web. The premade forms have been designed with form fields that are found in typical forms so that you have a good foundation from which to build. The Form Page wizard is a great tool for creating your own custom forms by answering several questions in a step-by-step manner.

THE FORM PAGE WIZARD

This wizard will walk you through the process of creating a custom form tailored to suit the needs of the form page for your web. To start the wizard:

- Select New from the File menu.
- Select Page or Web from the New menu.
- In the Task pane on the right, click the link to Page Templates. You will see the New Page dialog box. In it are many

options that you may wish to explore, one being the Form Page wizard (see Figure 3–6).

- You will be greeted with a dialog box that tells you that you will be walked through several questions to help you create your form. Click the Next button.
- The next step is to add the questions you want asked in your form. Click the Add button (see Figure 3–7a) in this dialog box to bring up the next screen, which has many options for the criteria of your form (see Figure 3–7b).

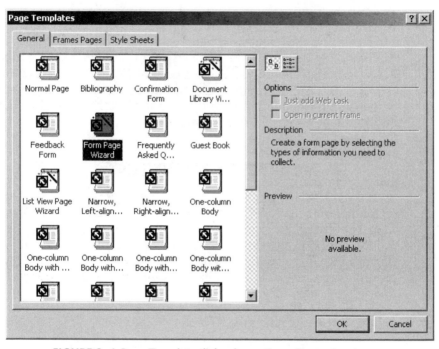

FIGURE 3–6 Page Template dialog box—Form Page wizard.

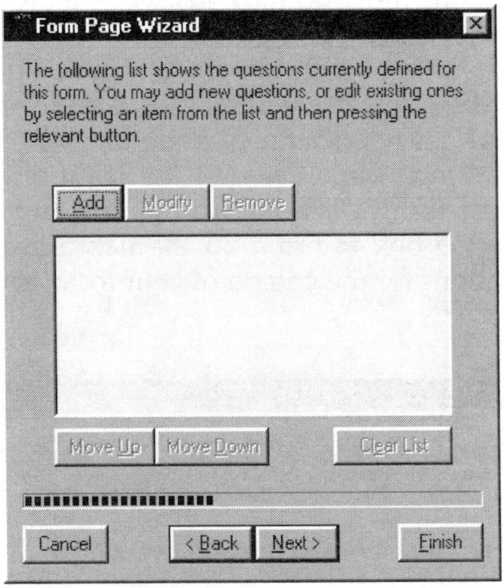

FIGURE 3–7a Click the Add button.

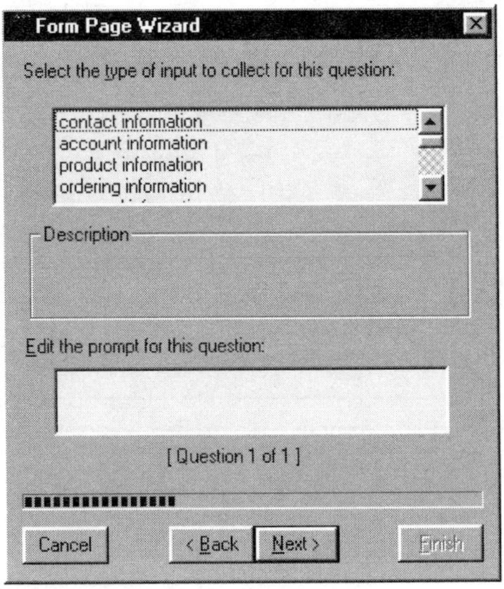

FIGURE 3–7b Form criteria.

- In the add questions screen, shown in Figure 3–7b, select the type of information you want added to your form and click the Next button. For example, select *contact information*.
- The next dialog box will allow you to choose the specific type of "contact information" to include in your form (see Figure 3–8).
- Click the Next button after selecting the specific contact information fields you want added to your form. You will then be taken back to the add questions screen shown in Figure 3–7a. You may repeat the steps of adding more questions from this dialog box until you are finished adding all of the questions and types of information you want to gather with your form. Once you have completed the process of adding all of the information to your form, click the Next button in the add questions screen (Figure 3–7a).
- The next step in the Form Page wizard is to select your presentation options. This step allows you to choose some formatting options for how you would like your forms page and form fields presented on your form Web page (see Figure 3–9).

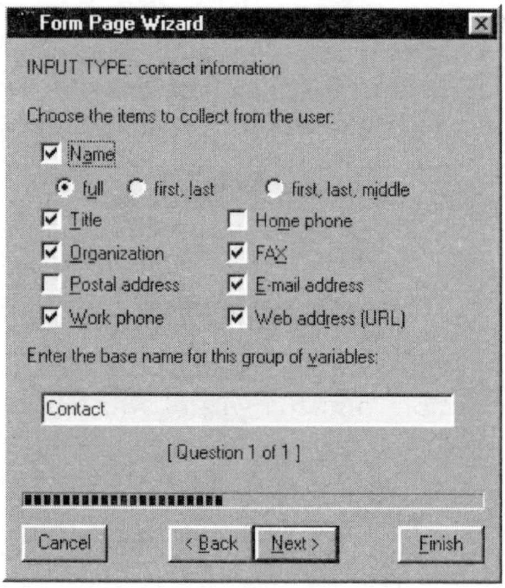

FIGURE 3–8 Input type screen—Form Page wizard.

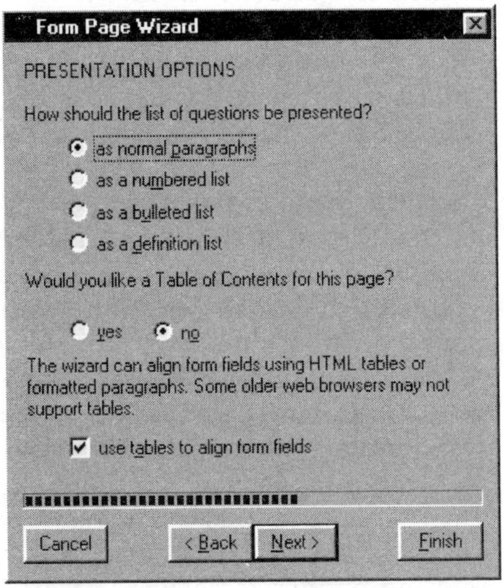

FIGURE 3–9 Presentation options screen—Form Page wizard.

- After you have made your selections in the presentation options screen, click the Next button.
- The next step is to choose where you want the results of your form sent. You may choose to have the results of your form sent to you by email after you have completed the Form Page wizard. This wizard gives you the options of saving the results to a text file or Web page on the server, or to use a custom CGI script (see Figure 3–10).
- For this example, we chose the save results to a Web page option. There are additional output formatting options that can be selected and customized after the form is completed. We will go over those options later in this chapter.
- Once you have selected your output options, click the Next button, and the wizard will tell you that you have completed all the questions for your form. Click Finish to see your new form page. The new form page will look something like Figure 3–11.

You may now format the look of your new form page to match the look of other pages in your web. Right-click on the page, choose Page Properties, and select the page background colors and hyperlink colors for your page, as well as the page title. From the Format menu, select Shared Borders to add any shared

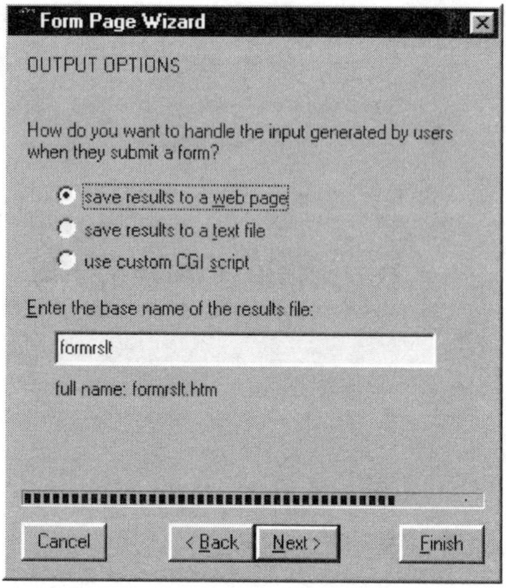

FIGURE 3–10 Output options screen—Form Page wizard.

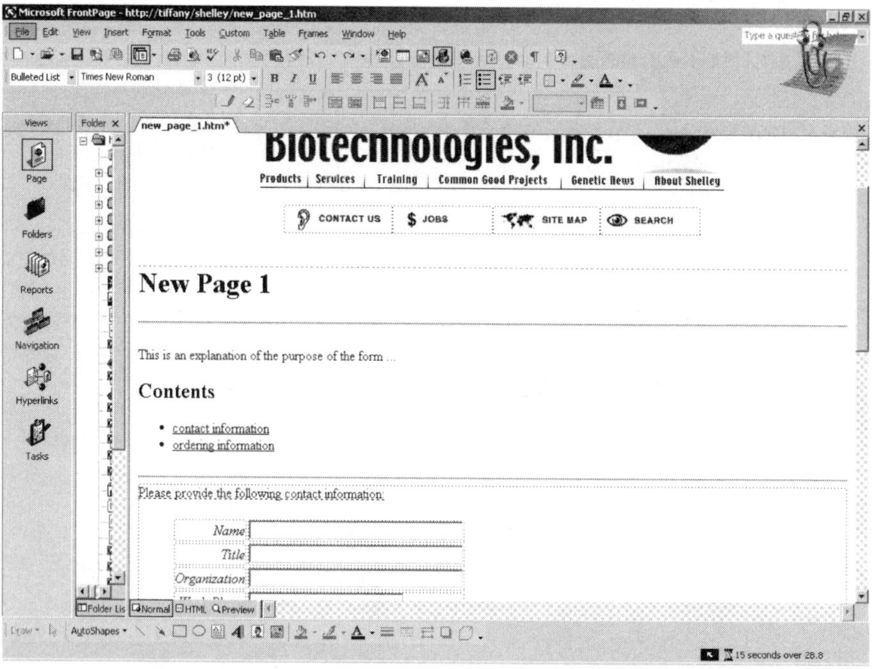

FIGURE 3–11 New form page.

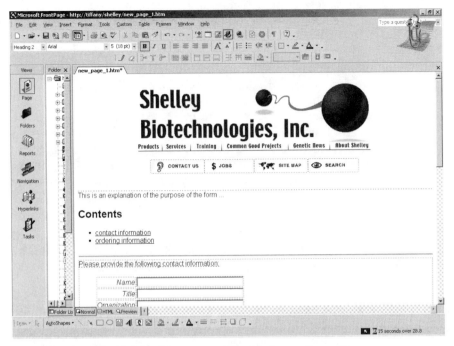

FIGURE 3–12 New form page with added page formatting.

borders to your page. For this example, we will add a white page background color and a top shared border (see Figure 3–12).

In the following section on the Feedback Form, we will review many ways of further customizing your form, including how to add specific fields to your form individually and how to customize a form's properties, such as sending the results of a form to an email recipient, adding subject and reply-to lines to an email form result, and incorporating other formatting options for results sent to text files and Web pages.

THE FEEDBACK FORM

A popular form is the Feedback Form. This form is very useful and can be a great way to interact with your viewers. You may want to start with the standard Feedback Form in FrontPage, then customize the input for your form.

- Select New in the File menu, then Page or Web.
- In the New Page dialog box, select Feedback Form.
- On the right in the NewPage dialog box is the Just add Web task option. Checking this box will not create the form when you click OK but instead will add this as a task in your task list, which is accessible by clicking the Tasks button on the Views toolbar. Notice the dashed line around all of the form fields (see Figure 3–13). This represents the "form" area. You may customize the page first by selecting or deselecting shared borders, background images, background colors, and/or themes for your page. All of these page options are available by right-clicking on the page and selecting the properties that you would like to choose for the page or from the Format menu at the top of the screen.

You may also highlight the text next to any form field (like the text next to the checkboxes at the top) and change the text

FIGURE 3–13 Create a Feedback Form from a template.

next to the selection. You will want the name of each form field to match the text next to it so that you understand the results of your form.

- Right-click on any form field and select Form Field Properties.
- Enter a short, descriptive name for your form field in the dialog box to match the text that you selected to describe this selection on the page. It is important that you do not include spaces in the form field name. Use lowercase text only for the name.
- Click on any form field to delete it if you do not want to include the field on this standard Feedback Form.
- You may add more fields of your choice to this form, as well.

Now, let's add a text box for names and email addresses to be entered. To add a form field text box:

- Place your cursor inside the form on your new form page.
- Type *Name:*, then press the spacebar to add one or two spaces.
- In the Insert menu, select Form, then select One-Line Text Box from the Form menu. The text box will appear next to *Name:*
- Now, right-click on the text box and select Form Field Properties to open the Text Box Properties dialog box (see Figure 3–14).

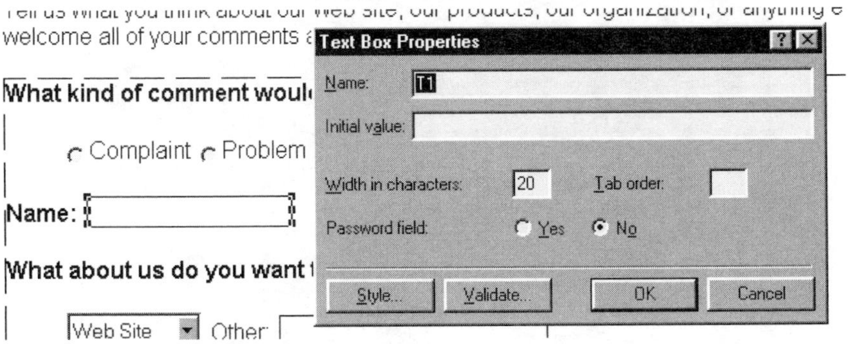

FIGURE 3–14 Adding a form field—Text Box Properties dialog box.

- In this Text Box Properties dialog box, you will assign a name to the form field. You have the option to enter an Initial value, set the box's Width in characters, choose the Tab order, and indicate whether it is to be a Password field. For this example, type in *Username* as the Name for this form field.
- Clicking the Style button gives you options that will add inline style tags to the HTML code, which may not be compatible with some browsers.
- The Validate button will allow you to set some parameters that will cause the user to be prompted with a warning if a field is not filled in using the criteria for the field (see Figure 3–15). Checking the Required box in the Text Box Validation dialog box will allow you to set options for required fields in your form. By adding numerical values in the Data length section of this dialog box, you can select maximum and minimum characters that the viewer must enter in this box. Because it is a Name box, we will leave this alone so that we do not limit the number of characters for any

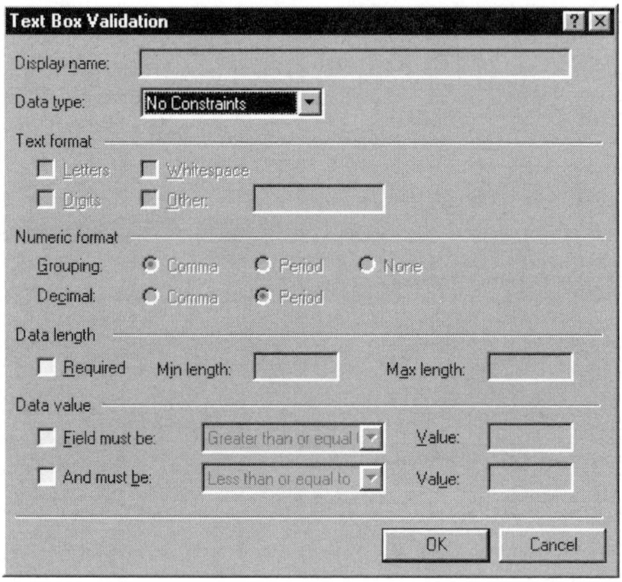

FIGURE 3–15 Text Box Validation dialog box.

viewer's name. You may limit the number of characters your viewer may enter in your text boxes; this comes in handy for text boxes that collect information such as Zip codes. Be careful not to limit the number of characters for email addresses, because you may not allow enough space for your viewer's email address.

- When you have the fields in your form selected and in place, you are ready to set up how you want the results of your form handled. By default, FrontPage forms are pre-configured to send the results of the form to a *.txt* file in the *_private* folder within your web.

SENDING THE RESULTS OF YOUR FORM

- Right-click inside your form and select Form Properties.
- This opens the Form Properties dialog box (see Figure 3–16).

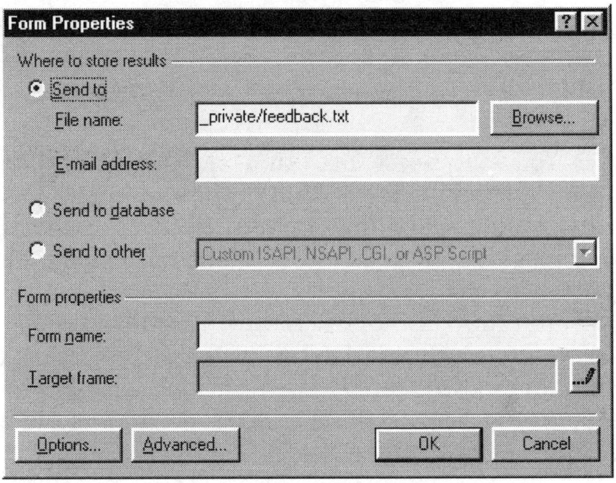

FIGURE 3–16 Form Properties dialog box.

- In this dialog box, you may add an email address to send results to, in addition to or instead of the default *.txt* file. To send the results via email instead of to the *.txt* file on your server, simply delete the path in the File name box and add the email address to the E-mail address box.
- You may add a name for your form in the Form name box and set more options for your form by clicking the Options button (see Figure 3–17).

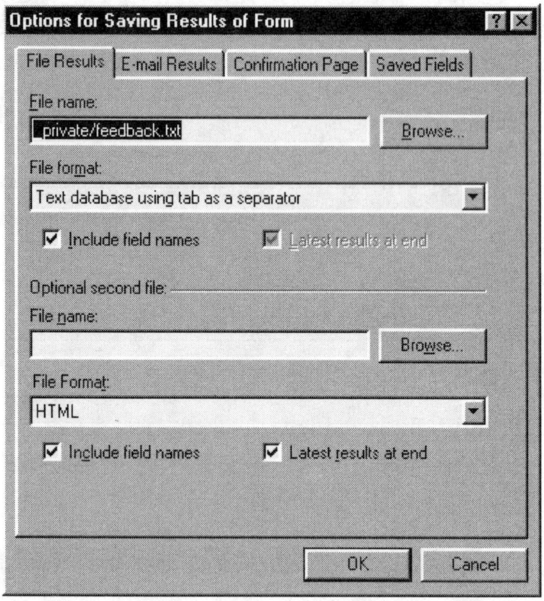

FIGURE 3–17 Options for Saving Results of Form dialog box.

You may select the format in which FrontPage displays your results using the File format dropdown menu. Make sure to check the Include field names option. This will display the results of the form fields next to the name of the form field that was selected by your viewer.

You may also opt to send the results to a second file on your server if you choose. Do this in the section below the first File format dropdown menu.

If you have chosen to send the results via email, click the E-mail Results tab in the Options for Saving Results of Form dialog box (see Figure 3–18). Select the format in which you wish to receive the results in the dropdown menu. Check the Include field names option to display the values of each entry in the results next to the name of the field. You may also enter the subject line for the results of the form. This will display in your email message's subject line.

You can implement a subject line to display with emailed results by entering a value in the Subject line box in the Email message header section, or you may choose simply to have the subject line be the value entered in one of the fields of your form.

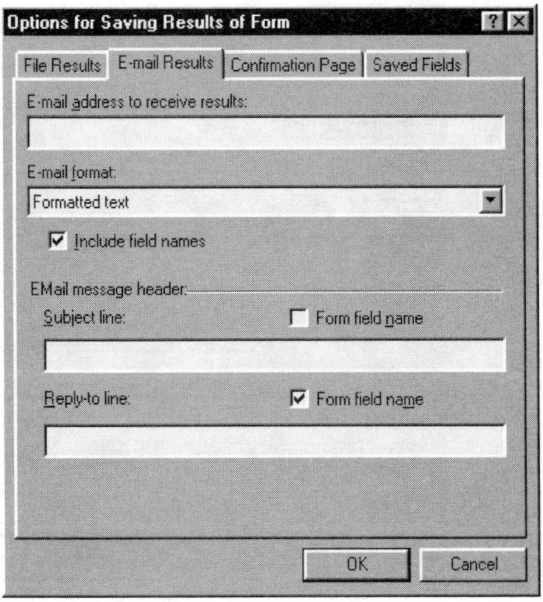

FIGURE 3–18 E-mail Results screen.

Further, you can configure the form to send the results with a reply-to line (which will allow you to click Reply to the results and have the reply go to the person who submitted the form). To do this, choose the name of the form field that collected the email address of your viewer; often, this field is simply named *email*.

Under the Confirmation Field tab, you have the option to use a custom confirmation page. FrontPage has a built-in confirmation page if you do not need a customized one. If you do want one, you may create it within your web, then use the Browse button to select that page from your web and configure FrontPage to use it as the confirmation page for this form. A custom confirmation page allows you to add any and all formatting options to the page so that it appears consistent with the theme of your Web site. We will create a custom confirmation form in the next section. If no custom confirmation page is selected, the default or built-in confirmation page displays the results of the form as submitted by the user and has a link at the bottom of the page that sends the user back to the form page.

Lastly, you have the Saved Fields tab (see Figure 3–19). Here, you may choose which fields within your form to "save" or send

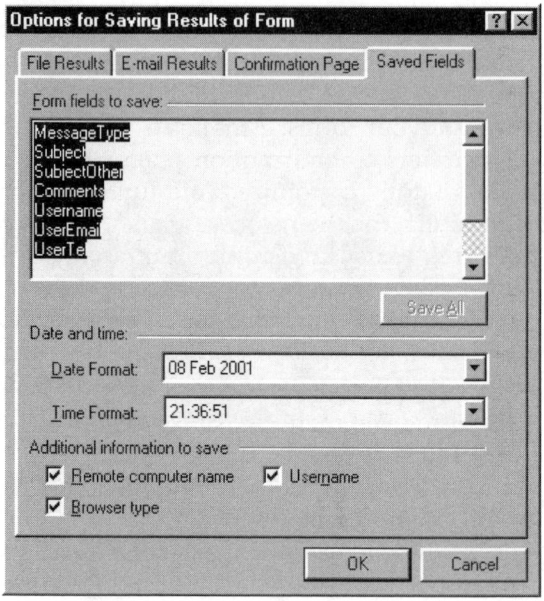

FIGURE 3–19 Saved Fields screen.

with the results. You may click the Save All button to save/send all of the fields and their results values. Included in the Saved Fields dialog box are options to include the Date, Time, Remote computer name, Browser type (of the user submitting the form), and Username. Some of this information can be valuable in determining your target audience.

To save all of the changes you have made in the Options for Saving Results of Form dialog box, click OK. Now save this page under a file name that is fairly easy to identify. It is also a good idea to keep your file names fairly short and all lowercase. NT servers are not case-sensitive, but UNIX servers are. To avoid any complications, it is a good idea to keep your file names all lower-case characters. For this exercise, we will name our page *feedback* and save it as a Web page (or with the *.htm* extension).

CUSTOM CONFIRMATION FORM

When visitors to your Web site submit a form on your site, they will be directed to a confirmation page. Usually, the confirmation page will thank visitors for filling out the form and show them the information they have submitted in the form. This also lets the visitors know that the form was submitted properly without errors.

FrontPage has a built-in default confirmation page that will be used if no custom confirmation page is selected in the form properties of your forms. Among its many new page templates, FrontPage offers a confirmation page template. This allows you to create a totally customized and functional confirmation page that can match the theme on your site.

Let's create a custom confirmation page from the FrontPage template and customize it to match the theme that we are working on with the Shelley Biotechnology Web site. After we create this confirmation page, we will select it as the confirmation page for the form we just created in the last section. To start:

- From the File menu select New, then select Page or Web to open the Task pane on the right.
- Under the New from Template section of the Task pane, select Page Templates.
- In the New page dialog box, highlight the icon labeled Confirmation Form and click the OK button (see Figure 3–20).

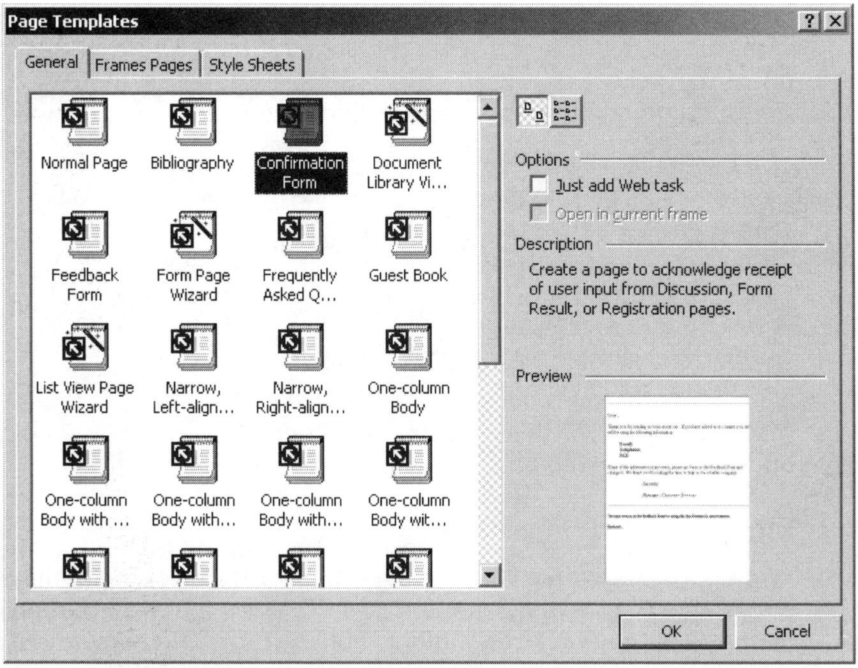

FIGURE 3–20 Page Templates dialog box—Confirmation Form.

FrontPage will create a new page with an example Confirmation form in the format of a letter. There will also be a comment at the top of this new page with information about a Confirmation form. The comment will not show in preview or in the browser, but you may just want to delete the comment anyway.

If you have set any specific shared borders for all pages of your web, the new page will be created with those shared borders; otherwise, you may add any shared border to the page that you like. If you have a theme selected for your site, that will be applied to the new page, too.

Let's begin customizing the Confirmation form to work with the Feedback form we created in the last section. To do this, it would be helpful to have the Feedback form open in FrontPage also, so that you can copy and paste the exact field names into the Confirmation form and be sure that your results will be accurate.

The default Confirmation form comes preset with Confirmation fields that match the default Feedback form, such as Username, MessageType, and so forth. These Confirmation fields match the form field names given in the Feedback form specifically, so that the FrontPage form component will know which information entered into the Feedback form should be placed on the Confirmation form (see Figure 3–21).

NOTE
On the Confirmation form are the Confirmation form fields. They are shown on the page in [brackets]. These are not plain text form field names enclosed in brackets. These form field names are actually FrontPage components. When you move your cursor over one of these, you will see the cursor change from the standard pointer to a hand holding a file. Right-clicking on any of these components or form fields will allow you to select Confirmation Field Properties from the menu, giving you the ability to change the name of the form field to confirm (see Figures 3–22 and 3–23).

The default Confirmation form comes preset to confirm the Username, MessageType, Subject, E-mail, Telephone, and FAX information, as entered by the user. Let's add to this form another field to confirm: the Comments field. This will show users what

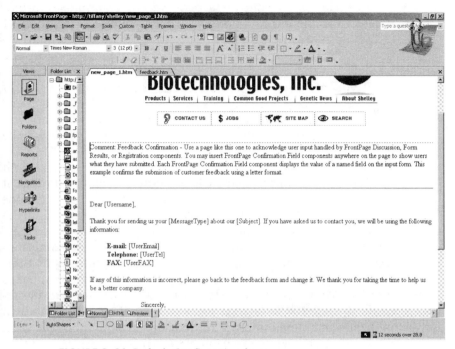

FIGURE 3–21 Default Confirmation form.

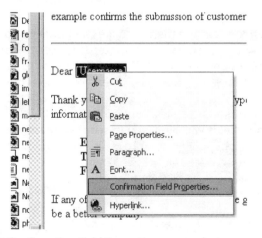

FIGURE 3–22 Confirmation Field Properties menu select.

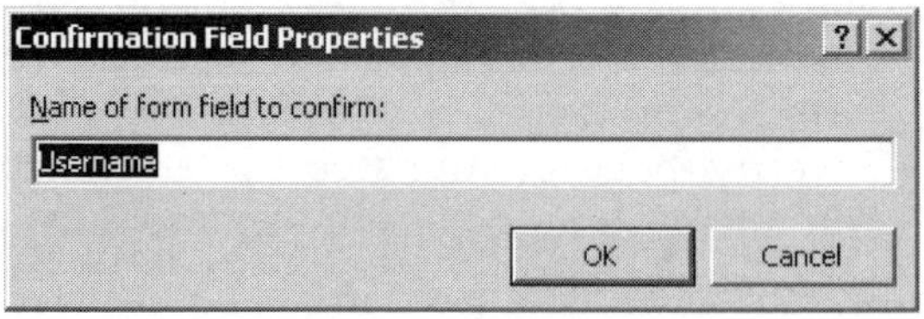

FIGURE 3–23 Confirmation Field Properties dialog box.

comments they entered and submitted to you through the Feedback form.

- Place your cursor on the page under the FAX Confirmation field.
- Type in the word *Comments:* and a space.
- From the Insert menu, select Web Components.
- In the Web Components dialog box, on the left pane, highlight Advanced Controls. Then on the right pane, highlight Confirmation Field (see Figure 3–24).
- Click the Finish button—This will launch the Confirmation Field Properties dialog box, where you will type in the name of the field you want to confirm.
- In the Feedback form, the Comments form field is named *Comments*; therefore, we will type in *Comments* exactly as it is named in the Feedback form with a capital C and click OK.

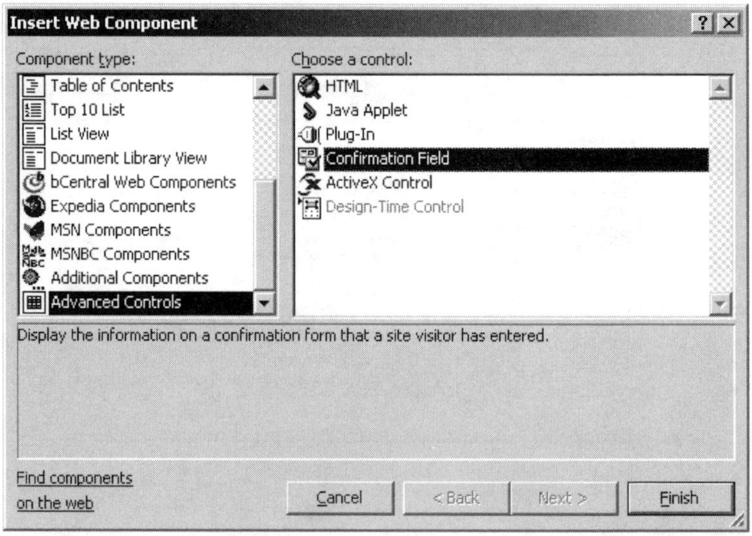

FIGURE 3–24 Insert Web Component dialog box—Advanced Controls.

- Repeat this process for any and all other form fields that you would like this page to confirm when the Feedback form is submitted.
- Save the page in your web by selecting Save As from the File menu and giving it a descriptive name, such as *confirmation.htm.*

To select this confirmation page as the custom confirmation page for your Feedback form:

- Open your Feedback form page and place your cursor somewhere inside the form on the page.
- Right-click and select Form Properties from the menu.
- Click the Options button.
- Click the Confirmation Page tab.
- In the Confirmation Page dialog box, click the Browse button and navigate to the *confirmation.htm* page you just created (see Figure 3–25).
- Click OK and save the page.

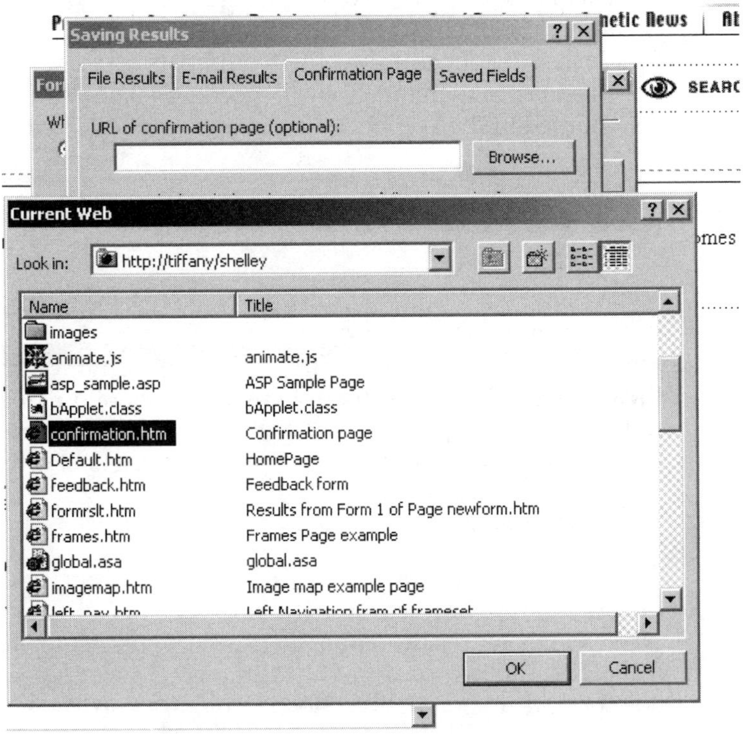

FIGURE 3–25 Configure a custom confirmation page.

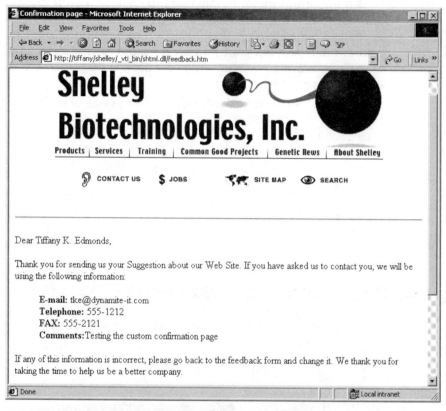

FIGURE 3–26 Submitted custom Confirmation form.

When a site visitor submits the Feedback form, the input values are paired with the Confirmation form fields. The FrontPage form handler generates a customized confirmation page using the Confirmation form you just created. Each of the Confirmation form fields are replaced by the value entered into the Feedback form by the site visitor (for example see Figure 3–26).

Discussion Webs

A FrontPage discussion web is another very easily created, maintained, and edited feature. It, too, depends on the FrontPage server extensions to function, as it should. In this section, we will walk through the process of installing your own discussion web to go along with your Shelley Biotechnologies web.

An important factor in creating a discussion web is to ensure that you create the discussion web as a subweb, which we will explain as we go along. This ensures that if you are publishing your changes to your web up and down, to and from a remote server, you will not overwrite any new posts made to your discussion web from Internet users.

Let's begin with creating a new folder, then converting it to a subweb for our discussion web (see Figure 3–27).

In the File menu, select New then Folder. Enter a name for it, such as *Discussion*. Right-click on this Discussion folder, either from the Folder List or from the Contents pane while in Folders view (as shown in Figure 3–27), and select Convert to Web from the menu. This will create a "nested subweb," meaning that it is a web all of its own. When you open the Shelley web, however, you will see this new subweb within the contents of the Shelley web, because they are associated with each other. When you

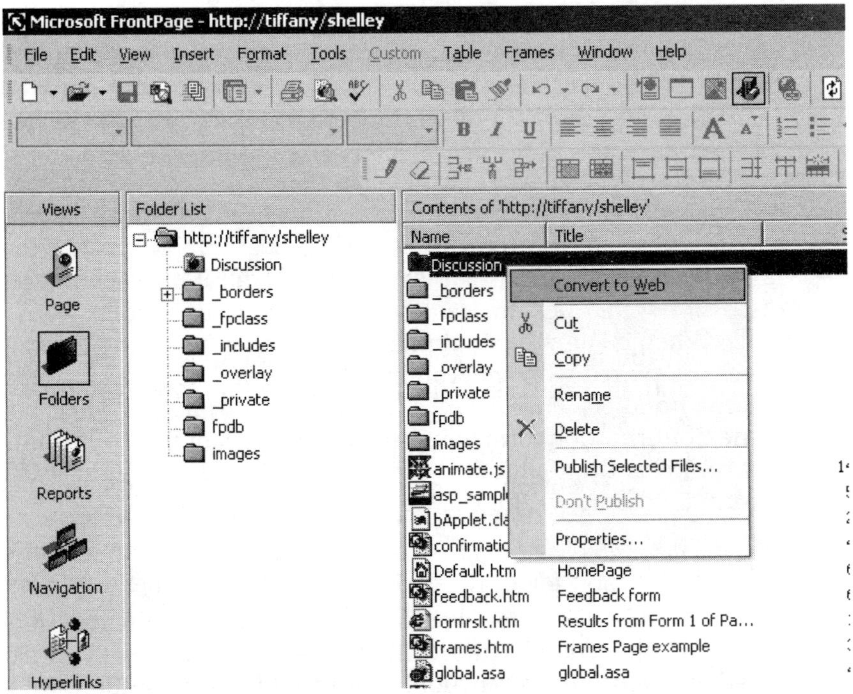

FIGURE 3–27 Convert a folder to a web.

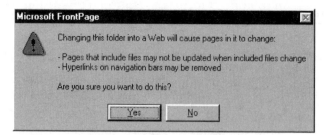

FIGURE 3–28 FrontPage Convert to Web alert box.

select Convert to Web, you will be prompted with an alert (see Figure 3–28). Click Yes to dismiss this alert box.

You will now see your subweb in the Folder List with a new icon that represents a FrontPage web, the folder with a World icon on it. Double-click this subweb from your Folder List to open it. We will add the discussion web to your subweb directly. FrontPage will launch the subweb in a new FrontPage window.

Now, confirm that you are working in the /shelley/Discussion web and select New then Page or Web from the File menu. In the New Web dialog box (see Figure 3–29), select the Discussion Web wizard, and on the right of this dialog box, check the Add to current web option.

The step-by-step wizard will begin the process of creating your new discussion web when you click OK. The first screen in this wizard will alert you that the wizard is beginning and that the answers to the questions will determine the final product of your discussion web. Click the Next button to begin the process.

1. In the first step of the Discussion Web wizard, select the options you would like to include within your discussion web, such as a Table of Contents, Search Form, Threaded Replies, and a Confirmation Page (see Figure 3–30). Click the Next button when you have made your selections.

2. Enter a descriptive name for the discussion web, such as *Shelley Biotechnologies Discussion*, and enter a name for the discussion folder (I usually leave this as the default folder name, _disc1, as shown in Figure 3–31). Click the Next button when you have made your selections.

3. Choose the appropriate set of input fields for your form. This is the form that your visitors will complete to post a reply or topic on your discussion board. The default choice is simply Subject and Comments, but it does allow

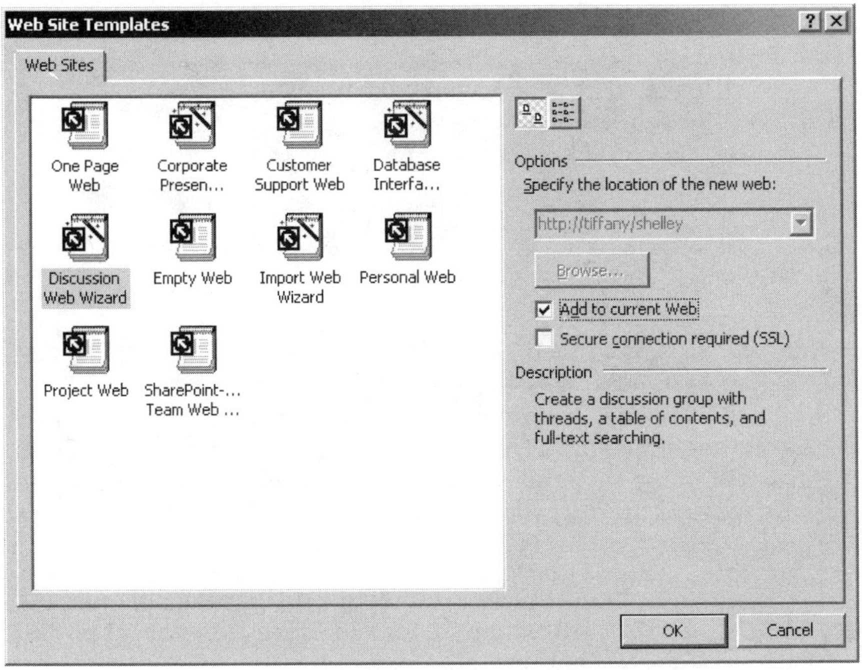

FIGURE 3–29 New Web dialog box—Discussion Web wizard.

FIGURE 3–30 Discussion Web wizard step one.

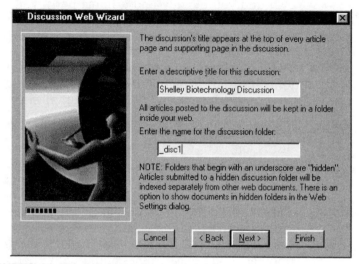

FIGURE 3–31 Discussion Web wizard step two.

the option to include an input field for category and product also, if appropriate for your discussion web. Then click the Next button.

4. Will the discussion take place in a protected web? This question is asking whether you will allow anyone to view and participate in the discussion web, or will password-protect it so that only registered members can participate. Another advantage to having placed the discussion web in a subweb as we have done is that you will be able to set permissions and security on this subweb, separate from the main web, if you choose. See Chapter 5, "Publishing Webs," for more on permissions. Click the Next button, once you have made your choice of protection options.

5. Choose the display of the new messages posted—oldest to newest or newest to oldest—then click the Next button to continue to the next step of the wizard. The default setting is oldest to newest, placing any new posts at the end of the Table of Contents. I have found that more people prefer to see what is new at the top of the page, instead of having to scroll down and search for new topics and replies.

6. In the next step, you may choose to make the Table of Contents the homepage for this subweb, because we created this as a web of its own. If this was not a web of its

own and you already had a home page, you would not want to overwrite that home page with the Table of Contents for the discussion web. Choose yes or no, then click the Next button.

7. The next step gives you options for the results the search form will show. These options are easily configured now or changed later. Click the Next button once you have made your selection.

8. The next step gives you the option to select a theme for this discussion web. Clicking the Choose Web Theme button will launch the Choose Theme dialog box. A theme can be selected during the wizard or at any time after the discussion web is completed (see Chapter 2 for more on themes). Click the Next button to continue to the final step.

9. The last step in the Discussion Web wizard is to choose the layout for your discussion web. I have found that this is another good use for frames and usually choose the Contents beside current article layout option because it allows users an easy way to click on a post or reply on the left and read that post or reply content on the right. This step allows you to choose a nonframes option or even an option to use frames if supported by the user's browser (see Figure 3–32). Click the Finish button.

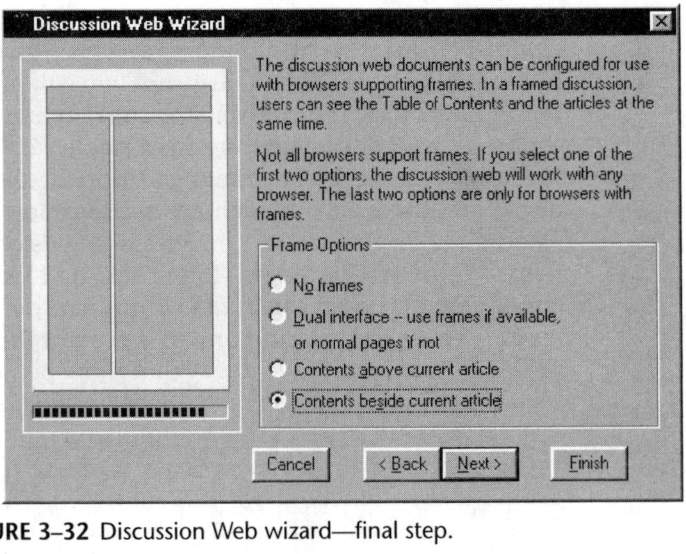

FIGURE 3–32 Discussion Web wizard—final step.

Once you have completed the wizard, you may open your *Default.htm* page and customize the discussion Web pages in any way that you like in an effort to continue the same look and feel of your main site. This can include images, navigation buttons, and/or a theme applied to the site. It is recommended that you do not use shared borders, however, in a frameset.

Hit Counters

Hit counters count how many times your page has been viewed. Each time the page is viewed or refreshed in the browser, the hit counter increments. FrontPage has a built-in hit counter script that will allow you to install a hit counter easily on any of the pages in your web. This is a great component for a personal Web site but is difficult to use in a professional environment. More professional and business-type Web sites rely on third-party Web statistics programs that are often included in a Web hosting package by the hosting company and already installed on the server. Check with your Web host provider to find out whether your hosting company provides a statistics program that will tell you more about your visitors than simply how many you have had on your site.

To add a hit counter:

- Select Web Component from the Insert menu, then choose Hit Counter in the left pane. Choose the desired hit counter from the right pane and click the Finish button (see Figure 3–33).
- This will launch the Hit Counter Properties dialog box (see Figure 3–34).
- Choose one of the available hit counter styles in the dialog box and click OK to insert it on the page. This component will need to be saved on the page before it can be viewed, and while in Normal mode, it will always appear as [Hit Counter].

USING CUSTOM COUNTER IMAGES

The Hit Counter Properties dialog box includes an option to add a custom hit counter. You can easily create a custom counter by creating a *.gif* image such as the one shown in Figure 3–35. It is a good idea to use a solid color background, then add numbers evenly spaced, for example: 0 1 2 3 4 5 6 7 8 9. Center the numbers on the background. Transparent *.gif* images do not work, and if you get the numbers too close together, they may not display correctly.

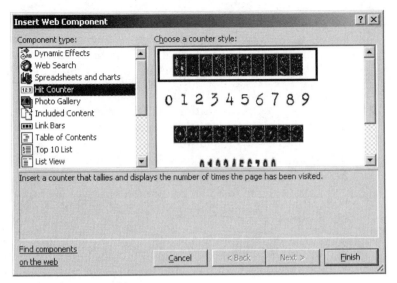

FIGURE 3–33 Insert a hit counter.

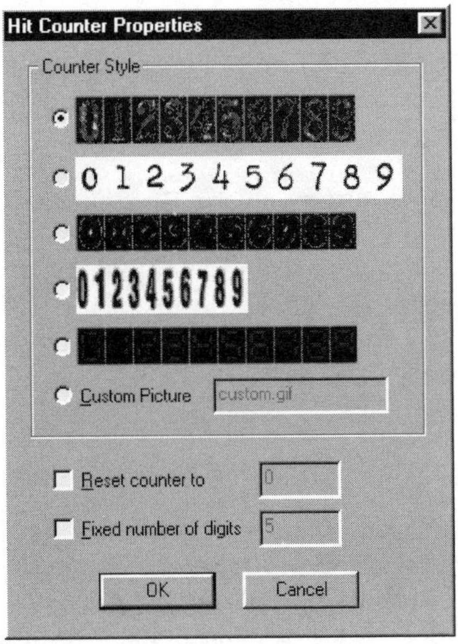

FIGURE 3–34 Hit Counter Properties dialog box.

0 1 2 3 4 5 6 7 8 9

FIGURE 3–35 Custom hit counter.

To add a custom counter, you must save your custom *.gif* image in your web. In the Hit Counter Properties dialog box (see Figure 3–34), select Custom Picture, then type the path to that custom image. Finally, click OK, and FrontPage will use your custom image as the hit counter.

Search Feature

FrontPage 2002 includes a premade search page that can be installed in your web by way of the Page Templates dialog box. Select New then Page or Web from the File menu. From the Task pane, click the link to Page Template under the New from Template section (see Figure 3–36).

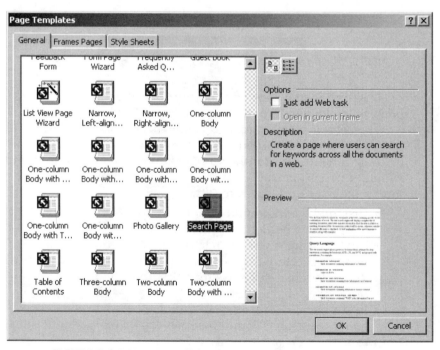

FIGURE 3–36 New Page dialog box—Search Page.

```
new_page_1.htm                                                                          ×

Comment: Text Search - This page lets you search through the default text index that is created whenever web pages
are saved or web links are recalculated. No customization is required.
```

Use the form below to search for documents in this web containing specific words or combinations of words. The text
search engine will display a weighted list of matching documents, with better matches shown first. Each list item is a
link to a matching document; if the document has a title it will be shown, otherwise only the document's file name is
displayed. A brief underline_explanation of the query language is available, along with examples.

Search for: [_____]

[Start Search] [Reset]

Query Language

The text search engine allows queries to be formed from arbitrary Boolean expressions containing the keywords AND,
OR, and NOT, and grouped with parentheses. For example:

```
information retrieval
     finds documents containing 'information' or 'retrieval'


information or retrieval
     same as above
```

```
Normal / HTML / Preview / |◄|                                                            |►|
                                                  |◄| ⌛ 1 seconds over 28.8        NUM
```

FIGURE 3–37 New search page.

Selecting Search Page and clicking OK will open a new search
page, ready for you to customize (see Figure 3–37).

The default search page has comments at the top, which are
not visible in Preview mode or in the browser. These comments
are only a reminder that the search feature is ready to run as is,
without any customization at all. For this example, we will customize the page and search results.

- First, add a background color to the page—white—then add
a top shared border.
- Next, configure the search results and how they appear
by right-clicking on the search box within the dashed
line. Select Search Form Properties from the menu (see Figure 3–38).
- In the Search Form Properties dialog box, you may choose
either the Search Form Properties tab or the Search Results
tab.

The Search Form Properties tab allows you to set the Label for
Input, which will change the text that is visible on the page next

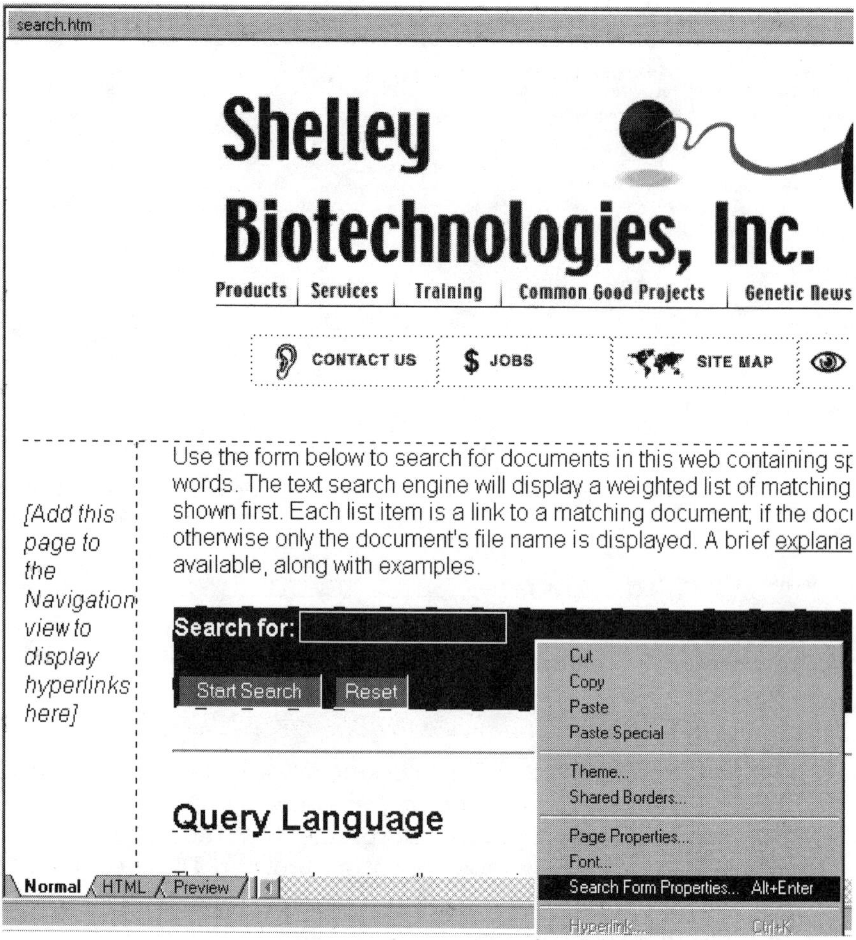

FIGURE 3–38 Select Search Form Properties from the menu.

to the input box. The Width in characters sets the length or width of the input box. The labels for the Start Search and Clear buttons fields will change the text of the buttons on the search page (see Figure 3–39).

Selecting the Search Results tab allows you to make several selections for the search results and display options (see Figure 3–40):

- Word List to search—By default, this is set to All, which sets the search feature to search all files and folders within the web except any folders that begin with an underscore.

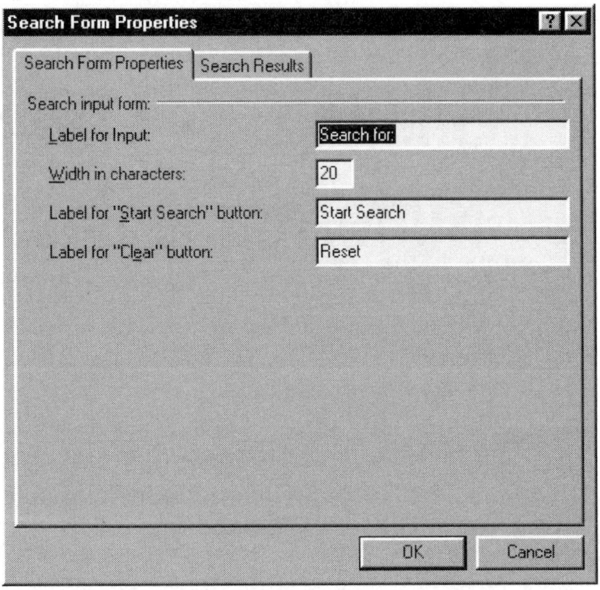

FIGURE 3–39 Search Form Properties dialog box—Search Form Properties tab.

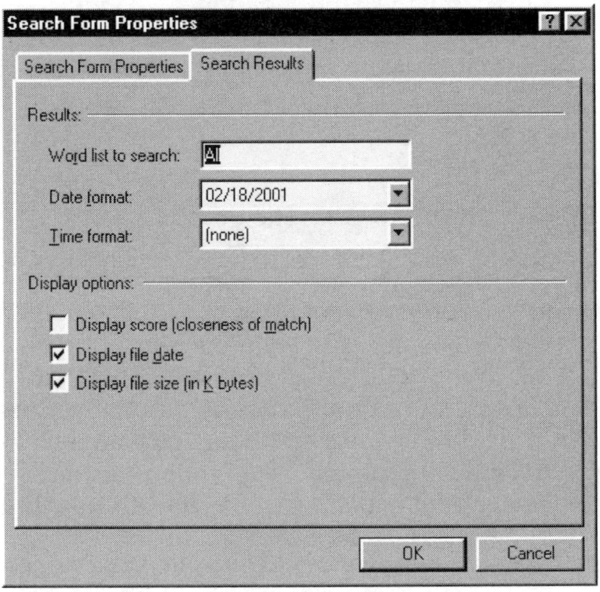

FIGURE 3–40 Search Form Properties—Search Results tab.

- Date format—If checked, along with the Display file date option, then this is the format in which the date will be displayed; that is, the date on which the file was last updated.
- Time format—This option is much the same as the date format, except that it shows the time at which the file was last updated.

Under the display options:

- Display score—This option adds a "score" or a closeness of match to the keywords used in the search.
- Display file date—Choosing this option will show the date the file was last updated next to the result.
- Display file size—This will show the file size of the result in Kb.
- Next, you may opt whether to leave the Query Language definitions on the search page. Save the page as *search.htm*.

You may also add a search component to an existing page by placing your cursor on the page where you want a search box inserted.

- Select Web Component from the Insert menu.
- Highlight Web Search in the left pane and Current Web in the right pane.
- Clicking the Finish button will launch the Search Form Properties dialog box for you to configure (see this chapter for more details on configuring the Search Form Properties).
- Click the OK button to insert the Search form on the page.

File Upload

The new FrontPage 2002 File Upload feature is as easy to use and configure as inserting any form field on a page. To use this feature, however, the server hosting your web must have the FrontPage 2002 server extensions installed.

File Upload does just what the name implies, it allows visitors to your Web site to upload a file to your Web server through a Web browser. Clicking the Browse button will open a dialog box that will allow your visitors to navigate on their hard drives to the files they want to upload. Submitting this form will then upload the file that the visitor selected to the directory that you have configured this form to send to.

We will configure a File Upload feature to allow visitors to the Shelley Biotechnologies Web site to upload files and documents to a folder on this web. First, we need to create a folder in the web for the files to be uploaded to. In most cases, you would not want these files to be indexed by search engines or by the FrontPage search component. To prevent the files from being uploaded by site visitors or team members, we can name the upload directory with an underscore in front of the folder name, such as _upload. The underscore in front of the folder name prevents the files in the directory from being indexed by search components or search engines. It also prevents visitors on the Internet from browsing the directory. If a visitor tried to browse this directory through a Web browser, he or she would be prompted for a username and password.

To create the new folder for the uploaded files:

- In the Folder List, right-click on the very top folder. If you are working against a server, this would be something like *http://localhost/shelley*; if you are working on a Disk-Based Web (DBW), this would be something like *C:\My Webs\shelley*.
- From the right-click menu, choose Folder from the New menu (see Figure 3–41).

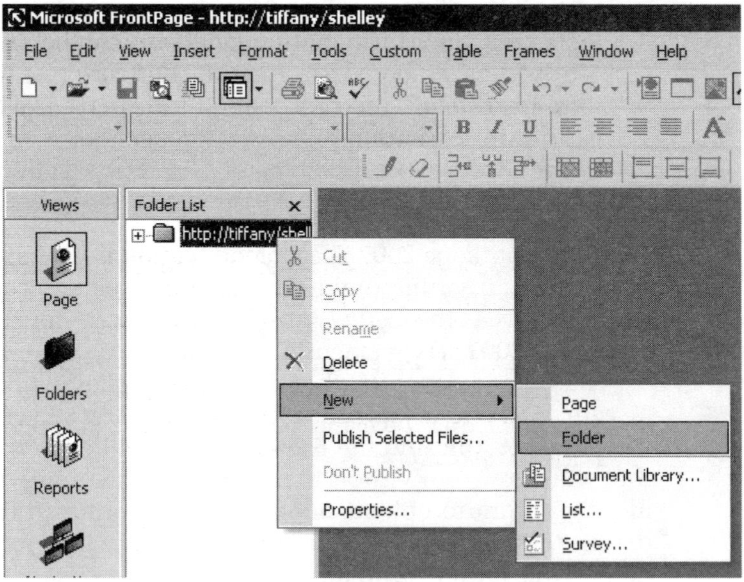

FIGURE 3–41 Create New Folder menu.

- A new folder will appear in your Folder List that is high-lighted blue. Type _upload, then click on the folder one time. This will assign the name upload with the underscore to the new folder.

If you are unable to see the folder in your Folder List after naming it, you will need to set FrontPage to show all hidden files and folders in the web. To do this:

- From the Tools menu, select Web Settings.
- Click the Advanced tab.
- In this Advanced screen, place a check next to the box to Show hidden files and folders. Click the OK button.
- You should now be able to see the folders in your web that begin with an underscore.

You are now ready to create your File Upload form.

- From the Task pane under the New section, click the link for Blank Page.
- At the top of the page, you can add some text, such as Upload a file.
- Place your cursor on the page where you would like to insert the File Upload form and select Form from the Insert menu
- Select File Upload from the Form menu (see Figure 3–42).
- Right-click on the text box form field on the page next to the Browse button and select Form field properties. Name this form field upload and click the OK button (see Figure 3–43).
- Next, right-click and select Form Properties.
- In the Form properties dialog box, click the Options button.
- Click the File Upload tab in the Saving Results dialog box (see Figure 3–44).
- Click the Browse button next to the Destination box and navigate in your web to the _upload folder that you created and click OK. Then click OK on the Saving Results dialog box, and click OK again on the Form Properties dialog box.
- Add any other formatting options you would like to add on this page and save the page. For this example, save the page as upload.htm.

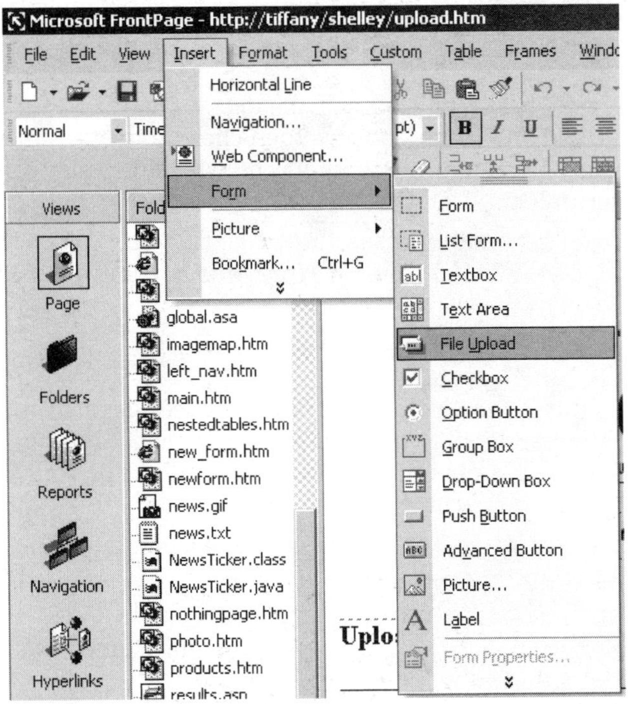

FIGURE 3–42 File Upload menu.

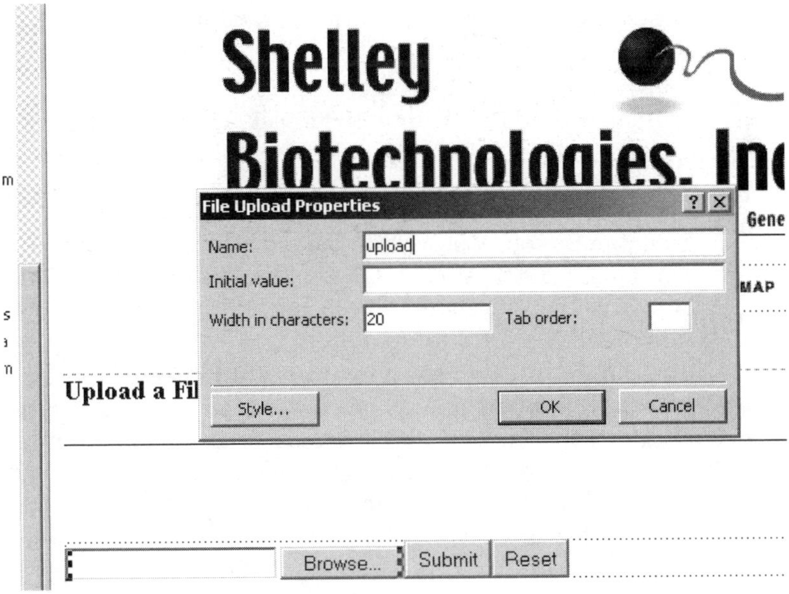

FIGURE 3–43 File Upload Properties.

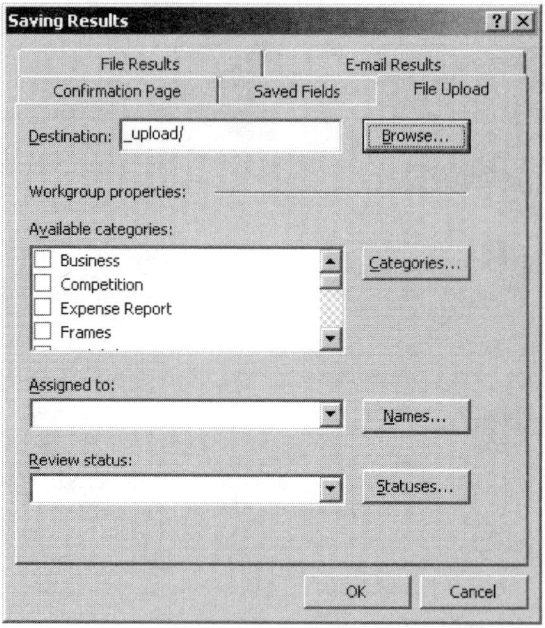

FIGURE 3–44 File Upload—Saving Results dialog box.

If you are working against a Web server, PWS, or IIS, you can test this form by opening it in your web browser using the *http://localhost/shelley* URL. Click the Browse button to choose a file on your hard drive to upload to the web and submit the form (see Figure 3–45).

FrontPage will generate the default Confirmation form when the form is submitted (see Figure 3–46). Remember, you can create a custom Confirmation form that matches the look and feel of your Web site if you like.

Table of Contents

To add a Table of Contents page that FrontPage automatically updates for you when new pages are added and old pages are deleted, select the Table of Contents icon from the Page Templates dialog box (see Figure 3–47). This feature will list all of the pages in your web that are linked from a starting point that you configure in the Table of Contents Properties dialog box in a bulleted list on the Table of Contents page.

FIGURE 3–45 Upload a file using the browser.

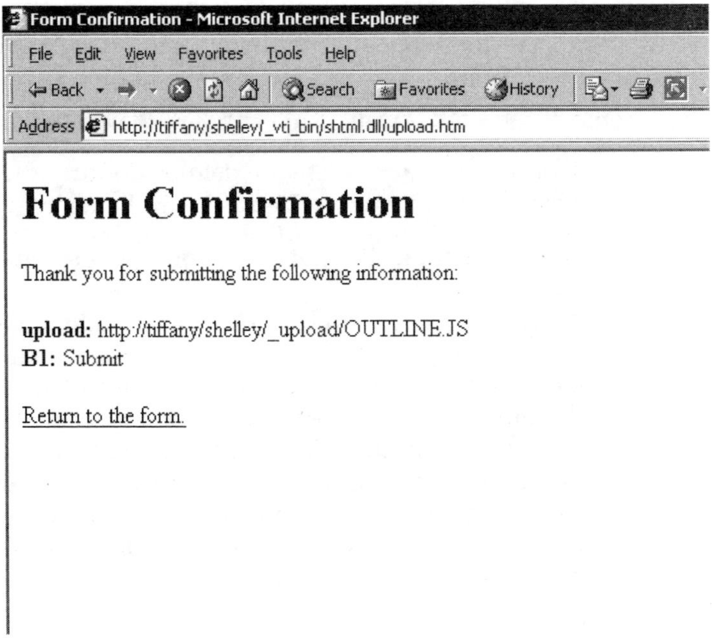

FIGURE 3–46 File upload default confirmation page.

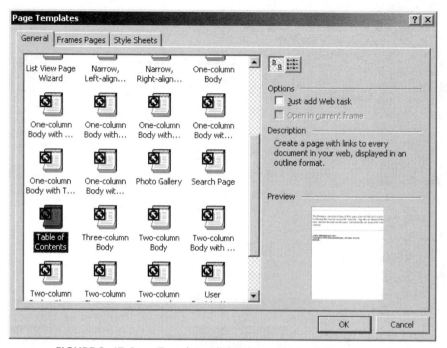

FIGURE 3–47 Page Templates dialog box—Table of Contents.

After selecting the Table of Contents icon from the Page Templates dialog box, you may customize the page to match the theme of the site, as well as to configure the display results of the Table of Contents.

- First, add the page background color—white—and a top shared border.
- Next, configure the Table of Contents display results (see Figure 3–48).
- Right-click on the Table of Contents Heading Page text that is on the page. Notice that when you place your mouse over the title or any of the items in the bulleted list, the pointer changes to a hand with an index card in it. This signifies that the item is a FrontPage component. Right-clicking while the pointer is changed to the hand holding a file will show a menu. From this menu, you can choose the Table of Contents Properties, which launches the component's Properties dialog box, as shown in Figure 3–49.

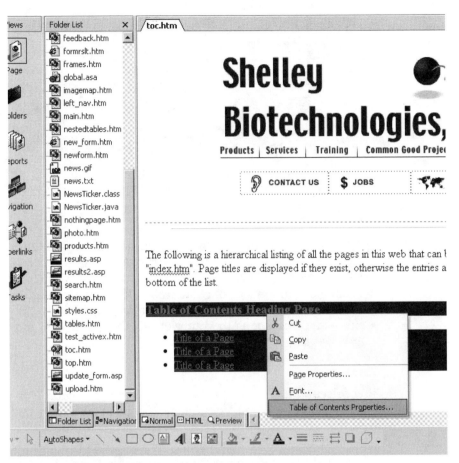

FIGURE 3–48 Table of Contents Properties menu selection.

- In the Table of Contents Properties dialog box (see Figure 3–49), select the starting point for your Table of Contents. This will be the page that is shown as the title on the Table of Contents page. The links displayed on the page will be the pages that are linked under the starting point page in the Navigation view. For instance, in our Shelley Biotechnologies web, we have set up a frameset, a Feedback form, and a search page. All of these have been dragged and dropped into the Navigation view in FrontPage to create a Navigation Tree view (see Figure 3–50), and this structure

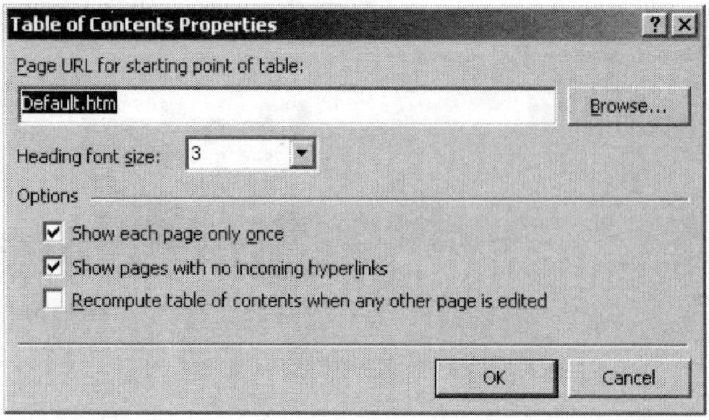

Table of Contents Properties　　　　　　　　？✕

Page URL for starting point of table:

Default.htm　　　　　　　　　　　　　　　Browse...

Heading font size:　3　▼

Options

☑ Show each page only once

☑ Show pages with no incoming hyperlinks

☐ Recompute table of contents when any other page is edited

OK　　　　Cancel

FIGURE 3–49 Table of Contents Properties dialog box.

will be outlined in text in the Table of Contents feature when the page is saved and viewed in the browser.

- The navigation structure in the Navigation view will create a Table of Contents display, as shown in Figure 3–51, if the default page, or home page, is chosen as the starting point.
- Now, save your page in your web. At this point, you may link to it from other pages in your web.

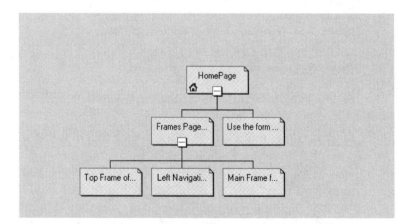

FIGURE 3–50 FrontPage Navigation view.

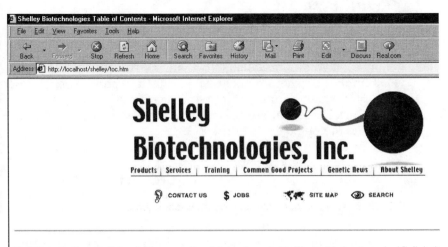

The following is a hierarchical listing of all the pages in this web that can be reached by following links from the top-level file "index.ht they exist, otherwise the entries are file names. Unreachable files are shown at the bottom of the list.

HomePage

- Frames Page example
    Top Frame of frameset page
    Left Navigation fram of frameset
    Main Frame for frameset page
- Use the form below to search for documents in this web containing specific words or combinations of words
- Feedback form
- Shelley Biotechnologies Table of Contents

FIGURE 3–51 FrontPage Table of Contents display.

Hover Buttons

Hover buttons are Java applets that are easily configured using FrontPage 2002. The first thing you should know about Java applets is that they are not supported by many of the older browsers, such as IE 3 and NN 3 or older. As a result of not being supported by the older browsers, they simply do not appear on the page when a viewer is using one of these browsers. With that in mind, you may want to reconsider using them for navigational purposes. If you do choose to use them, you should be sure to add text hyperlinks to the other pages on your site.

Java applets also take a little longer to load than a standard button or small image. Until they are fully loaded, a gray box will appear on the screen of the viewer whose browser supports them.

GETTING STARTED

First, explore the Hover Button Properties dialog box.

- Open a page in your FrontPage Editor.
- Select Web Components from the Insert menu.
- Highlight Dynamic Effects in the left pane and choose Hover Button in the right pane (see Figure 3–52).
- Click the Finish button to launch the Hover Button Properties dialog box (see Figure 3–53).
- In the Hover Button Properties dialog box, you can choose from a variety of options:
  - Button text—This text will appear on your button.
  - Link to—Enter a URL for your button to link to when clicked, or click the Browse button and navigate to a file in your web to link to from your Hover button.
  - Button color—Choose the color of the button upon load.
  - Effect—Choose from a variety of effects that you wish to occur when the cursor is moved over the button. Glow is the most popular effect.

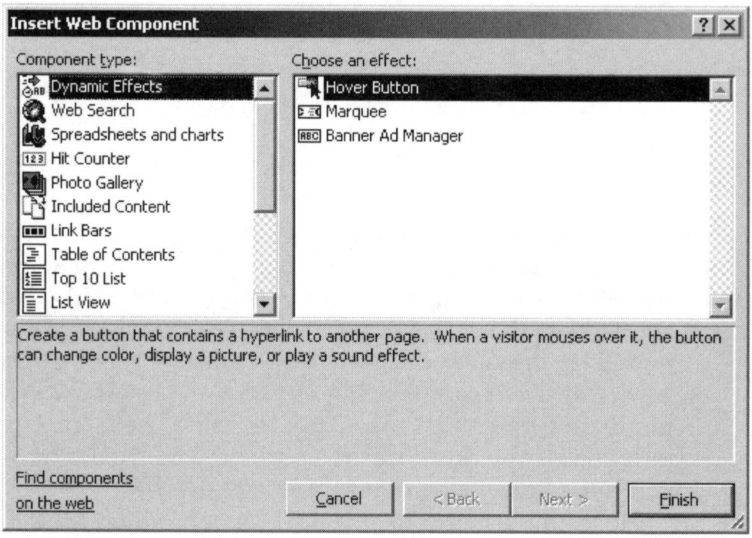

FIGURE 3–52 Hover Button menu selection.

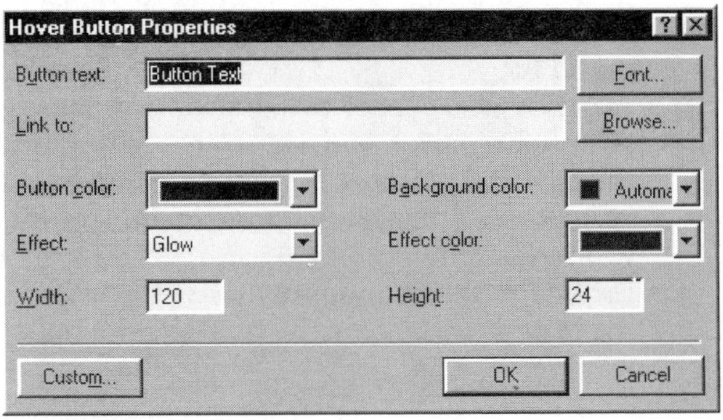

FIGURE 3–53 Hover Button Properties dialog box.

- Effect color—Choose the color that you wish the effect to be when the cursor moves over the button.
- Width and Height—These default to the sizes shown in Figure 3–53. You may make them larger or smaller, according to your taste and/or needs.
- You also have the option to choose the font style and color by clicking the Font button next to the Button text box.

CUSTOM BOX

- In the Hover Button Properties dialog box (Figure 3–53), click the Custom button at the bottom of the box. You will then see the Custom dialog box (see Figure 3–54).

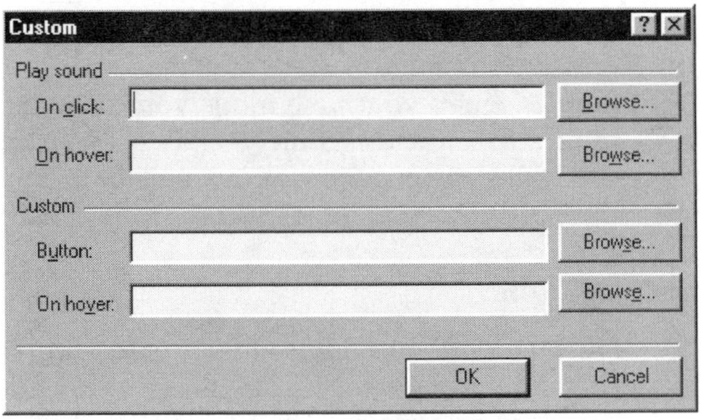

FIGURE 3–54 Custom Hover Button dialog box.

- In this box, you may add sound to your button when it is clicked or hovered over. To do this, you must use an *.au* sound file.
- You may also choose two of your own images to use for the button and hover. You can select the size, width, and height in the Hover Button Properties dialog box to match your images' sizes. You should use two images that are the same width and height.
- For any of the above options, use the Browse button next to the appropriate box to navigate to the image or sound you would like to use.

FINISHING UP

To save these additions to your page, click OK on the Custom dialog box and/or on the Hover Button Properties dialog box. Save the page, and you are ready to preview and/or upload your new page.

Date and Time

To add the date and/or time that your page was last edited to your page(s), FrontPage has a built-in Date and Time script that can be added from the Insert menu (see Figure 3–55).

This Date and Time script is not the current date and time; it is the date and/or time that the page was last edited in FrontPage. Configure the date and time display in the Date and Time Properties dialog box (see Figure 3–56).

Use the dropdown menus to choose the format for the date and/or time, then choose a Display option from this dialog box, either Date this page was last edited or Date this page was last automatically updated.

Click OK when you have made your selections. You can add text around the date and time display on your page if you wish. Something like "This page was last edited on _____." You can also highlight the text and format the font size, style, and color.

Include Pages

A powerful yet often underused feature in FrontPage is a component called the *include page.* I use it for quickly adding navigation bars, repeated addresses, or recurring strings of HTML. The great feature of using this component is if you decide to add or change the navigation of your site, the changes have to be made only

FIGURE 3–55 Insert Date and Time.

one time. For organization, I store my include pages in a folder called _includes. Adding the underscore also prevents the pages from being indexed in the search results in a local search within the web or by search engines and Web crawlers. This feature does not require the FrontPage server extensions.

For this example, we will create an include page for the bottom of the pages on the Shelley Biotechnologies Web site. This include page will have a set of text navigation links, copyright

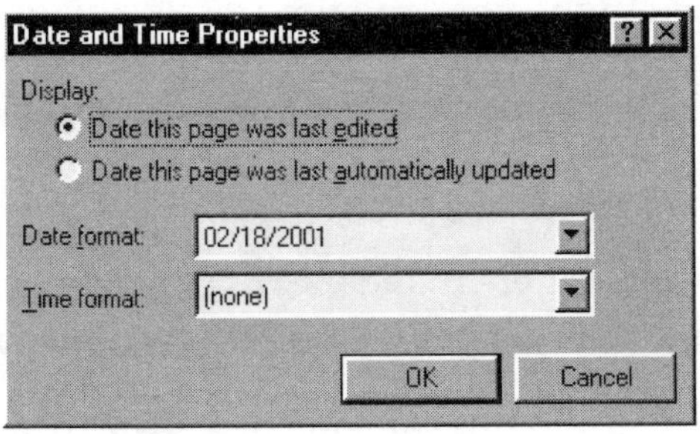

FIGURE 3–56 Date and Time Properties dialog box.

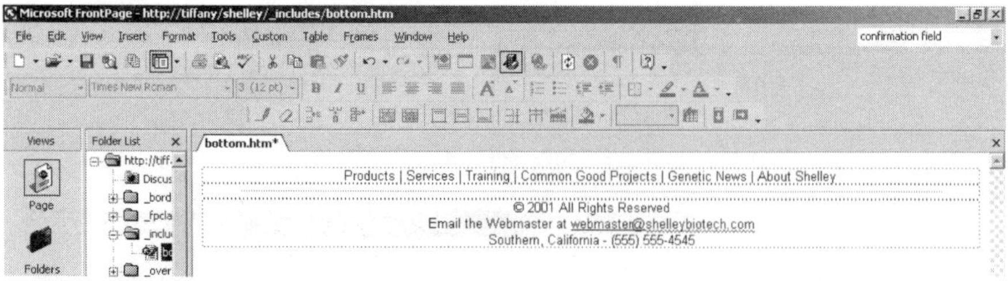

FIGURE 3–57 Bottom include page.

information, and contact information. Let's start with a blank white page, add our links and contact information in a table on the page, and save the include page (see Figure 3–57).

We can now insert this include page on the bottom of any or all of our Web pages by selecting Web Components from the Insert menu. In the left pane, choose Included Content, and in the right pane, choose Page (see Figure 3–58), then click the finish button to launch the Include Page Properties dialog box.

In the Include Page Properties dialog box (see Figure 3–59), you may use the Browse button to browse to the _includes_ folder and select the *bottom.htm* page to be inserted into an existing page.

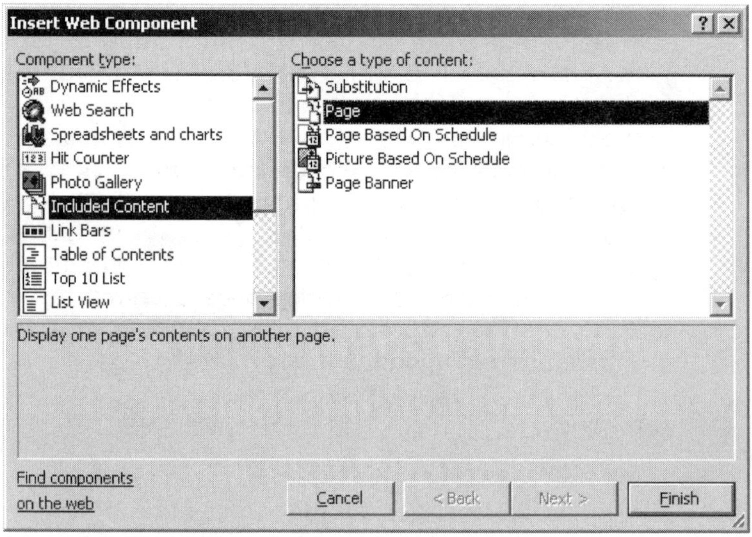

FIGURE 3–58 Insert Web Component—Include Page.

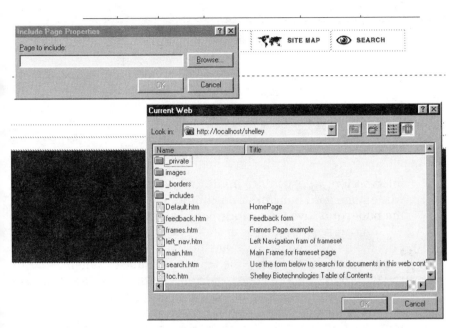

FIGURE 3-59 Include Page Properties dialog box and Current Web dialog box.

Unlike shared borders, an include page may be inserted at any place on a page. It is not limited to being used on the top, bottom, or sides. You can create a table on your page and select a background color for the cell or table, then insert an include page in the table.

Like shared borders, when you want or need to make a change to information that is repeated on all or many pages of your web, you have to make that change or update to only one page, and FrontPage will append that change to all of the pages that share that border or include page. For navigation and contact information purposes, include pages can save you a lot of maintenance and updating time.

Image Maps

FrontPage 2002 has a built-in image-mapping tool that allows you to add "hotspots" to an image on a page. Hotspots are hyperlinks that are added to a "spot" on an image, rather than simply making the whole image a hyperlink. Several hotspots can be added to the same image, which then creates an image map.

To add hotspots to an image:

- First, insert the image into your Web page.
- Select the image by clicking on it one time. This will high-light the Image Formatting toolbar at the bottom of the FrontPage Editor, as shown in Figure 3–60 (see also Appendix A, "FrontPage Image Tools").
- The Image Formatting toolbar at the bottom of the Editor has four hotspot tools from which to choose (see Figure 3–61):
  - Rectangular hotspot
  - Circular hotspot
  - Polygonal hotspot
  - Highlight hotspot

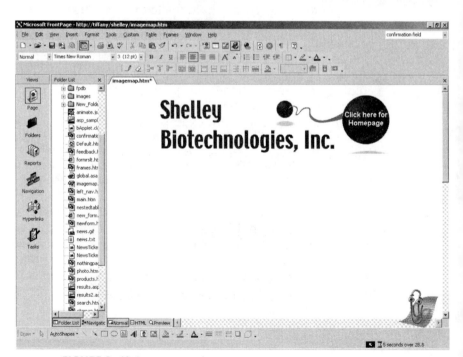

FIGURE 3–60 Image mapping.

FIGURE 3–61 Image map tools—Image Formatting toolbar.

- Each hotspot tool works in a similar fashion, except for the highlight hotspot tool, which simply highlights any hotspots already on an image. For this example, we will choose the rectangular hotspot tool to create hyperlinks on each title that appears to be a button but is actually one wide graphic. We will add hotspots to this image so that it will work as though it has separate buttons.
- Click the rectangular hotspot tool on the Image toolbar.
- Click once at the top left corner of where you want the first hotspot to be placed and hold the left mouse button to drag the hotspot rectangle to the bottom right corner of where you want the hotspot (see Figure 3–62).
- Once you have created the rectangle and let go of the mouse, FrontPage will prompt you with the Insert Hyperlink dialog box. Here, choose the page or hyperlink that you want for this hotspot (see Figure 3–63).
- For the first hotspot in this example, we will select the *products.htm* page for the hyperlink. Any URL can be added as a hyperlink for a hotspot, as well as any Mailto hyperlink.

FIGURE 3–62 Adding a hotspot.

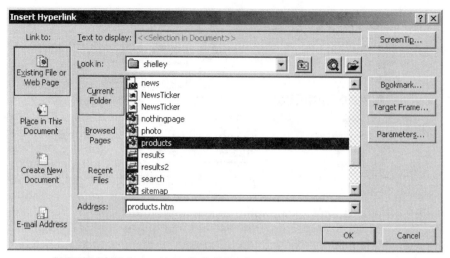

FIGURE 3–63 Insert Hyperlink dialog box.

- Repeat the process of adding hotspots for each hyperlink hotspot you want created on this image map. You may view the page in your browser or in the Preview view of FrontPage 2002 to test the hyperlinks.
- Each hotspot can also be dragged and dropped on the page in case you want to move it slightly on the image. To do this, just highlight the image, move your mouse over the hotspot you want to move, left-click on that hotspot outline, and drag it to the location you want.
- You may also adjust the size of your hotspots by left-clicking on any node on a hotspot outline and dragging that node to make the outline bigger or smaller.

◆ Photo Gallery

The Photo Gallery feature in FrontPage 2002 is a great way to display galleries of photos for which FrontPage will automatically format the layout, based on the layout selection you configure. Choose from several preset layouts, add your photos to the gallery with descriptions and captions, and let FrontPage manage the design formatting and thumbnail creation for you. Photo Gallery is a great tool for product displays, employee bio pages or

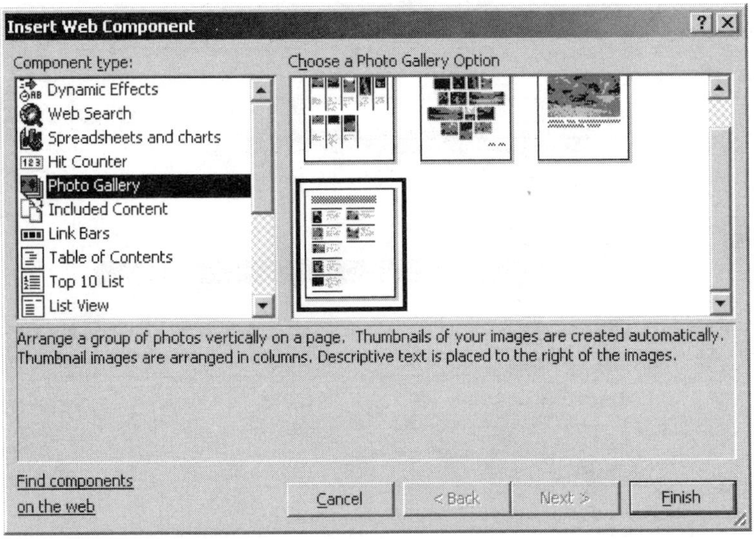

FIGURE 3–64 Insert Web Components—Photo Gallery.

just for personal photographs to share with family and friends through your Web site.

To create a Photo Gallery, follow these simple steps:

- From the Insert menu, select Web Components.
- Choose Photo Gallery on the left pane, then select one of the styles from the right pane and click the Finish button to launch the Photo Gallery Options dialog box (see Figure 3–64).
- In the Photo Gallery Properties dialog box, you can add photos to the gallery by clicking the Add button (see Figure 3–65).
- Add your photo or graphic selection to the Photo Gallery and customize this photo in the gallery. With the image file name selected in the left pane of the Photo Gallery Properties dialog box, you will see a preview of that graphic in the right pane.
- Chose to Use font formatting from page or Override and use custom font formatting. If you choose to override the font formatting, you can use the font formatting tools above the caption entry box in the Photo Gallery Properties dialog box to choose the font style, size, color, and more.

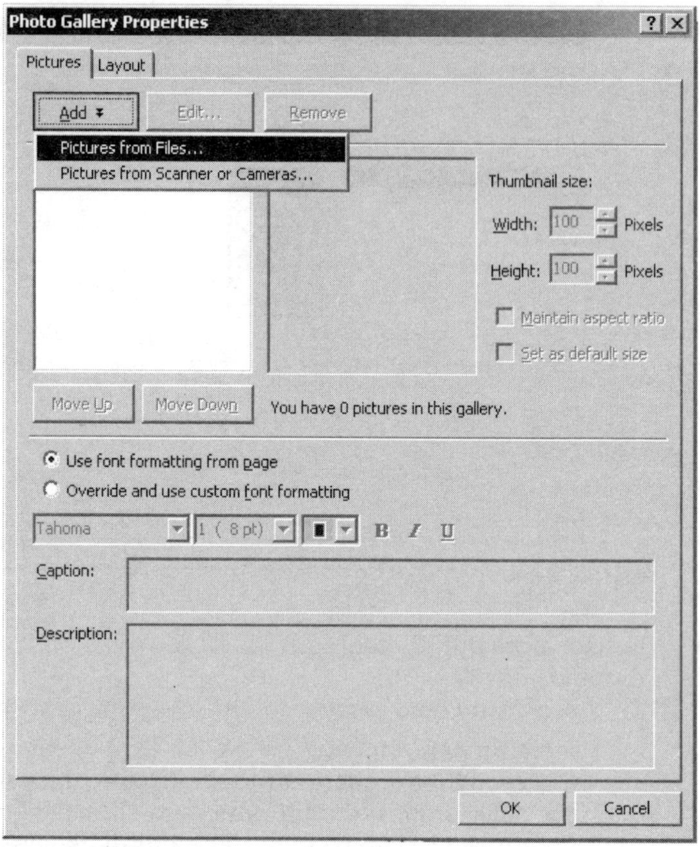

FIGURE 3–65 Add pictures to a Photo Gallery.

- Type in a Caption for your graphic and a description (see Figure 3–66).
- Repeat the above steps to add more graphics with captions and descriptions, then click the OK button to insert the new Photo Gallery on your Web page (see Figure 3–67).
- You may change the Photo Gallery properties any time by right-clicking over the Photo Gallery in Normal view and selecting Photo Gallery Properties from the menu.

FIGURE 3–66 Customizing photos in Photo Gallery Properties dialog box.

- In the Photo Gallery Properties dialog box, you can change any of the text captions and descriptions for individual graphics, add more graphics to the gallery, or remove graphics from the gallery.
- Clicking the Layout tab at the top of the Photo Gallery Properties dialog box gives you the option to change the layout style of the selected Photo Gallery.

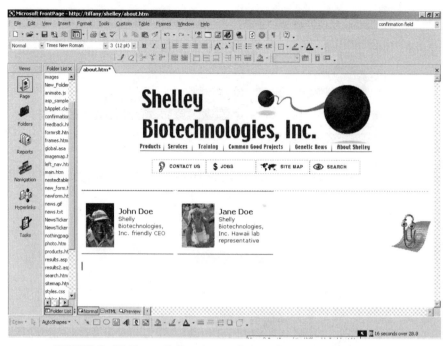

FIGURE 3–67 Photo Gallery inserted on page.

◆ Interactive Content

Adding interactive content to your Web site pages has never been easier than it is now with FrontPage 2002. Interactive content, such as weather forecasts and news headlines from MSNBC, Web searches and stock quotes from MSN, maps from Expedia, and several features from bCentral, can now be added to your Web pages by selecting the content you want to add right from the Web Components dialog box.

Add interactive content from the Web Components dialog box (see Figure 3–68).

Under Component, type on the left scroll down to see:

- bCentral Web Components
- Expedia Components

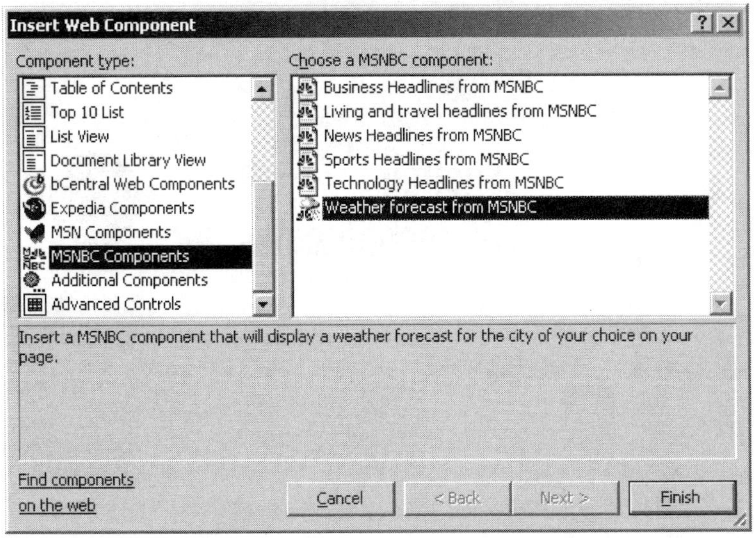

FIGURE 3–68 Insert Web Components dialog box—Interactive Content.

- MSN Components
- MSNBC Components

When you highlight the components in the left pane, the respective component features are listed in the right pane. You can highlight any of those features in the right pane to see a description of that component. When you select a component and click the Finish button, the Component Properties dialog box or configuration utility will open and give you step-by-step help screens to configure the component to suit your needs.

The bCentral components are membership based; however, when you opt to insert any of those components, you will be able to sign up for a membership from the step-by-step wizard within FrontPage.

See Figure 3–69 for an example of a page with interactive content from MSNBC inserted on it in the FrontPage 2002 Normal view.

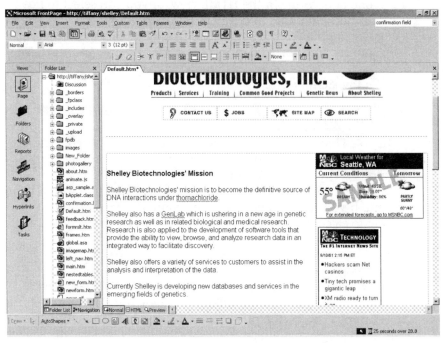

FIGURE 3–69 Sample interactive weather and news headlines components.

◆ Global Site Editing

FrontPage 2002 has a new interface that is much more like the other programs within the Microsoft Office suite. It includes some of the editing tools that you might expect to find in MS Word, for example.

Some of the global site-editing tools in FrontPage include:

- Find and Replace tools—These tools are able to find text on a current page or in all pages of the web. You may also select only a few pages in which to find and/or find and replace.
- Spell Check—This can be run on one page, several selected pages, or all pages in the web.
- Find in HTML option—this option can be extremely helpful and was new to FrontPage 2000. It, too, may be run against

one page while in the HTML view, or you can select to have it check all pages in a web in HTML view.

- Go To Line Number in HTML find—Use this feature if you are looking for something on a specific line in the HTML code. This option is very useful when trying to troubleshoot a JavaScript error.

Find and Replace Tools

Both the Find and Replace tools are found in the Edit menu. These tools are very easy to use and have been improved over previous versions of FrontPage (see Figure 3–70).

Simply type in the Find what box the text that you would like to find. If you have a page open in FrontPage, you will have the option to select the direction in which to search the page—either All, Up, or Down the page from the point where the cursor is placed on the page.

Choose the search options you would like to specify. If you have selected the All pages option, the Find in HTML option will be available. Otherwise, FrontPage will look only in the page, in the current view for the open page. If you have selected the Current page option and the current page is in HTML view, FrontPage will search the HTML code.

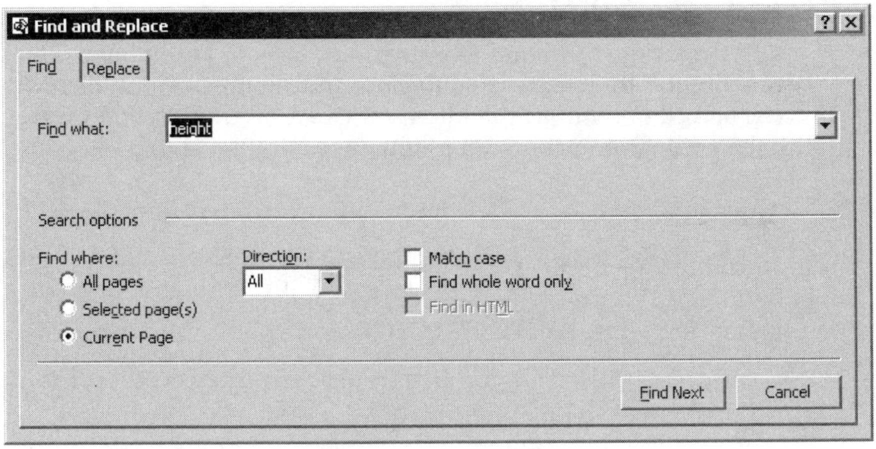

FIGURE 3–70 Find dialog box.

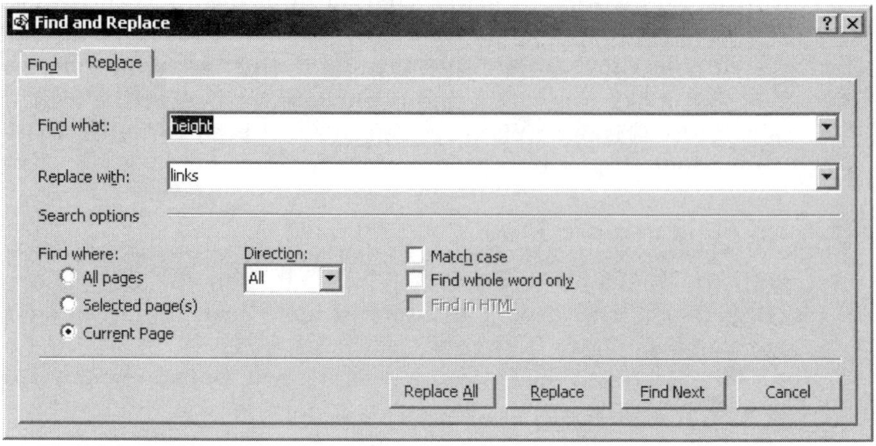

FIGURE 3–71 Replace dialog box.

The Replace tool is similar to the Find tool, with the exception that there is an additional entry box for what you would like to replace the found text with (see Figure 3–71).

The Replace dialog box also allows you to choose to replace each instance it finds one at a time or to replace all instances found.

In previous versions of FrontPage, if the All pages option is chosen, FrontPage would work only one page at a time, prompting you to save each page it edits before launching a new page and running a Find and Replace on it. New to FrontPage 2002 is the ability to choose the Replace All option—FrontPage will replace all instances in your web without prompting you to open each page and save it individually. This can be a big time saver!

Spell Check

To run the Spell Check tool against all pages or selected pages in FrontPage, you must first select the Folders view from the Views list on the left pane. While in Folders view, the Spell Check tool can be selected by choosing Spelling from the Tools menu (see Figure 3–72).

To select several pages to run the Spell Check tool on, hold the <Ctrl> key while clicking on the files that you want to spell-check or simply choose to run the Spell Check tool on all pages in the web.

FIGURE 3–72 Spelling dialog box.

If no pages have been selected in the Folders view, the default, Entire web, will be selected in the Spelling dialog box. You may also select the option to add the found spelling errors to the Tasks view and assign the spelling corrections/edits to someone else or schedule the corrections for later. FrontPage will add the files with misspellings to the Tasks view instead of correcting the spellings.

Go to Line Number in HTML

On any particular page, you may find a specific line number in the HTML code. To accomplish this, simply do the following:

- Open the desired HTML file in FrontPage.
- Click the HTML View tab at the bottom of the page.
- Right-click anywhere in the page in HTML view.
- Select Go To from the menu (see Figure 3–73).
- Enter the line number you want to find in the code (see Figure 3–74).
- Click OK, and FrontPage will place your cursor on the line you selected to find in the HTML view.

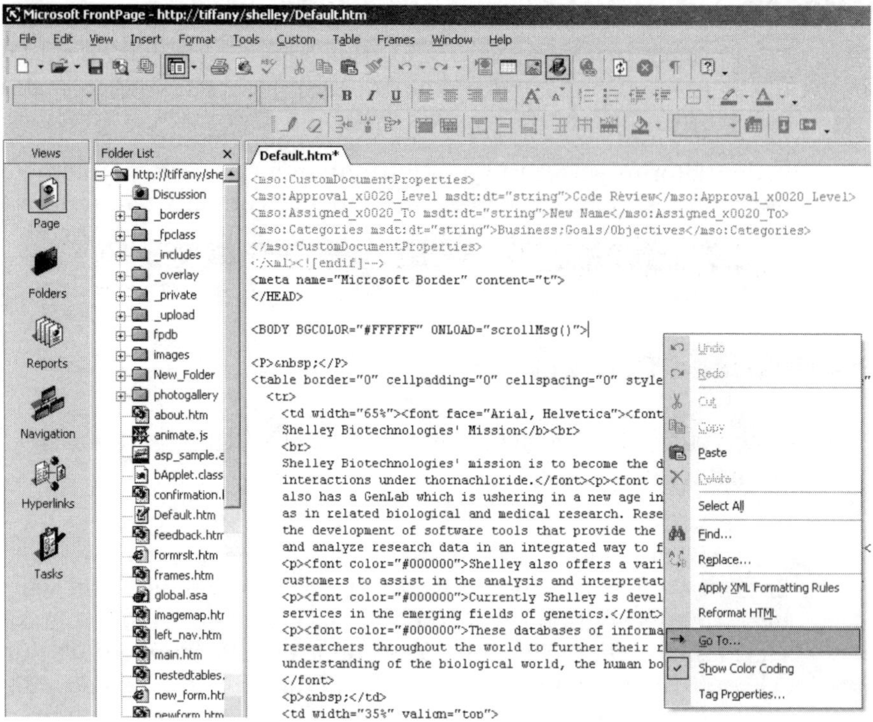

FIGURE 3–73 Go To menu selection in HTML view.

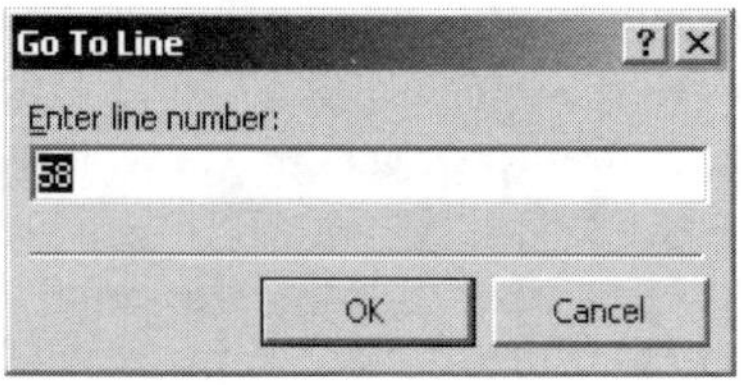

FIGURE 3–74 Go To Line dialog box.

◆ Recap

We have now learned how to open a saved web and begin editing existing pages and adding new pages. We learned to configure many of FrontPage 2002's components and features, such as Feedback forms with custom Confirmation forms, search, interactive contents, photo galleries, and table of contents features, as well as creating a discussion web as a subweb within the Shelley Biotechnologies web.

◆ Advanced Project

Open your Shelley Biotechnologies Web site. Using the skills you learned in this chapter:

1. Create a Feedback form, Search form, and Table of Contents page.
2. Create and set up at least one include page and one custom Confirmation form.
3. Ensure that you have your pages correctly structured in your Navigation view.
4. Create a discussion web.
5. Run the Spell Check tool on all the pages in your web.

4 Advanced FrontPage Features

IN THIS CHAPTER

- Built-In FrontPage DHTML Effects and Events
- JavaScripts and Java™ Applets
- Macro Add-Ins
- Cascading Style Sheets
- Recap
- Advanced Project

You have become familiar with FrontPage 2002, managing your Web pages and files and you're ready to add more advanced features and components to your Web. This chapter describes adding scripts and special effects to your FrontPage Web, adding and using third-party FrontPage add-ins and an overview of cascading style sheets.

◆ Built-In FrontPage DHTML Effects and Events

Dynamic HTML (DHTML) is not one specific technology like Java-Script™ or VBScript; rather, it uses several technologies to create

HTML that can change and/or move, even after a page has been loaded in the browser:

- JavaScript
- VBScript
- Document Object Model (DOM)
- Layers
- Cascading Style Sheets (CSS)

FrontPage 98 had just a few built-in DHTML effects. Something that users of FrontPage 98 seemed to ask for the most was a built-in onMouseover, or image swap script. FrontPage 2002 complies with the DHTML image swap feature (see Table 4–1).

DHTML features built in with FrontPage include:

- Image swap
- Text formatting options:
  - Fly in, Fly out, Spiral, Wave, Bounce, Wipe, Wave, Zoom, Spiral, Drop in by word
- Events options
  - onMouseover, onPageLoad, onClick, and onDoubleClick

The image swap effect is typically done using an onMouseover event, which is when the user places the cursor over an image and it changes to a new image. This is also called a *rollover effect* and is often achieved using JavaScript, as well.

To get started using FrontPage DHTML effects, choose Dynamic HTML Effects from the Format menu (see Figure 4–1).

This will launch a Dynamic HTML toolbar in the FrontPage Editor (see Figure 4–2).

The DHTML toolbar is composed of cascading dropdown menus. You choose an event from the first menu (On), then the Apply menu is populated with a set of options based on the choice you made in the event dropdown (first dropdown). The final dropdown menu is populated according to the choice you made in the previous dropdown menu. The toolbar also has a Remove Effect button, which removes a DHTML effect that has been applied to an image with one click.

We will create a DHTML text effect for this example using the following steps:

- On a test Web page or the *Default.htm* page, type in the words *Welcome to our site.*
- Drag your mouse over this text to highlight it.
- In the first dropdown menu (On), choose Page Load.

TABLE 4–1 Built-In DHTML Features

Event	Effect	Settings	
onClick	Fly Out	To Left To Top To Bottom Left To Bottom Right To Top Right To Top Left	To Top Right by Word To Bottom Right by Word
	Formatting	Choose Border—launches the Borders and Shading Properties dialog box Choose Font—launches the Font Properties dialog box	
onDoubleClick	Fly Out	To Left To Top To Bottom Left To Bottom Right To Top Right To Top Left	To Top Right by Word To Bottom Right by Word
	Formatting	Choose Border—launches the Borders and Shading Properties dialog box Choose Font—launches the Font Properties dialog box	
onMouseover	Swap Picture (image)	Choose Picture—launches Picture dialog box so that you may select the image to use for the onMousever image	
	Formatting (text)	Choose Border—launches the Borders and Shading Properties dialog box Choose Font—launches the Font Properties dialog box	
onPageLoad	Drop in by Word		
	Elastic	From Right From Bottom	

TABLE 4–1 Built-In DHTML Features (Continued)

Event	Effect	Settings	
	Fly In	From Right	From Top Right
		From Left	From Top Left
		From Top	Along Corner
		From Bottom	From Top Right by Word
		From Bottom Left	From Bottom Right by Word
		From Bottom Right	
	Hop		
	Spiral		
	Wave		
	Wipe	From Left to Right	
		From Top to Bottom	
		From Middle	
	Zoom	In	
		Out	

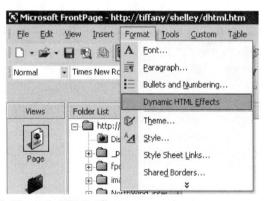

FIGURE 4–1 Dynamic HTML Effects menu selection.

FIGURE 4–2 Dynamic HTML toolbar.

Products | Services | Training | Common Good Projects | Genetic News | About Shelley

CONTACT US $ JOBS   SITE MAP   SEARCH

site

our

Welcome to

FIGURE 4-3 DHTML Drop in by word effect.

- In the next dropdown menu (Apply), choose Drop in by word.
- Now click the Preview tab to see the effect in action (see Figure 4–3).

It is that simple to add text DHTML effects in FrontPage 2002. To create an image swap effect, you must have the two images in your web that you will use for this effect. The first image is the one that will display initially, and the second image is the one that will show when your site visitors move a mouse over the initial image.

- First, insert the initial image on the page.
- With the image selected (click once on the image in the FrontPage Editor), choose OnMouseover from the first dropdown menu in the DHTML toolbar (see Figure 4–4).
- In the next dropdown menu, choose Swap Picture.
- In the final dropdown menu, select Choose picture. This will launch the Picture dialog box with the *images* folder as the look-in folder by default (see Figure 4–5).
- Choose the image that you want to appear on the final page when the mouse is placed over the initial image and click the Open button.
- It is best to use two images of the same width and height.

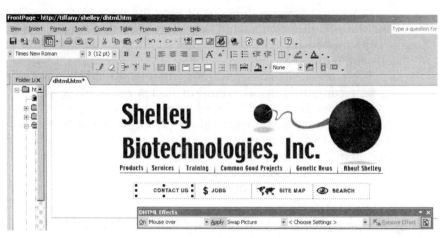

FIGURE 4–4 Applying the DHTML image swap effect.

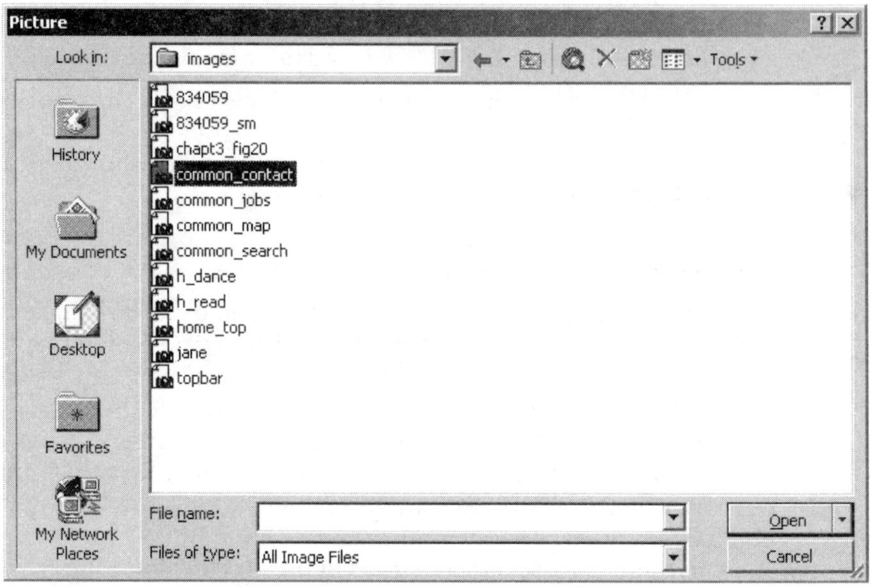

FIGURE 4–5 Picture dialog box.

When you preview the page or view the page in the browser, you will see this effect in action. It can be applied to several images on one page, adding a rollover effect to navigation buttons, for example.

There are some considerations when using DHTML, such as browser compatibility. The built-in image swap effect works in both Internet Explorer (IE) 4 and newer and Netscape Navigator (NN) 4.7 and newer browsers. Many, if not all of the text effects, such as the Drop in by word, do not work in Netscape browsers as they do in IE. For instance, the Drop in by word effect in Netscape drops in the whole sentence at once.

For more on DHTML and browser compatibility issues, see the following Web sites:

- *http://webopedia.internet.com/TERM/d/dynamic_HTML.html*
- *http://www.dhtmlzone.com/*

DHTML Resources:

- *http://www.dynamicdrive.com* (This site is created at least in part with FrontPage.)
- *Essential CSS and DHTML for Web Professionals,* 2d edition, by Dan Livingston.

◆ JavaScripts and Java™ Applets

JavaScripts

JavaScript, commonly believed to be the same as *Java technology,* is Netscape's cross-platform, object-based scripting language for client and server applications. With JavaScript, you can create applications that run over the Internet. Client applications run in a browser, such as NN or IE, and server applications run on a server. Using JavaScript, you can create DHTML pages that process user input and maintain persistent data using special objects, files, and relational databases.

Microsoft has developed support for JavaScript, and most JavaScripts will run fine in both browsers, but they should be fully tested in both browsers before being sure of the browser compatibility issues with any particular script.

There are literally thousands or more JavaScripts readily available for free on the Internet for you to copy and paste into your Web pages. Some of the more popular resources for JavaScript examples and scripts are:

- *http://www.javascripts.com*
- *http://javascript.internet.com/*
- *http://www.gamelan.com*

Some of the most commonly asked-for JavaScripts among FrontPage users are located at *http://www.at-frontpage.com/scripts.htm*

Using JavaScripts in FrontPage has never been easier, now that FrontPage 2000 and 2002 protect your source code. This is a big help for users who like to add JavaScripts without worrying that FrontPage will alter some part of that code and render a non-working JavaScript that causes browser errors.

To insert a JavaScript into your page in FrontPage, simply open your page in the FrontPage Editor. Click the HTML View tab and paste your script into the HTML view. Many scripts consist of two parts: one part going into the HEAD section of the page, and the other part going into the BODY section of the page. Most sites that offer JavaScripts for free also clearly state which part to paste where. We will work through two simple JavaScript examples and add them to the pages on our Shelley Biotechnologies site.

SCROLLING STATUS WINDOW MESSAGE

NOTE
When copying and pasting code from Web pages, HTML, or rich text format (RTF), be sure to paste it first into a blank Notepad file (or simple ASCII text editor file). Trying to paste RTF or HTML directly into the FrontPage HTML view creates a lot of extra code that will prevent your scripts from working correctly, unless it is pasted into the Editor as plain text.

Reminder
You may download all files used in this book from the companion Web site to this book. You may copy and paste source codes from this site as well: *http://www.phptr.com/essential/frontpage2002.*

Add the following in the <HEAD> </HEAD> section in your HTML view, just above the closing </HEAD> tag (see Figure 4–6):

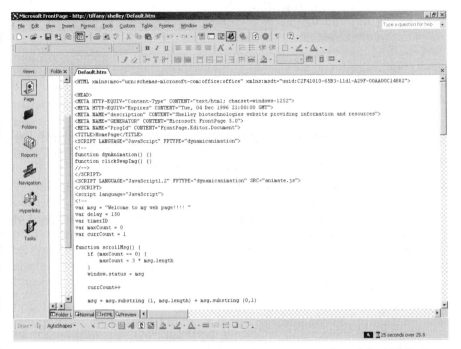

FIGURE 4-6 Inserting a JavaScript in the `<HEAD>` section of the HTML view.

```
<script language="JavaScript">
<!--
var msg = "Welcome to my web page!!!! "
var delay = 150
var timerID
var maxCount = 0
var currCount = 1

function scrollMsg() {
    if (maxCount == 0) {
        maxCount = 3 * msg.length
    }
    window.status = msg

    currCount++

    msg = msg.substring (1, msg.length) + msg.substring
(0,1)

    if (currCount >= maxCount) {
        timerID = 0
```

```
        window.status = " "
        return
    }else{
        timerID = setTimeout("scrollMsg()",delay)
    }
}
}
// -->
</script>
```

Change only the text near the top of this script "Welcome to my web page!!!!". Next, add this short line to your <BODY> tag in your HTML view:

```
onLoad="scrollMsg()"
```

Do not change anything in this line. Your <BODY> tag should now look like this:

```
<body onLoad="scrollMsg()">
```

Although it may have several other attributes in the tag already, that is fine; don't remove the other attributes. Just add this line before the closing wicket symbol (see Figure 4–7).

```
}
// -->
</script>
</HEAD>

<BODY BGCOLOR="#FFFFFF" onLoad="scrollMsg()">
```

FIGURE 4–7 Adding the OnLoad attribute to the <BODY> tag.

This script will create a scrolling message from right to left in the status bar of the browser at the bottom left of the browser window (see Figure 4–8).

Another sample script that is simple to add and popular at the time of this writing is the Add to Favorites link, which is described next.

ADD TO FAVORITES LINK

This very simple script will add your page to the viewer's Favorites (or bookmark your site) automatically when the link is clicked. This works only for IE users. This script is on the *http://www.at-*

FIGURE 4–8 JavaScript status menu script.

frontpage.com homepage, in the right column, if you would like to see it in action.

To add this to your page, create a hyperlink like the following:

```
<a HREF="Default.htm#" ONDRAGSTART="return false"
ONCLICK="window.external.AddFavorite(location.href,
document.title);return false"
ONMOUSEOVER="window.status='Add to
Favorites';return true">CLICK HERE</a>
```

In your FrontPage Editor, assuming that you are using the text *CLICK HERE* as the link:

- Type the text *CLICK HERE*.
- Copy the code above.
- Highlight the text *CLICK HERE* and click the HTML View tab at the bottom of your screen.
- In the HTML view, the text *CLICK HERE* should be high-lighted. Paste the code over it or type it into the HTML view.

- Now, change the *Default.htm#* to the actual file name of the page on which you are creating this link. For this example, we are adding this to the *Default.htm* page in your Shelley Biotechnologies web.
- Save your page.
- This is now ready to preview in your IE browser and use on your pages.

Java Applets

Java, unlike Netscape's JavaScript, is a programming language like C®, C++®, Visual Basic®, and COBOL. Introduced to the market by Sun Microsystems, Java is very popular, mainly because of its interactive multimedia capabilities.

A Java applet, a small program written in Java, runs in the viewer's browser. When a visitor to your Java-powered Web page visits the page, the applet is copied to the visitor's browser and executes there. This is in contrast to the way that, for example, that CGI (Common Gateway Interface) scripts run, because they are executed on the server. Java programs can display slick animations, invite users to play games, show step-by-step tutorial instructions, and create an array of effects using standard *.gif* and *.jpg* images.

Each Java applet consists of at least a *.class* file and the code that you place on the Web page to call that *.class* file. The applet is run by inserting the `<applet></applet>` tags within the `<parameter>` tags, which will place the applet in the page and enable you to customize its features. As an example, we will walk through the steps of importing some *.class* files and inserting the code for a scrolling news applet on a Web page in FrontPage.

This scrolling news applet requires the following files to work properly:

- *news.txt*—This file holds the text information that will scroll on the page.
- *news.gif*—This is the image over which the text will scroll.
- *NewsTicker.class.*
- *NewsTicker.java.*
- *bApplet.class.*

These files can be downloaded for this example from the Web site *www.phptr.com/essential/frontpage2002*

Once the files have been imported into your Shelley Biotechnologies web in FrontPage, we will add the code to the home page on which to run the scrolling news applet. To insert the applet on the home page:

- Place your cursor on the page where you would like to insert the Java applet.
- Choose Web Components from the Insert menu.
- In the Web Components dialog box, highlight Advanced Controls in the left pane, then highlight Java Applet in the right pane. Click the Finish button to proceed (see Figure 4–9).
- This opens the Java Applet Properties dialog box, in which you will add specific information about your applet (see Figure 4–10).
- In this case, the Applet source is *NewsTicker.class*.
- Nothing needs to be added in the Applet base URL because the *.class* files needed are imported into the main folder in your web, as opposed to being run from a remote server.
- You may add a message for the viewers who do not support Java, or you may choose to turn off Java support in their browser.
- Next, set Width to 136 and Height to 137.

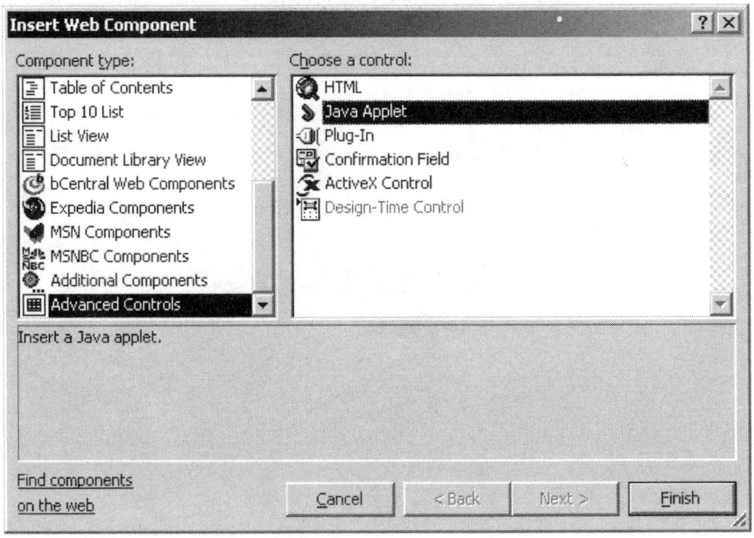

FIGURE 4–9 Insert a Java applet.

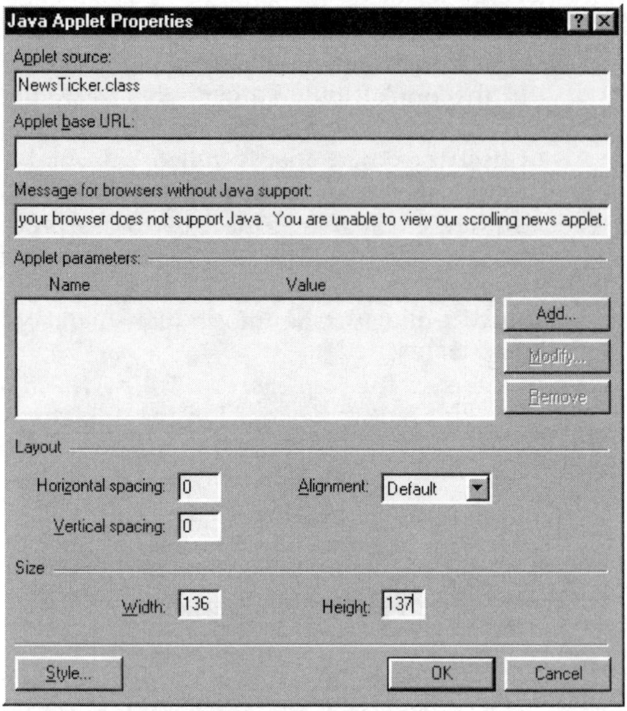

FIGURE 4–10 Java Applet Properties dialog box.

- Click the Add button, bringing up the Set Attribute Value dialog box (Figure 4–11), to add the parameters necessary to run the applet with this text and image file.

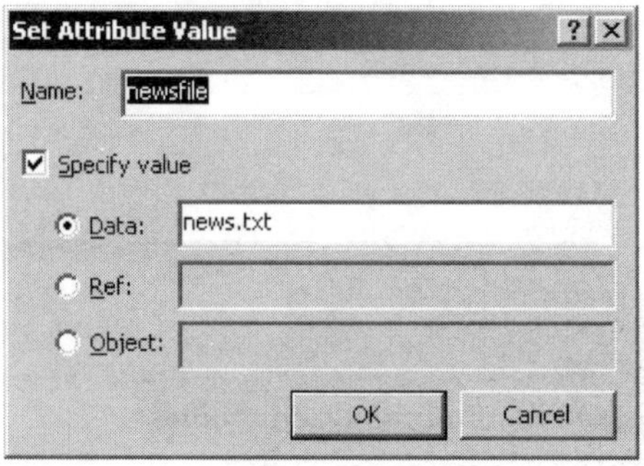

FIGURE 4–11 Set Attribute Value dialog box.

- We will first add the parameter for the newsfile so the applet will know to look to the *news.txt* file for the actual news text to display in the applet.
  - In the Set Attribute Value dialog box, enter the word *newsfile* in the Name box.
  - Check the box to Specify Value.
  - Next to Data: enter the text *news.txt* and click the OK button.
- Repeat this process for each of the following parameters individually by clicking the Add button in the Java Applet Properties dialog box for each one (each of the values should be inserted as Data):

```
<param name=newsfile value="news.txt">
<param name=x value=25>
<param name=y value=25>
<param name=cx value=140>
<param name=cy value=140>
<param name=background value="news.gif">
<param name=bgcolor value="102,102,153">
<param name=hilitecolor value="007FFF">
<param name=pause value="true">
```

Or you may copy all of the above parameters to a plain text editor (such as Notepad) file and simply paste them all in the HTML view of the page, inside the <APPLET></APPLET> tags (see Figure 4–12).

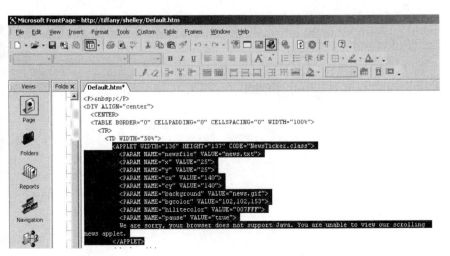

FIGURE 4–12 HTML showing the <APPLET> code.

- Either method, pasting/writing directly in the HTML view or adding each parameter via the Java Applet Properties dialog box, will produce the same end result, as shown in Figure 4–12.
- Save your page and view it in a Java-enabled browser such as NN 2 or newer or IE 3 or newer. The contents of the scrolling news may be edited easily within the *news.txt* file.

Resources

- *http://javaboutique.internet.com/*
- *http://www.javashareware.com/CFScripts/Japplets.cfm*
- *http://www.online-magazine.com/java2_s.htm*

◆ Macro Add-Ins

A macro is a shortcut or a way to perform a command that might otherwise take several keystrokes to perform in one step. New to FrontPage 2000 was the ability to use macros and create them using the Visual Basic Editor. FrontPage 2002 is equally as capable in making use of macros and the Visual Basic Editor.

FrontPage 2002 comes with the Visual Basic Editor, so that you may use it to create macros. If you are familiar with programming, you should have no problem with using this feature to create many useful and helpful macros and add-ins. If you are not familiar with programming, you may want to get your feet wet first by downloading and installing some macros created by other FrontPage users. There are macros available for free from Web sites on the Internet. One popular FrontPage 2000 and FrontPage 2002 macro Web site is *http://www.jimcoaddins.com*. On this site, you can download ready-to-run macro add-ins and code samples that may help you become familiar with creating your own.

Some of the things you can do with macros are:

- Save All—This macro is used to replace the Save All command that was written out of FrontPage 2000 from FrontPage 98. When run, it will save all open pages within your web. This is an example, because FrontPage 2002 came with a Save All command in the File menu.

- Case Changer—This is a macro that changes the case of the files in your web from uppercase to lowercase or from lowercase to uppercase.
- Netscape Margins—This is a very handy macro that codes the margin attribute into the `<BODY>` tag, which FrontPage doesn't automatically do when you set the page margins in the page properties.

These are just a few examples to give you an idea of some of the things that can be done with macros in FrontPage 2002.

◆ Cascading Style Sheets

Cascading Style Sheets (CSS), in a nutshell, are a simple way to gain more control of the overall "style" of your Web pages than with HTML alone. There are three ways to use CSS:

- External style sheets—A *.css* file can be linked from any or all pages in a web. The style code in this external style sheet will be read by the browser from the link in the `<HEAD>` section of the code, and the "styles" will be applied correctly to your Web page by a browser that supports CSS.
- Embedded styles—The coding for the style tags in the `<HEAD>` section is nearly the same as what you have in the external style sheet. Styles in the `<HEAD>` section can be used in conjunction with a link to an external style sheet, but all styles in the `<HEAD>` section will override any from the external style sheet.
- Inline styles—This is the least desirable of the three ways to use CSS if you are coding pages for cross-browser compatibility. Inline styles are nearly completely unsupported in Netscape browsers up to NN 4.7; however, any inline style tag will override any other style code applied to the page. An inline style tag is a style code added "in" an HTML tag within the body of the page, for instance:

```
<p style="padding-left: 40">
```

CSS support begins as early as IE 3, although IE 4 and NN 4 and newer offer more support for CSS. IE, at the time of this writing, continues to offer more support for CSS than do the Netscape browsers. It is important to know the limitations of support and what the result of any unsupported code will be within your target audience. See the resources listed at the end of this chapter for some Web sites that offer browser compatibility charts.

For this section, we will work with a simple set of CSS code and walk through all three of the above methods: external style sheets, embedded styles, and inline styles. Let's begin with a few sample CSS elements that will add some style to your pages:

```
BODY {font-family: Arial; font-size: 10pt; color: 770000}

A:link {font-family: Verdana; font-size: 10pt; color: 000000;
font-weight: bold}
A:visited {font-family: Verdana;
font-size: 10pt; color: 808080; font-weight: bold}
A:hover {font-weight:bold; color:maroon;}


H1 {font-family: Verdana; font-size: 17pt; color: maroon}
H2 {font-family: Verdana; font-size: 16pt; color: maroon}
H3 {font-family: Verdana; font-size: 14pt; color: maroon}
H4 {font-family: Verdana; font-size: 13pt; color: maroon}
H5 {font-family: Verdana; font-size: 12pt; color: maroon}
```

You may use the above style sample in the style sheets that we will add in FrontPage. We will start with an external style sheet.

External Style Sheets

- In FrontPage, open the New page dialog box.
  - From the File menu select New then Page or Web.
  - In the Task pane under New from templates, click the link to Page Templates.
- Click the Style Sheets tab (see Figure 4–13).

NOTE
Choosing any of the style sheet icons except the Normal Style Sheet will open a preconfigured style sheet in FrontPage for you. These style sheets are similar to the formatting styles that you see in the themes of the same names. For this example, we will choose Normal Style Sheet, which is basically a blank, plain text page that FrontPage will save as a style sheet or add the *.css* file extension instead of the *.htm* file extension used with your HTML files (Web pages).

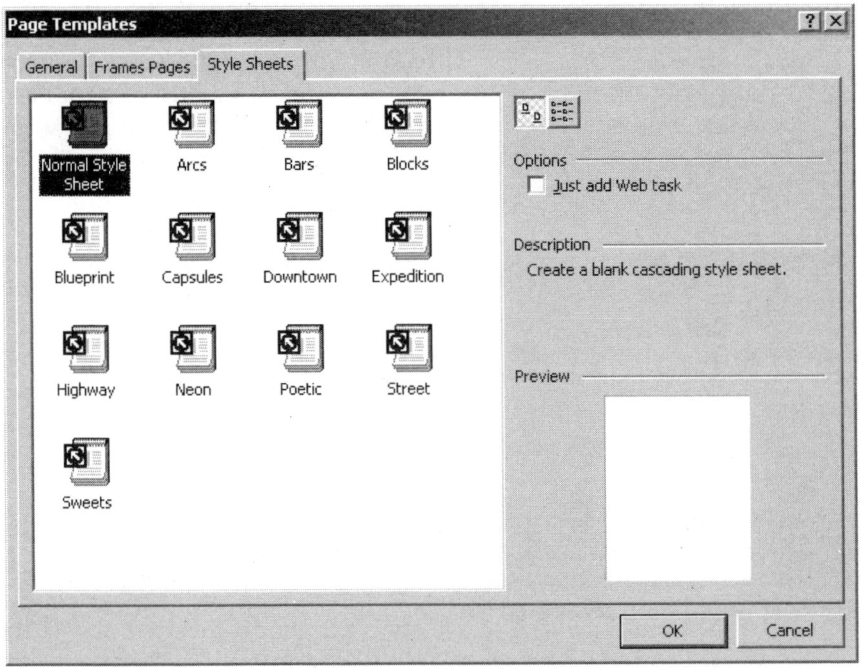

FIGURE 4–13 New page dialog box—Style Sheets tab.

- Copy the CSS code from above into this new .css file. (You can download this file or copy and paste the code from the companion Web site at *www.phptr.com/essential/frontpage2002*)
- Save the page as *styles.css* by selecting Save As from the File menu (see Figure 4–14).
- In the Save As dialog box, at the bottom in the Save as type field is a selection for Hyper Text Style Sheet. Saving the page as this type adds the .css extension.

Now we just need to link the style sheet into our pages so that they pick up our styles in the formatting. FrontPage allows you to link the style sheet to any or all pages in the web.

To link a style sheet to all pages in a web:

- Choose Style Sheet Links from the Format menu (see Figure 4–15).
- In the Link Style Sheet dialog box, choose the All pages option at the top.
- Click the Add button (see Figure 4–16).

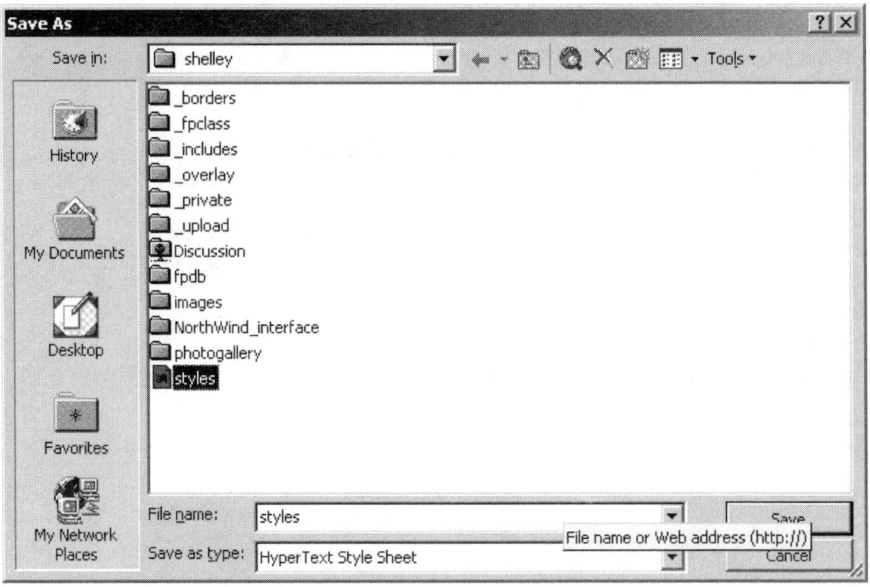

FIGURE 4–14 Save As dialog box.

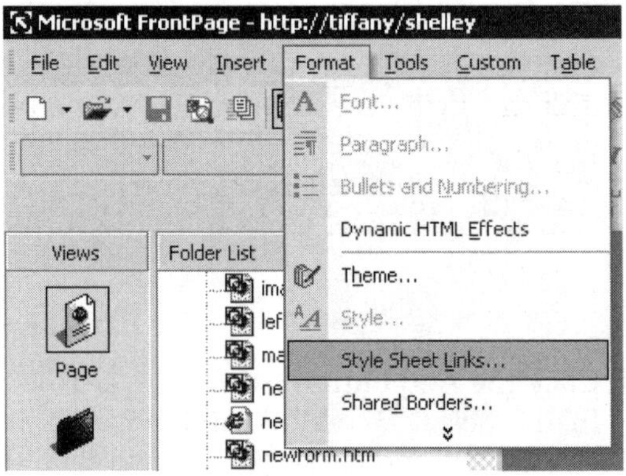

FIGURE 4–15 Style Sheet Links selection of Format menu.

- In the Select Hyperlink dialog box, select the *styles.css* file we created and click OK. This will add the style sheet to the Link Style Sheet dialog box.
- Lastly, click OK. This will cause FrontPage to add a line of code in the <HEAD> section of each HTML page in your web

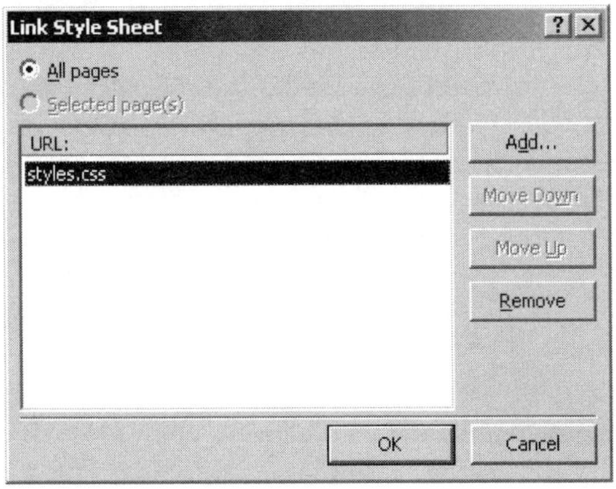

FIGURE 4–16 Link Style Sheet dialog box.

to tell the browser to look for style definitions in your *styles.css* page. This line of code will look like the following:

```
<LINK REL="stylesheet" TYPE="text/css" HREF="styles.css">
```

To link a style sheet to one page or a few selected pages:

- Choose Folders View from the Folder List on the left of FrontPage interface.
- Choose the file to which you want the style sheet linked. To link the style sheet to more than one page, select all of the pages you want the style sheet linked to by holding the <Ctrl> key while left-clicking on each file you want.
- Choose Style Sheet Links from the Format menu (see Figure 4–15).
- In the Link Style Sheet dialog box, choose the Selected pages option at the top.
- Click the Add button (see Figure 4–16).
- In the Select Hyperlink dialog box, select the *styles.css* file we created and click OK. This will add the style sheet to the Link Style Sheet dialog box.
- Lastly, click OK. This will cause FrontPage to add a line of code in the <HEAD> section of each HTML page in your web to tell the browser to look for style definitions in your *styles.css* page. This line of code will look like the following:

```
<LINK REL="stylesheet" TYPE="text/css" HREF="styles.css">
```

Embedded Styles

For this example, we will use a very simple bit of CSS code in the <HEAD> section of the Web page. We will use a bit of code that formats the styles for your hyperlinks. One of the most common questions asked by new FrontPage users and web designers is how to remove the underline from a hyperlink. For this example, we will use the following code:

```
<style><!--
A {text-decoration: none;}
--></style>
```

This bit of code is added in the HTML view of FrontPage, just above the closing </HEAD> tag. Notice above that the styles information is enclosed in:

- <style></style>—the style tags. These are HTML tags that tell the browser that the elements between them contain style formatting for the HTML page.
- <!-- -->—the comment tags. Nesting these inside the <style> tags hides the styles from older browsers that do not support CSS and prevents any errors in trying to read this code in a browser that does not have CSS support.

You can add as much or as little CSS as you wish in the embedded styles in the <style> tags. Any styles you add in the embedded styles will override any styles that may be linked to the HTML page in an external style sheet.

Inline Styles

Inline styles are very easily added in FrontPage to nearly any element within the code and can be added from the Normal view. Often, new users are not even aware that the formatting tools they have stumbled across in FrontPage are indeed adding inline styles behind the scenes that could cause problems in how a page is viewed in older browsers and in Netscape browsers particularly.

In this section, we will discuss how inline styles are added in FrontPage for two reasons:

1. To demonstrate how to add them.
2. To demonstrate how to prevent inline styles from being added accidentally or without understanding what is happening "under the hood" in the HTML code.

The easiest way to add inline styles in your Web page is by using the tools and menus in the Format menu, such as the Paragraph menu. In the Paragraph dialog box (see Figure 4–17), you are given options such as:

- Indents and Spacing Alignment—choose from Left, Right, Center, and Justify.
- Indentation—specified in numerical values.
- Spacing, Line Spacing, and Word Spacing—specified in numerical values.
- Preview Pane—allows you to preview how changes will appear.

These options offer more control for your content on your Web pages, control that is not available by using HTML elements. They make use of inline styles, so you need to be aware of your audience and understand that browsers other than IE may not support the use of inline styles.

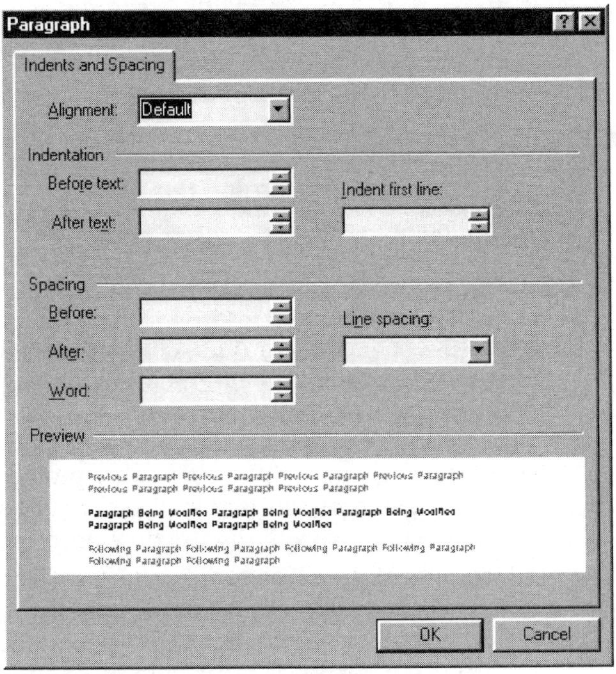

FIGURE 4–17 Paragraph Formatting dialog box.

Of course, if you are creating pages for an intranet or for an audience that uses IE only, you should be fine in using the inline style tags.

Resources

- *http://html.tucows.com/designer/intertut/csstut2.html*
- *http://wdvl.com/Authoring/Languages/XSL/Example/css.html*
- *http://builder.cnet.com/Authoring/CSS/*
- *Essential CSS and DHTML for Web Professionals*, 2d edition, by Dan Livingston.

◆ Recap

In this chapter, we looked at several advanced scripting and Web editing tools often used in Web site design. We also covered methods of using these technologies in your web with FrontPage and offered some resources for further reading, learning, and free scripts and applets to use on your own Web sites.

◆ Advanced Project

Using the skills, resources, and technologies you have learned in this chapter:

1. Create at least one DHTML effect using FrontPage's built-in DHTML features.
2. Insert at least one of the test JavaScripts in the examples in this chapter in one of the pages of your web. You may also wish to explore some of the resource sites listed, learn more about JavaScript capabilities, and see how readily available scripts of all kinds are on the Internet.
3. Visit the Microsoft Web site listed in this chapter and install the *Save All* macro.
4. Begin creating an external style sheet and use FrontPage to link that style sheet on all pages in your web. View your pages in a browser that supports CSS, then make some key changes in your style sheet and view how those changes affect all pages in your web that are linked to that style sheet.

5 Publishing Webs

IN THIS CHAPTER

- Search Engine Readiness
- Publishing Options
- NT versus UNIX
- Subwebs
- Recap
- Advanced Projects

There are several things to consider in preparation for publishing your web to the Internet. In this chapter, we will review some of these considerations and review the differences in servers that one commonly publishes to. We will also review preparing your Web site for search engine readiness so that your published Web site can be found in major search engines.

◆ Search Engine Readiness

Once you are comfortable with the content of your Web pages and you have a nice Web site ready to be viewed by the world, you will want to prepare the main pages for search engines. After all, what good will it do to have a fabulous Web site that no one can find? In this section, we will discuss some of the techniques used for preparing sites for search engines.

Good Content

First and most important is good content on your Web pages. A nice balance of visual effects and solid text content is optimal, not just for search engine rankings, but for keeping the interest and attention of your viewers. Your text content should include as many of the keywords that you believe will be used to find your site as possible. These keywords will be repeated in your META tags and weighed against the content on your page.

Good Title Tag

A good page title can be the most important factor in good search engine placement in some of the major search engines. Your page title should not exceed 100 characters and should be a good descriptive title that uses as many keywords as possible. It should never read like an advertisement for the site, using words and phrases such as "the best" or "awesome."

To add a title tag to your page:

- Right-click on the page in the FrontPage Editor.
- Under the General tab (which is the selected tab by default), enter your page title in the Title text box.

A good title tag, used in conjunction with the description and keyword META tags, is a big factor in getting listed advantageously in the search engines.

META Tags

META tags are used as a way for Web authors to provide more information about a Web site, the company, its location, keywords, and a description, among other things. These generally give the Web author more control over the description shown in search engine results and allow for more information to be found by search engines.

It is important to mention that not all search engines or indexes use META tag information. Crawler-based search engines such as AltaVista®, NorthernLight, and Hot Bot® are more likely to use META tag information, whereas human-based search engines, such as dmoz and Yahoo!®, may not look at META information at all. Each search engine handles META information differently, and the rules and standards change often to prevent search engine spamming. The following information describes how to add META tags in FrontPage. It also describes some of the basics of META tags. Detailed information and current standards should be looked up on some of the search engine resource sites listed at the end of this section.

META tags can be added to your HTML code in several ways:

- Directly in the HTML view, in the <HEAD> section of the code—To do this, you will want to have a good reference on META tags, so that you are sure to enter the META tags correctly in the HTML view (see Figure 5–1).
- By way of the Page Properties dialog box's Custom tab— This method also requires a good basic knowledge of META tag structure, because you must provide the META name, then add the value you would like to the Custom window. To add META tags this way:
  - Open your page in FrontPage.
  - Right-click on the page and select Page Properties from the menu.
  - Click the Custom tab (see Figure 5–2).
  - You need to know which META tags are system variables and which are user variables. Most of them are user variables. User variables are NAME variables, meaning that they look something like:

```
<META NAME="description" CONTENT="Shelley biotechnologies website
providing information and resources">
```

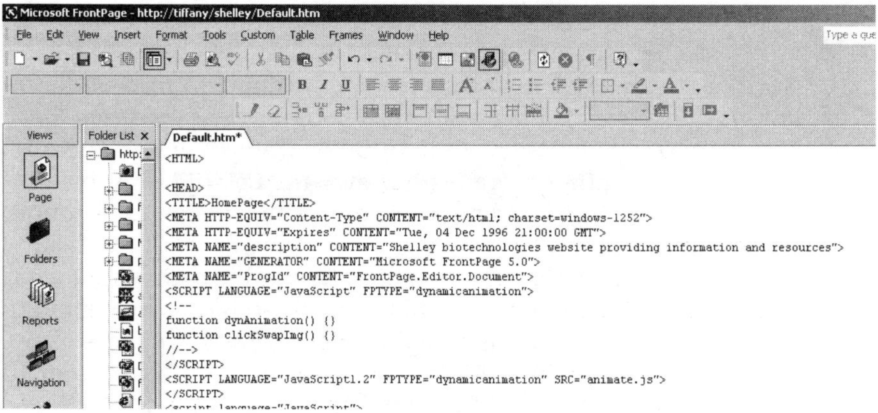

FIGURE 5–1 HTML view showing META tags.

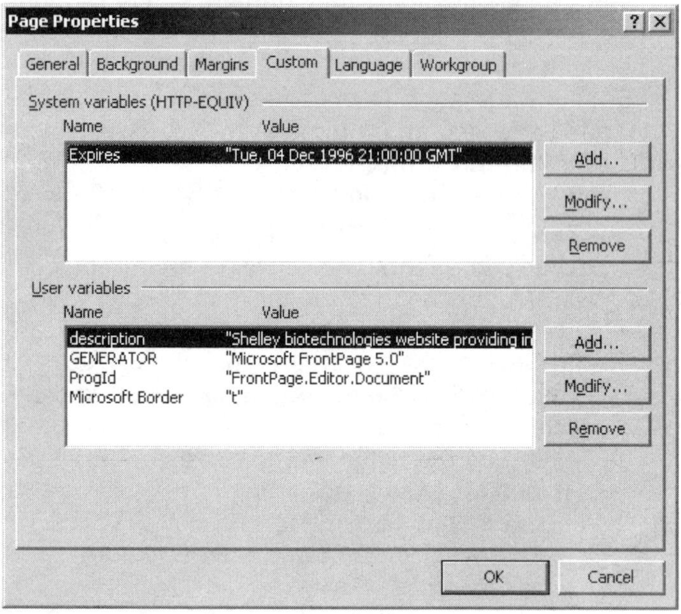

FIGURE 5–2 Page Properties dialog box—Custom tab.

System variables are HTTP-EQUIV variables. These are often used for the more technical details of a document, and they look something like:

```
<META HTTP-EQUIV="Content-Type" CONTENT="text/html;
charset=windows-1252">
```

– In the Custom Page Properties dialog box, under the User variables section, click the Add button to bring up the User Meta Variable dialog box (see Figure 5–3).

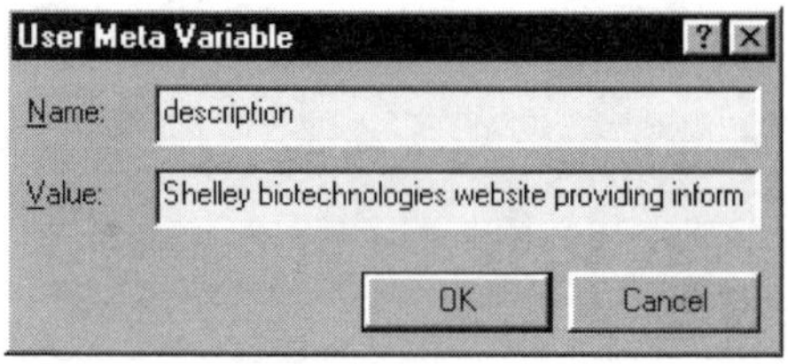

FIGURE 5–3 User Meta Variable dialog box.

- Type description as the Name and enter your description for the Web page in the Value text box.
- Repeat this process to add a Keywords box. Separate each keyword you want to use for your Web page by a comma.

• You can use a third-party tool, such as J-Bots® Meta Tag generator or HiSC's Tag Gen®, both of which are add-ins that integrate right into the FrontPage interface (see *http://www.at-frontpage.com/hisc.htm* and *http://www.at-frontpage.com/j-bots.htm*).

Some rules of thumb for acceptable lengths for your META description and keywords tags are:

• Description—The description value should be no longer than 200 characters.

• Keywords—The keywords value should be no longer than 1,000 characters. Each keyword should be separated by a comma, without spaces, and no particular keyword should be repeated more than six times.

The best order for the tags in the <HEAD> section of your HTML view is: The <TITLE> tag should appear just after the <HEAD> tag, the keywords META tag should follow the <TITLE> tag, and the description tag should be just after the keywords tag. Each META tag should be on one line, without line breaks in the code.

Again, each search engine handles META information differently. Many of them do not care what order the tags are listed in the <HEAD> section, as long as the keywords and description META tags are in the <HEAD> section.

Other uses for META tags are, for instance: for page transition effects, to refresh page content, and to perform page redirects.

A good reference for valid META tags and tutorials is: *http://www.searchenginewatch.com/webmasters/meta.html.*

KEEP YOUR PAGES FROM BEING STORED IN THE BROWSER'S CACHE

You can use a META tag to keep your page content from being stored in a user's cache. This can be used if you have content that changes often on a particular page, to help ensure that your viewer is not looking at a cached page. The downside to this is that the page will not load as quickly on subsequent visits because the browser is being forced to reload the page content and images used on the page.

To add the `refresh` tag, use a system variable tag or an `HTTP-EQUIV` META tag. For example:

```
<meta HTTP-EQUIV="Expires" CONTENT="Tue, 04 Dec 1996 21:00:00 GMT">
```

To accomplish this in the FrontPage Editor:

- Right-click on the page.
- Select Page Properties from the menu (see Figure 5–2).
- Click the Add button in the Systems Variables (HTTP-EQUIV) group.
- Enter *Expires* into the Name text box (see Figure 5–4).
- In the Value text box, enter a date in a format similar to: Tue, 04 Dec 1996 21:00:00 GMT (see Figure 5–4).
- Click OK in both dialog boxes.

FrontPage will add this META tag to your HMTL code in the <HEAD> section. This will force the browser to refresh the page each time it is loaded in the user's browser, rather than allowing the page to load from a version that may have been stored in the user's cache.

Some alternatives to using the META `refresh` tag include using server-side scripting, such as ASP™ (Active Server Pages), PHP (recursive acronym for PHP: Hypertext Preprocessor), or JSP (JavaScript Pages) for pages that have information that changes often. This would require that the site have an alternative static page that includes META tags to be included in search engines, because search engines do not index dynamic pages that are updated on the server side.

TRANSITION EFFECTS FOR A PAGE OR WEB

You can create special effects that are displayed when a visitor enters or leaves any page in your Web site, or browses to or from a specific page. Used on a personal-type Web site, such effects can

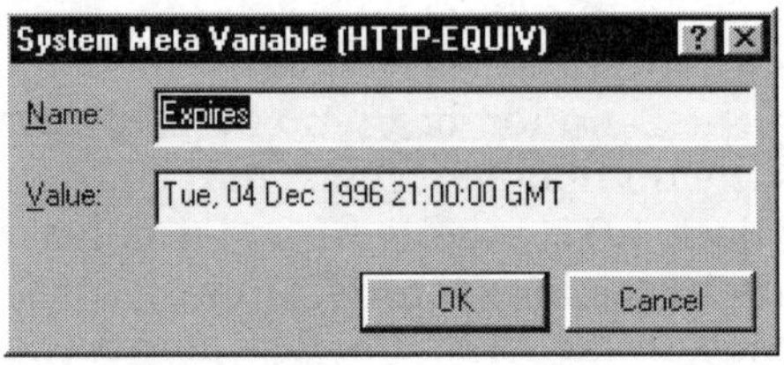

FIGURE 5–4 System Meta Variable dialog box.

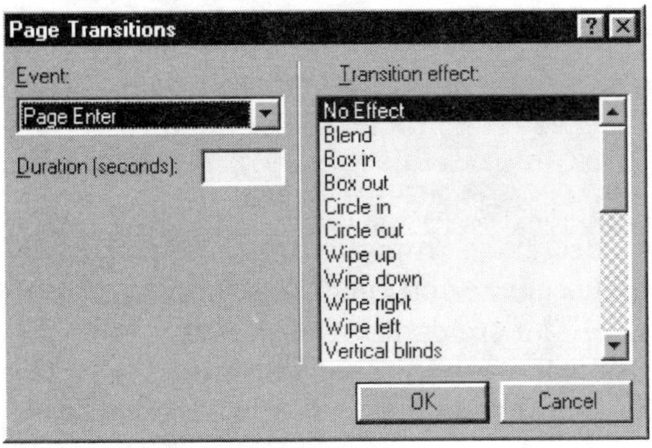

FIGURE 5–5 Page Transitions dialog box.

be used for fun or to jazz up a page or site. By applying transition effects consistently throughout your web or a section of your web, you can create a slide-show-type presentation with professional-looking transitions between pages.

- Open the page on which you want to display a transition effect. Select Page Transition from the Format menu (see Figure 5–5).
- In the Event dropdown menu, select the event you wish to use to trigger the transition effect. Options include:
  - Page Enter—This effect will be applied when the user enters the page or loads the page in the browser.
  - Page Exit—This effect will be applied when the user exits the page or loads a new page in the browser.
  - Site Enter—This effect will be applied when any page within your Web site is entered.
  - Site Exit—This effect will be applied when any page within your Web site is exited, unless the browser window is closed.
- In the Transition effect frame, on the right side of the Page Transitions dialog box, you are given a full selection of all page transition effects from which to choose.
- In the Duration box, enter a numerical value. This number is the number of seconds that you want the transition effect to last. 1.0 is usually a good number. More than one second can be too long for users to wait for the next page to load.
- Click on the effect you wish to apply, then click OK.

TO MAKE A PAGE AUTOMATICALLY "JUMP"
TO A NEW PAGE

To redirect the user to a different page, use the system variable META "refresh" tag. It looks like this:

```
<META HTTP-EQUIV="refresh"
CONTENT="15;URL=http://www.domain.com">
```

The value in quotes after CONTENT is the value that you change. The numerical value is the time in seconds before the browser will redirect to the following URL that you specify.

To accomplish this in the FrontPage Editor:

- Right-click on the page.
- Select Page Properties from the menu (see Figure 5–2).
- Click the Add button in the Systems Variables (HTTP-EQUIV) group.
- Enter *refresh* into the Name text box (see Figure 5–6).
- In the Value text box, enter the value 15;URL=http://www.domain.com (customized for your needs) (see Figure 5–6).
- Click OK in both dialog boxes.

FrontPage will add this META tag to your HMTL code in the <HEAD> section. This will force the browser to redirect to the page specified each time it is loaded in the user's browser.

This META tag is good for pages or Web sites that have moved to a new location with a new URL.

Resources

- *http://www.at-frontpage.com/meta.htm*
- *http://www.at-frontpage.com/searchengines.htm*

FIGURE 5–6 System Meta Variable dialog box.

◆ Publishing Options

When you have completed your Web site and are ready to put your site up on the Internet for the world to see, you have several things to consider:

- Domain name
- Web host provider
- Whether or not the Web host provider has FrontPage extensions installed on the server

The domain name you choose will be the URL that visitors use to find you or your business on the Internet; for example, the domain name *shelleybio.com* will become the URL of the Web site, once the domain is hosted on a Web host provider's server and the Web site pages are uploaded on the server.

The Web host provider is the service that will store your Web pages and configure your domain name correctly to point to your files when the domain name is called up from the browser.

Whether or not the Web host provider supports FrontPage extensions will determine several factors for you:

- How you will go about publishing your files
- Which FrontPage components you will be able to use in your Web site

If you are not building a Web site for a company or organization that already has a Web host provider that does not or will not support FrontPage extensions, I suggest looking for a provider that supports FrontPage extensions. Two places to look for a Web hosting company that supports FrontPage extensions are:

- *http://www.microsoftwpp.com/wppsearch/*
- *http://www.at-frontpage.com/links.htm#hosts*

If you are in the market for a Web hosting company and need some guidance as to what to look for, several hundred FrontPage users got together to create a Web host checklist that you may find helpful in this process. It can be found at *http://www.at-frontpage.com/hostchecklist.htm*.

Once you have your Web space secured, you are ready to publish your work. We will start with describing the FrontPage publish feature, which uses HTTP, or Hypertext Transfer Protocol, to transfer the files from your hard drive to the server that will host your pages for the world to see.

Publishing to a FrontPage Extended Server

- Open your web in FrontPage.
- Select Publish Web from the File menu (see Figure 5–7).
- In the Publish Web dialog box (see Figure 5–8), type the URL where you are publishing your files. Your Web host provider will supply you with the information you need for this purpose. On every subsequent publish, FrontPage will remember the address you previously published to, and the default, "Specify the location to publish your web to," will automatically be filled in with that address.
- For the first time you publish, type in the destination URL and click the OK button. FrontPage will prompt you for the username and password (see Figure 5–9), let you know that a Web does not exist on the destination, and ask whether you want to create one. Click OK, and FrontPage will load the Publish Web dialog box with a view of the local Web on the left and the remote Web on the right. For subsequent publishing, you will not need to type in a URL in the Publish Destination dialog box. FrontPage will compare the destination files, or remote files, to the ones you are pub-

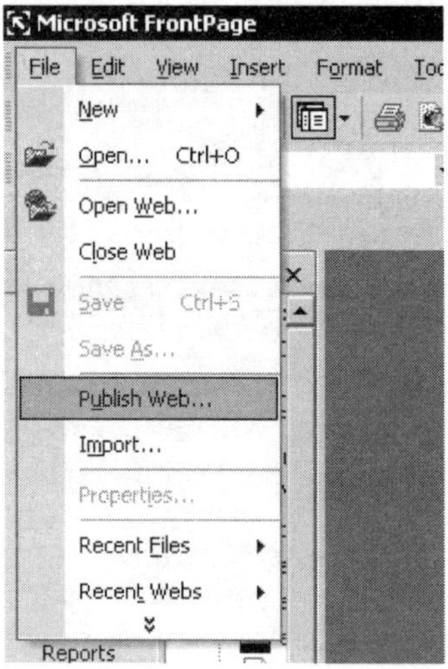

FIGURE 5–7 Publish Web menu.

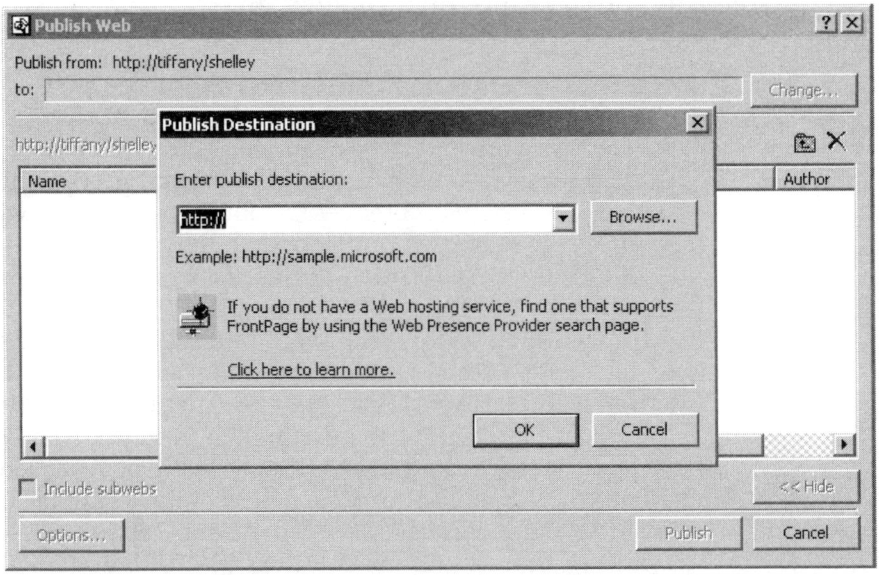

FIGURE 5–8 Publish Web dialog box.

lishing and transfer only files that have changed since the
last time you published (see Figure 5–10).

- For the first time you publish, you may want to include
  subwebs. In the example web we have built, *shelley*, we created a discussion subweb. This subweb would need to be
  included in the first publish. Subsequent publishes would

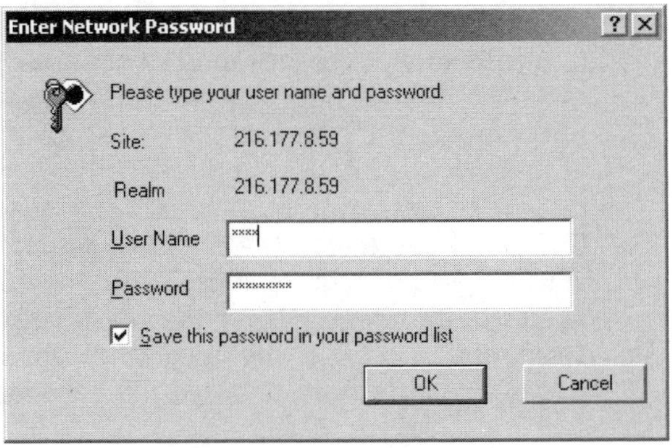

FIGURE 5–9 Enter username and password.

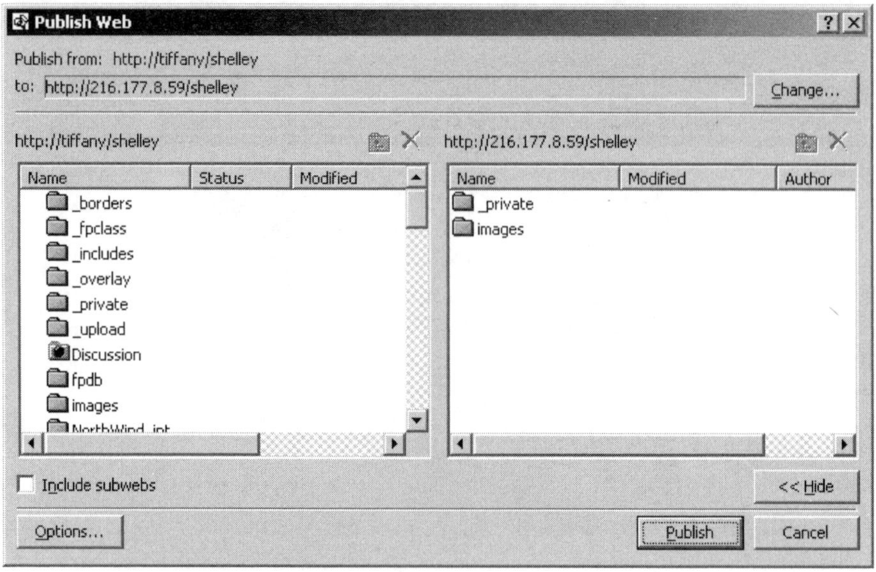

FIGURE 5–10 Publish Web dialog box.

not have the Include subwebs option checked unless you wanted to overwrite the remote files. To include subwebs in your publish, check the Include subwebs box under the left pane in the Publish Web dialog box.

- In the Options dialog box, accessible by clicking the Options button under the left pane in the Publish Web dialog box, you may change publish options to suit your needs (see Figure 5–11).
- Choose to publish changed pages only or All pages, and overwrite any pages that may exist on the server or destination Web. If you choose to publish all pages, FrontPage will not compare the pages on the local copy of the web to those of the remote or destination web.
- Choose to determine changes by comparing source and destination webs (default) or to use source file timestamps, which does not require comparing any files on the remote or destination web. Using the file timestamp means that FrontPage will read the local publish logs and publish pages that have been updated since the last publish.

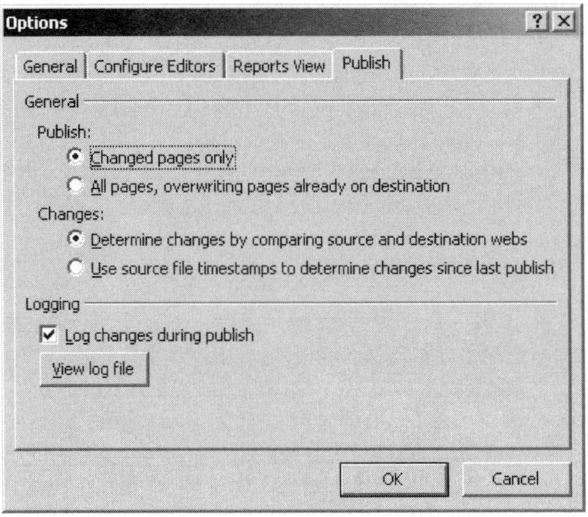

FIGURE 5–11 Options dialog box—Publish.

- Choose whether to log changes during publish.
- Click the OK button to return to the Publish Web dialog box.
- Click the Publish button to begin publishing your Web site

FrontPage will transfer all of your web files from your hard drive up to the remote server. When complete, you will get a prompt from FrontPage, alerting you that the publish was successful and allowing you to click on a link to view the Web site in the browser at the location to which you just published.

A nice addition to FrontPage 2002 is the built-in background publishing. Previous versions of FrontPage did not allow for continued page editing while the web was being published, but FrontPage 2002 now publishes in the background so that you may continue editing pages in the web.

Another very time-saving addition to FrontPage 2002 publishing features is the single-page publishing. The ability to publish a single page or just a selected group of pages to the web can save a lot of time, because it eliminates the need for FrontPage to compare a large web to a remote or destination web each time you want to publish pages.

Publish a Single Page

- With the web open in FrontPage, highlight the file you want to publish in the Folder List and right-click on this file.
- Select Publish Selected Files from the menu (see Figure 5–12).
- In the Publish Destination dialog box, ensure that the proper URL is in the text box or type in the correct URL and click the OK button to begin the publish (see Figure 5–13).

Publish a Selected Group of Files

- With your web open in FrontPage, switch to Folders view.
- Hold the <Ctrl> key while highlighting the group of pages that you would like to select to publish.
- Right-click and select Publish Selected Files from the menu (see Figure 5–14).
- In the Publish Destination dialog box, ensure that the proper URL is in the text box or type in the correct URL and click the OK button to begin the publish.

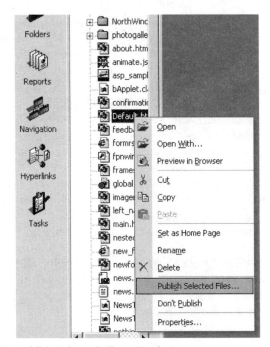

FIGURE 5–12 Publish Selected Files—Single Page.

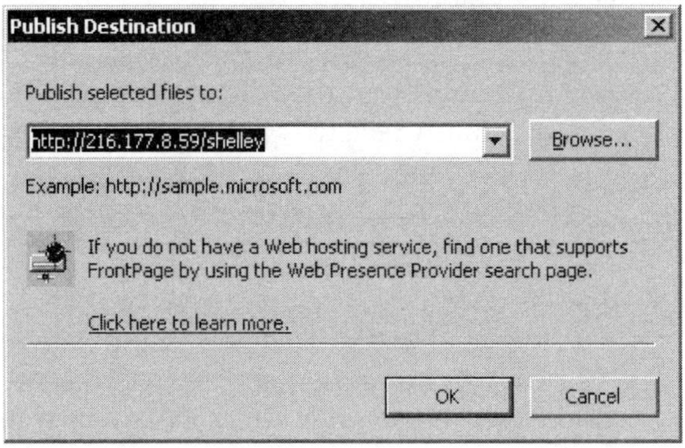

FIGURE 5–13 Publish Destination dialog box.

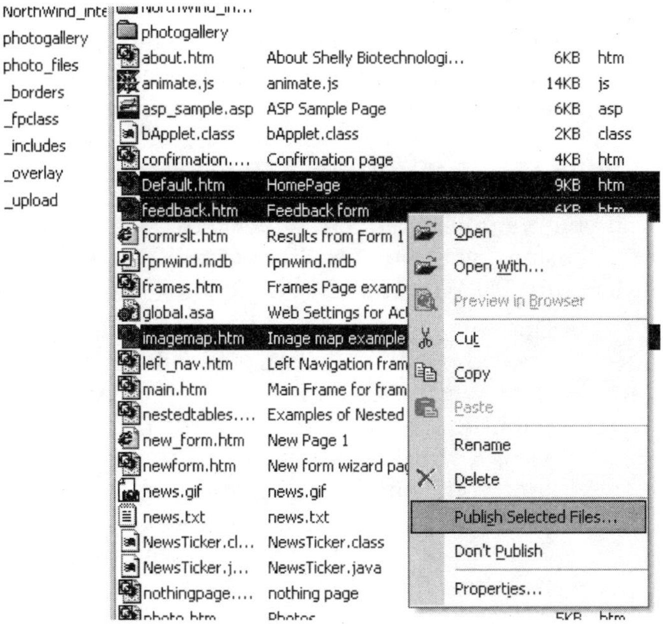

FIGURE 5–14 Publish Selected Files—Group of files.

Selective Publishing

This is a feature that was included in FrontPage 2000—the ability to exclude specified files from being published. If you have files within your web that you are not yet ready to publish to the remote location, you may select an option for the file to be excluded from the next publish. To do this in FrontPage 2002:

- With your web open in FrontPage, right-click on the file that you want excluded from publishes.
- Select Don't Publish from the menu (see Figure 5–15).
- The file will be marked for exclusion from future publishes, and a red circle with an *x* in it will mark the file in the Folder List so that you can easily see which files are excluded. (see Figure 5–16).
- To remove the mark for exclusion, simply right-click the file and select Don't Publish from the menu again. This will toggle the feature off.

See Chapter 6 for more information on publishing from a remote server to the localhost or hard drive.

Publishing a Web Using FTP Locations

If you are publishing to a server that does not support FrontPage extensions, you may use FrontPage 2002's FTP locations to publish with FTP (File Transfer Protocol).

- Open your web in FrontPage and select Publish Web from the File menu. This opens the Publish Web dialog box.
- Type the FTP address of the FTP server to which you are publishing. After you have done this once, you will be able to pick this location from a list of FTP locations the next time you want to publish your web. Your Web hosting company will provide an FTP address to you (see Figure 5–17).
- You will be prompted for a username and password; your web hosting company provides this information to you. Enter the username and password, and click the OK button.
- If this is the first time you have published to this destination, FrontPage will alert you that a web does not exist at this location and ask whether you want to create one. Click the OK button to proceed (see Figure 5–18).

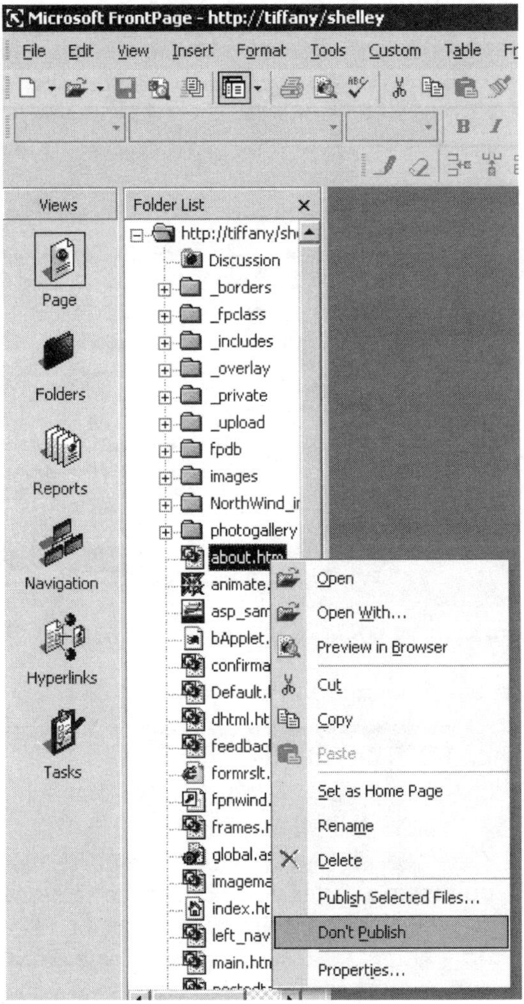

FIGURE 5–15 Excluding a file from publishes.

- In the Publish Web dialog box (see Figure 5–19), you will see options to publish all pages or only changed pages in the Options dialog box (accessible by clicking the Options button below the left pane). You can also opt to publish subwebs in this dialog box by checking the Include subwebs checkbox under the left pane.

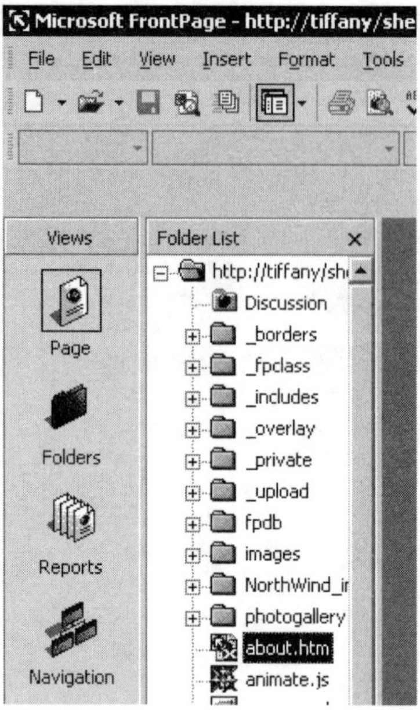

FIGURE 5–16 Excluded file.

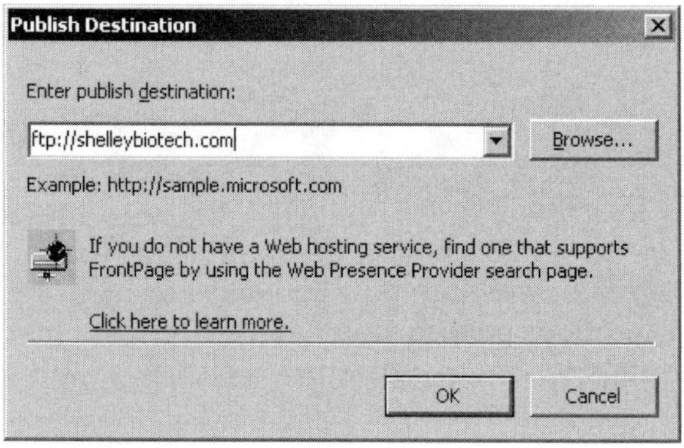

FIGURE 5–17 Publish Destination dialog box.

• Click the Publish button, and when the upload is complete, FrontPage 2002 will display the URL and an option to view the site to verify that the upload was successful.

FrontPage 2002 remembers where you last published your web to and makes this location the default destination on subse-

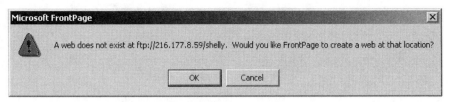

FIGURE 5–18 FrontPage publish alert.

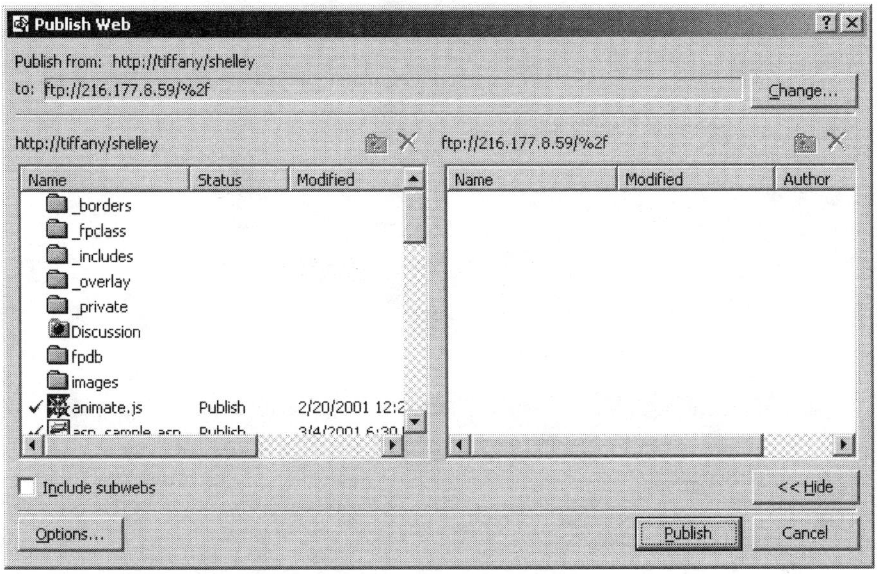

FIGURE 5–19 FTP Publish Web dialog box.

quent publishes, but you can add FTP locations and view prior FTP locations published to.

- In FrontPage, select Publish Web from the File menu (see Figure 5–20).
- Next to the destination location URL to publish your web, click the Change button. This opens the Publish Destination dialog box
- Next to the destination location URL in this box, click the Browse button to launch the New Publish Location dialog box (see Figure 5–21).
- At the top of this screen is the Look in dropdown menu. Click the down arrow to see the FTP locations at the bottom.

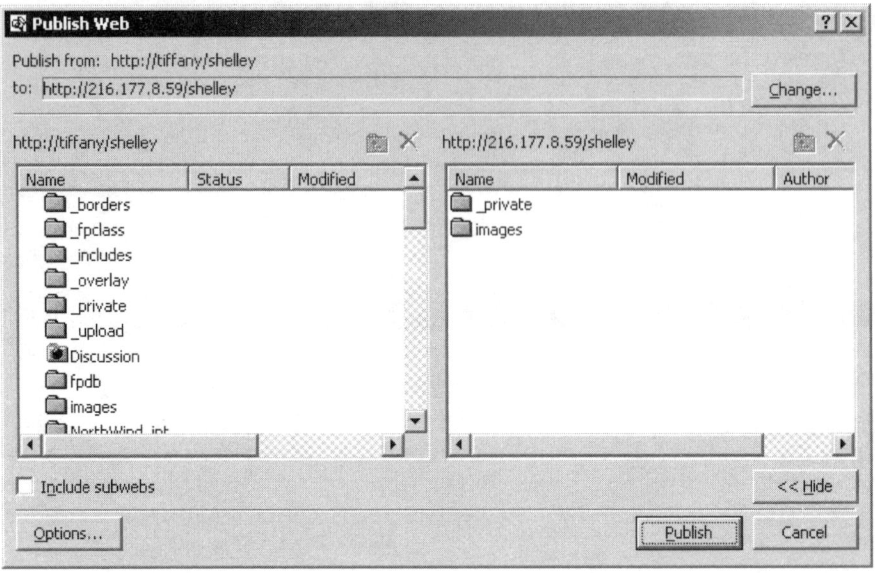

FIGURE 5–20 Publish Web dialog box.

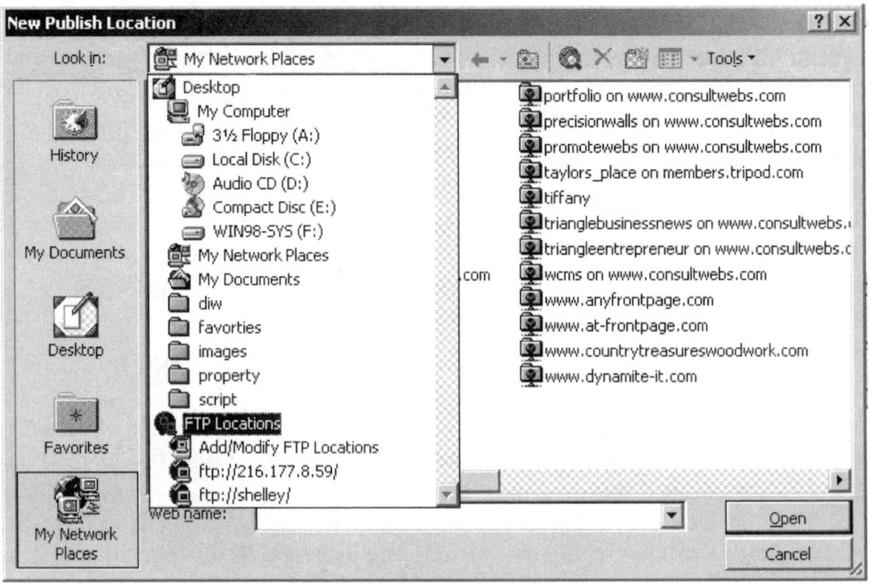

FIGURE 5–21 New Publish Location dialog box.

Previously published to FTP locations will be listed here, as well as the Add/Modify FTP Locations option.

- Select Add/Modify FTP Locations, enter the FTP address, your username and password, and click OK.
- FrontPage2002 will store this login information for you. When you select this FTP location from the list the next time you publish using an FTP location from the Publish Web dialog box, FrontPage will not prompt you for the username and password information. It will just publish the pages for you.

Another option for publishing pages using FTP is to use a third-party FTP program, such as WS FTP or Cute FTP.

◆ NT versus UNIX

There are two main types of operating systems used on servers hosting Web pages:

- Microsoft NT
- UNIX-based operating systems

There are several differences between these two with regard to how files are treated, how default pages are named, and the features that are used in FrontPage.

First and foremost, let's look at the default page names. The default page is the page that is called to the browser first when the URL is entered without specifying a file name; for instance, *www.shelleybio.com*. On an NT-based server, the default page is *Default.htm*. On a UNIX-based server, the default page is *index.html*, and *index.htm* is secondary if *index.html* is not found. If a user types the URL *www.shelleybio.com*, the browser will detect the server that the Web pages are stored on and look for the appropriate default page, either *Default.htm* or *index.html*. If you are unsure of the operating system your hosting company uses or the default page, ask the system administrator so that you know what to name your home page.

NT-based servers support Active Server Pages (ASP) in most cases, but UNIX-based servers do not have support for ASP without the aid of very costly solutions. What is ASP? It is a Microsoft technology that utilizes ActiveX scripting—usually VBScript or JavaScript. It is a server-side script that generates HTML pages when a page is requested and sends the HTML-generated page to the browser. ASP is similar to CGI scripts but enables Visual Basic programmers to work with familiar tools.

A big advantage of ASP is that any browser can read ASP or *.asp* pages without having to download a plug-in. It is also very fast. It does, however, have to be run on a server with ASP capability, such as an NT server. There is software available, such as ChiliSoft, that will enable ASP to run on a UNIX server, but it can be expensive.

Some of the many exciting uses for ASP are:

- The ability to highly customize generated HTML pages. Because the pages are created dynamically and upon request from the user's browser, an *.asp* page can be customized for each individual user based on the browser with which they are viewing the HTML-generated page, the date and time, whether or not they have viewed the page previously, and more.
- Database connectivity that allows data from your database to be dynamically written to an HTML page and opens the door for many powerful and exciting possibilities, including e-commerce solutions.

Chapter 8, "Database Connections in FrontPage," has more information on the database connectivity features built into FrontPage 2002.

ASP Resources

- *http://www.asp101.com/*
- *http://asp-dev.aspin.com/*
- *http://www.web-savant.com/users/kathi/asp/*

There are also differences in how a Web author is able to set permissions on subwebs. We will discuss subwebs in the next section and setting permissions in Chapter 6, "Collaborating on Project/Team Webs."

◆ Subwebs

The term *subweb* is a specific term used with FrontPage. For all intents and purposes, it is nothing more than a directory or folder within a Web site; however, in FrontPage, it has a whole new meaning when used with FrontPage extensions.

As we discussed in Chapter 3, "Adding and Using FrontPage Components and Features," with the discussion web example, converting a directory or folder to a subweb in FrontPage prevents the publishing of the parent web from publishing any changes to the subweb. Converting a directory or folder to a subweb in FrontPage creates a virtually independent web. FrontPage treats a subweb as though it were a web of its own. You can publish a subweb independently from the parent web. A subweb can have a theme separate from the parent web. A subweb cannot, however, share borders with a parent web.

FrontPage 98 server extensions supported only a parent web and subwebs one level away from the parent web. FrontPage 2000 upgraded the server extensions to support nested subwebs, or subwebs not limited to the root level.

◆ Recap

In this chapter, we learned about publishing our pages and the servers to which we are publishing. We also learned more about FrontPage subwebs.

◆ Advanced Projects

Using the skills, resources, and technologies you have learned in this chapter:

1. Secure a Web hosting service provider.
2. Determine the operating system of your Web host provider and whether the server has installed FrontPage extensions.
3. Publish your Web pages to your remote server using either FrontPage's publish feature or its FTP locations feature.

6 Collaboration on Project/Team Webs

IN THIS CHAPTER

- Working "Live" on the Server
- Development Web
- Source Control
- Publishing Down from a "Live" Web
- SharePoint Team Services
- Recap
- Advanced Projects

With only FrontPage 2002, you can create an effective environment for collaboration on project or team webs; but with the addition of SharePoint Team Services, you can create even more ways to interact and collaborate through surveys, discussion boards, document libraries and more. Tools such as source control, work groups and task lists aid collaboration and help ensure the work on a team or project web is not overwritten by other members and that tasks assigned by a project leader can be completed by the appropriate team member. In this chapter, you will learn more about the team management features and effective ways to collaborate with others on a project or team web.

199

◆ Working "Live" on the Server

You must have FrontPage extensions installed on the server to be able to open a web and work "live" on the server. By *live*, we mean that you are working on the copy of the web remotely hosted and visible to the world via the Internet (World Wide Web) or your intranet server. There are some clear advantages and disadvantages to working on a remote server with FrontPage. We will discuss these in this chapter.

To work *live*, as it is referred to among FrontPage users, discussion groups, and newsgroups, first open FrontPage 2002:

- In the File menu, select Open Web.
- In the Open Web dialog box, next to the Web Name box, type the URL of the remote web. For this example, we will use the fictitious URL of *shelleybio.com* (see Figure 6–1).
- Click the Open button.
- FrontPage will now locate the remote server and prompt you for your username and password. Once entered, click OK, and FrontPage will load the remote web on which you may work.

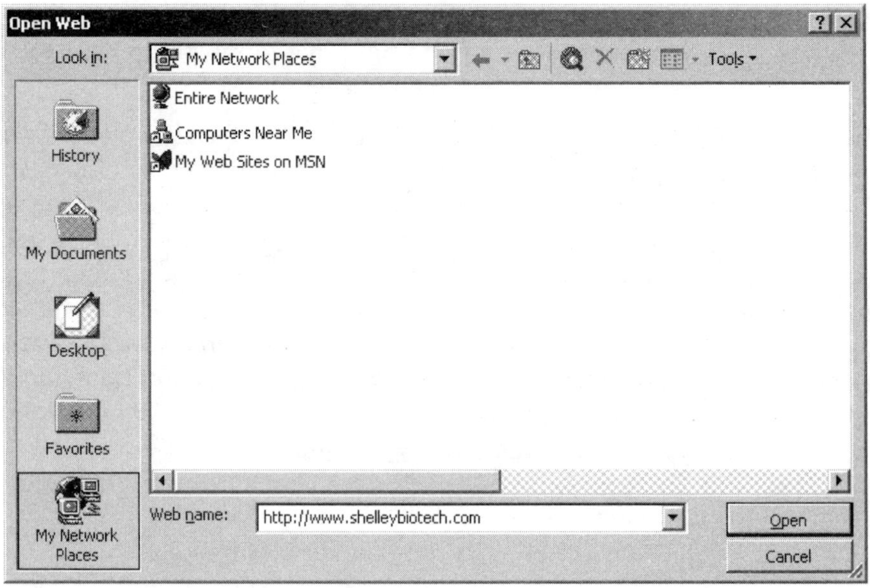

FIGURE 6–1 Open Web dialog box.

FIGURE 6–2 Open Web dialog box—shortcut to previously opened webs.

- After you successfully open a remote web in FrontPage, a shortcut to the web will be added to the My Network Places window so that you do not have to retype the URL in the Web name box (see Figure 6–2).

Remember that you are now working on a live copy, so any page that you open, edit, and save on the server will be immediately visible to the world through the browser. You do not need to publish any of these changes unless you want to publish the changes to a local copy as a backup. I always recommend keeping a backup copy of your webs in case you inadvertently save work that you would rather you hadn't.

Some advantages to working live on the server are:

- Instant changes on the web without having to publish the web up to the server.
- The ability to make quick changes on the remote server.
- The possibility of collaborating with teams on one project through a remote server.

Some disadvantages to working live on the server are:

- Instant changes that may be in error will be live.

- Working on a remote server can be slower in opening and saving pages.
- Unless source control is used, it is possible to overwrite another's work when working with a team. We will discuss source control later in this chapter.

◆ Development Web

When working primarily live on a server or on a remote host with a team of people on a project, it is a good idea to have a development web. The development web is simply a copy of the live web that is used by the team to develop and test new works and changes before actually publishing to the live or production web. Particularly if you are working with teams of developers, it is a good idea to use a development web and copy changes that have been tested over to the live web.

The processes of publishing a development web, then opening that web on a remote server are the same. You may publish a site from one remote server to another remote server, as well, which is helpful when working on a development web.

Setting Up Permissions and Security

As the project manager or site administrator, you may want to set up your security and permissions on the development web before opening it up to the team. For work tracking, source control, and task assignment, you may want to set up individual permissions for each member of the team, as well as make the development web visible only to registered users.

UNIX SERVER

Adding users and setting permissions on a UNIX server are quick and easy to do, provided that your Web host provider has not restricted these capabilities. Most Web host providers do not restrict these capabilities unless they are a free hosting company, such as Geocities or Tripod®.

SETTING PERMISSIONS ON A UNIX SERVER RUNNING FRONTPAGE 2000 EXTENSIONS

- Open the remote web in FrontPage.
- Once the web is fully loaded in FrontPage, select Server from the Tools menu.
- Select Permissions from the Server menu (see Figure 6–3).

This will launch the Permissions dialog box (see Figure 6–4).

- First, click the Use unique permissions for this web option.
- Click the Apply button.
- Click the Users tab (see Figure 6–5).
- By default, the main user is listed in the Users window, with full Administer, Author, and Browse permissions.
- Click the Add button to add new users and passwords (see Figure 6–6).

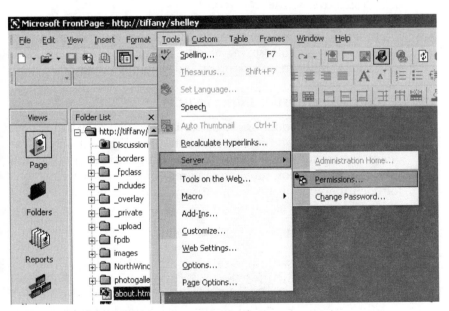

FIGURE 6–3 Permissions menu selection.

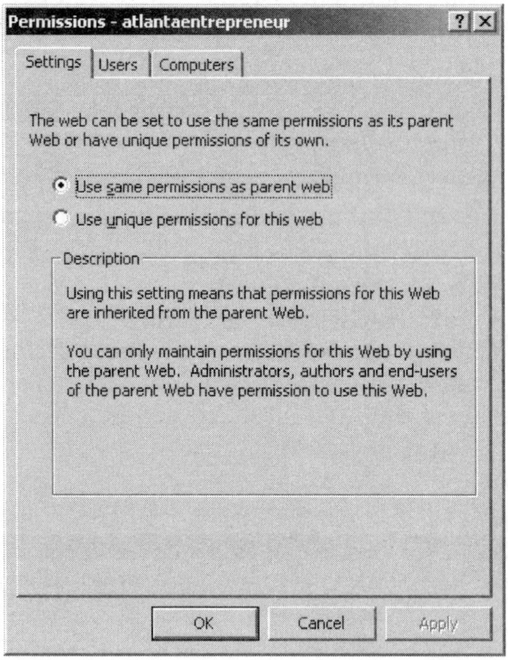

FIGURE 6–4 Permissions dialog box.

- In the Add Users dialog box, enter a username and password, then confirm the password.
- Next, choose the permissions you are assigning to the user from the following three options:

1. Browse this Web
2. Author and Browse this Web
3. Administer, Author, and Browse this Web

- Click OK.

To secure a development web so that only registered users may browse it, check the Only registered users have browse access option in the main Permissions dialog box (see Figure 6–4).

SETTING PERMISSIONS ON AN NT SERVER RUNNING FRONTPAGE 2000 EXTENSIONS

The process on an NT server is very similar up to the point of adding the users. On an NT server, the NT server administrator must add the users on the server side first. After that is complete, users

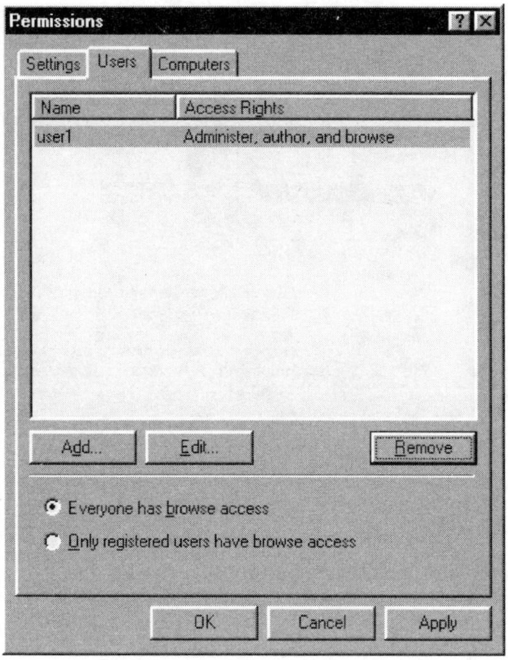

FIGURE 6–5 Permissions dialog box—Users tab.

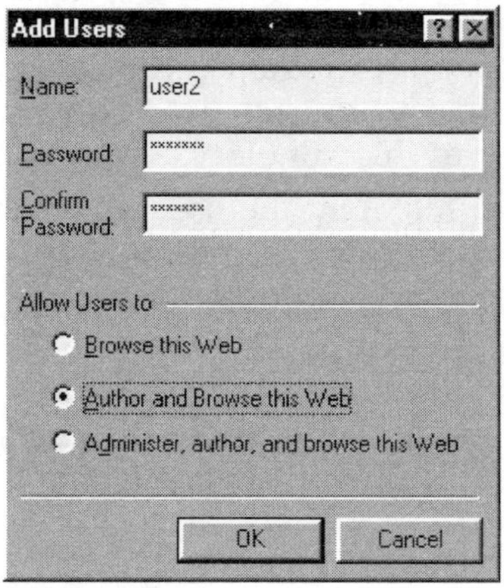

FIGURE 6–6 Add Users dialog box.

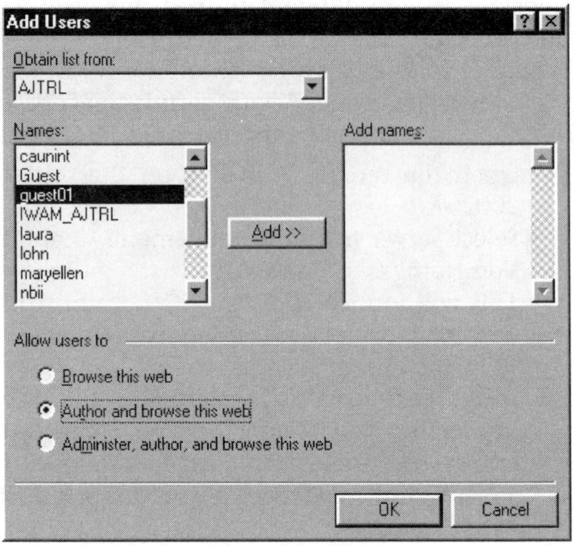

FIGURE 6–7 Add Users dialog box—NT server.

are added by clicking the Add button in the Permissions dialog box. The Add Users dialog box on an NT server differs from the UNIX server, as shown in Figure 6–7.

- On the NT server, choose a user to whom you want to give permissions from the main list of users that is shown in the left pane of the Add Users dialog box. To do this, highlight the user in the left pane and click the Add button in the middle. This will place that user's name in the right pane.

- Next, highlight the username in the right pane and select the permissions you would like for that user from the following three options:

  1. Browse this Web
  2. Author and Browse this Web
  3. Administer, Author, and Browse this Web

- Click OK.

SETTING PERMISSIONS ON AN NT SERVER RUNNING FRONTPAGE 2002 EXTENSIONS

With the addition of the SharePoint Team Services (SPTS), setting up permissions on an NT server running FrontPage 2002 server extensions is very different than it has been with previous versions. The administration of permissions, users, and groups is now done via the Web browser and forms. In this section, we will review the steps involved with permissions administration on an NT server running the FrontPage 2002 extensions.

- Open the remote Web live on the server with FrontPage 2002.
- Select Server from the Tools menu, then select Administration Home (see Figure 6–8).
- This will launch the Web site administration page for this web in your browser (see Figure 6–9).
- Click the link to Manage Users.
- In the Manage Users screen, click the link to Add Users to launch the Add Users screen (see Figure 6–10).
- Enter a username in this screen, along with a password. You will need to retype the password in the Confirm Password box, as well.
- Under the User Role section, set the authority you wish this user to have. The options include:
  - Administrator—This gives the user full rights to all aspects of this web, including the ability to add and delete users.
  - Advanced Author—This gives the user full authority of the pages in the web but not the ability to change security settings or user roles for this web.
  - Author—The user has the ability to view, add, and change pages and documents in the web. This user cannot change the theme of the site or settings to security.

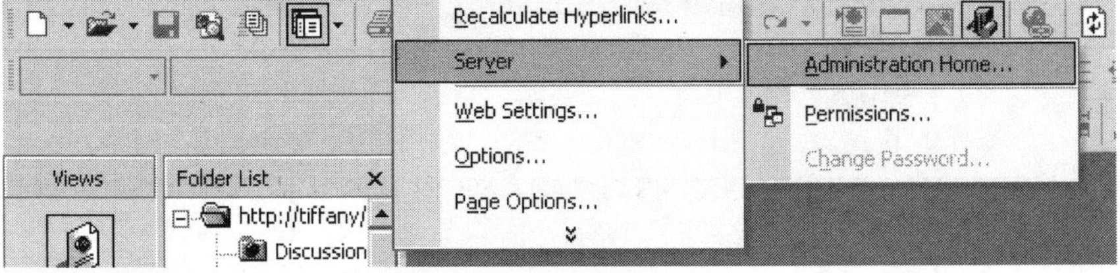

FIGURE 6–8 Server Administration menu.

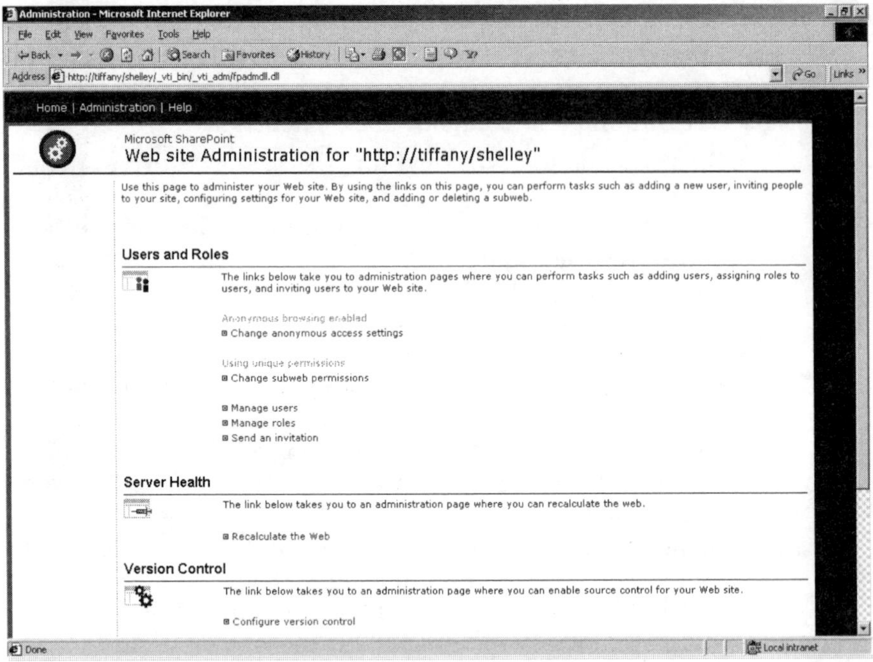

FIGURE 6–9 Web site Administration screen.

- Contributor—A contributor is able to view pages and documents of the web and participate in discussions
- Browser—This limits the user to browse-only rights.
- You may check more than one of the roles for a user, then click the Submit button to be returned to the Add a User screen, where you will see the new user added under the administrator.
- Once you have added all of the users you want to add, click the Administrator link at the top of the screen. The users you have added will now be able to access the web using the login information (username and passwords) that you set up for them.

If you have a subweb that you would like to have unique permissions from the root web, you can do this in the administration section:

- Open the subweb in FrontPage 2002 and select Server from the Tools menu, then select Permissions from the submenu.
- This will launch the Permissions Administration page for this web in your browser (see Figure 6–11).

FIGURE 6-10 Add a User screen.

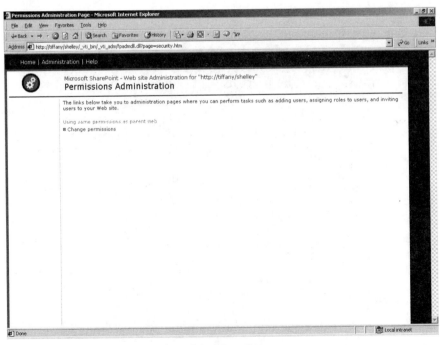

FIGURE 6-11 Permissions Administration screen.

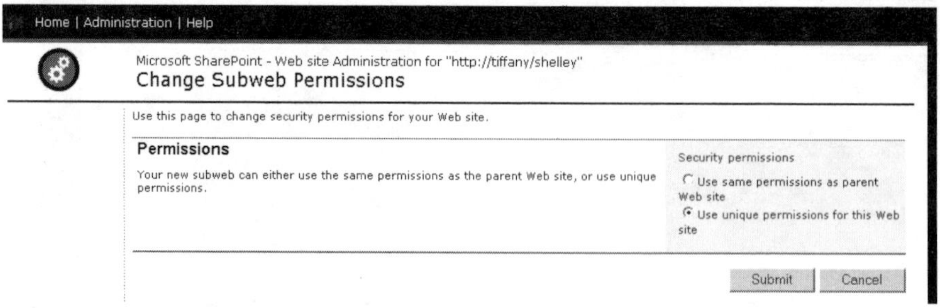

Home | Administration | Help

Microsoft SharePoint - Web site Administration for "http://tiffany/shelley"
Change Subweb Permissions

Use this page to change security permissions for your Web site.

Permissions

Your new subweb can either use the same permissions as the parent Web site, or use unique permissions.

Security permissions

○ Use same permissions as parent Web site

◉ Use unique permissions for this Web site

Submit   Cancel

FIGURE 6–12 Change Subweb Permissions screen.

- Click the link on this page to Change permissions, which will bring you to the Change Subwebs Permissions page.
- On this page, check the option to Use Unique Permissions for this Web site, and click the Submit button (see Figure 6–12).
- Now click the Administration link at the top of this screen to open the Administration page for this subweb and add or remove users specifically for this subweb.

Tasks and Tasks View

A development web is ideal for making use of the Tasks view in FrontPage 2002, which is one of the many management tools built into the application. Once you have added users and set permissions for the users in your team, you can assign tasks in the Tasks view to each of those users by name.

Tasks can be added directly in the Tasks view via the Edit menu or from any page within the web. First, we will add a task in the Tasks view by selecting Add Task from the Edit menu (see Figure 6–13).

You may also assign a task to a user by name without having individual permissions set for each member of the team by simply typing the name of the member into the menu box next to the Assigned to dropdown menu (see Figure 6–14).

In the New Task dialog box (see Figure 6–14), we will add the following information:

- Name of the task
- The priority level: High, Medium, or Low
- The task for the team member
- A description of the task, if applicable or desired

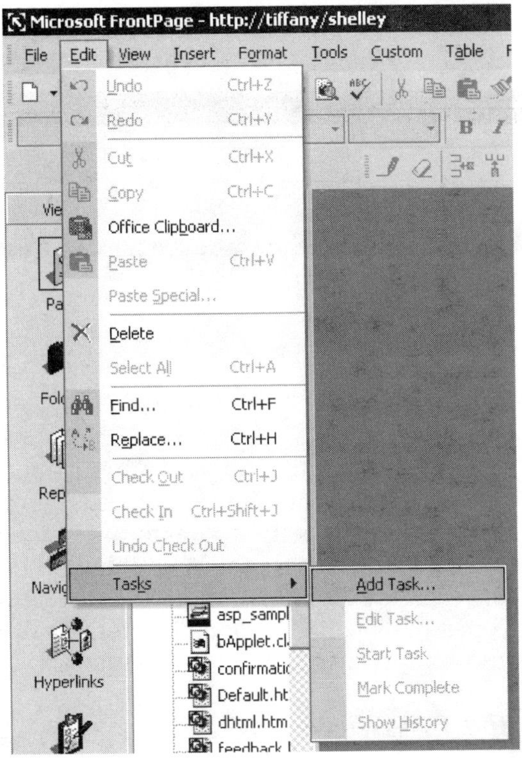

FIGURE 6–13 Add Task menu selection.

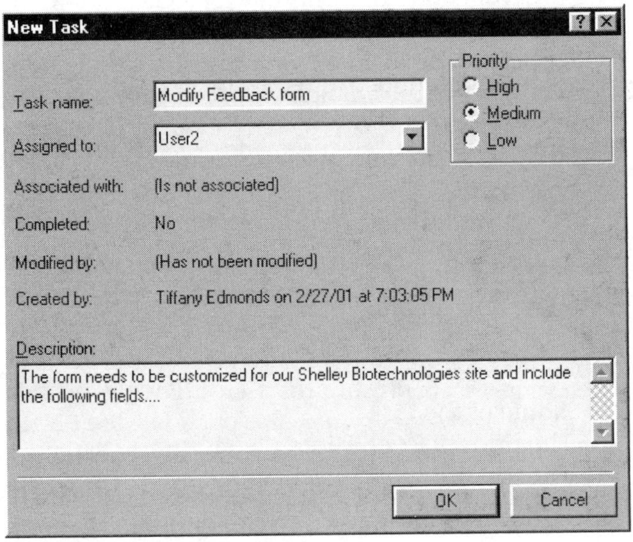

FIGURE 6–14 New Task dialog box.

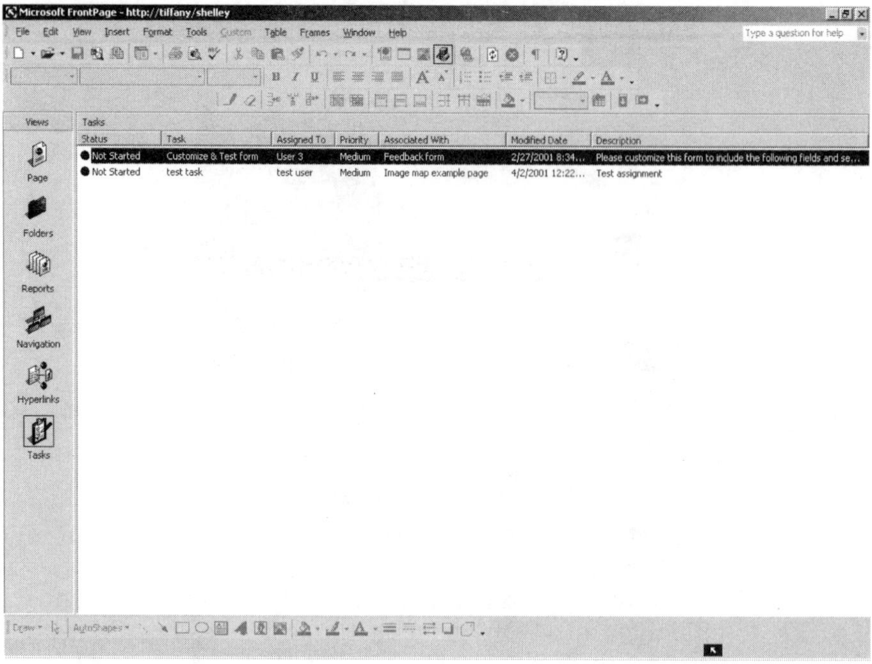

FIGURE 6–15 Tasks view.

- Once you add this information, click OK to see the task added in the Tasks view (see Figure 6–15).
- To open a task in Tasks view to read, simply double-click on it. When the user assigned to the task has completed it, it can be marked as completed by right-clicking on the task in the Tasks view and selecting Mark as Completed. At any time, a task may also be deleted by right-clicking on the task in the Tasks view and selecting Delete (see Figure 6–16).

If the task that you want to assign is associated with a particular page that already exists within the web, it may be best to add the task from the page. Doing this will associate the task in the Tasks view with that page and allow the page to launch from the Tasks view to begin the task. FrontPage will update the task report in the Tasks view when the page is edited if it is launched from the Tasks view. This can be done two different ways: Either:

- Open the page that you wish to associate with a new task.
- Choose Task from the Edit menu, then choose Add task from the Task menu.

or:

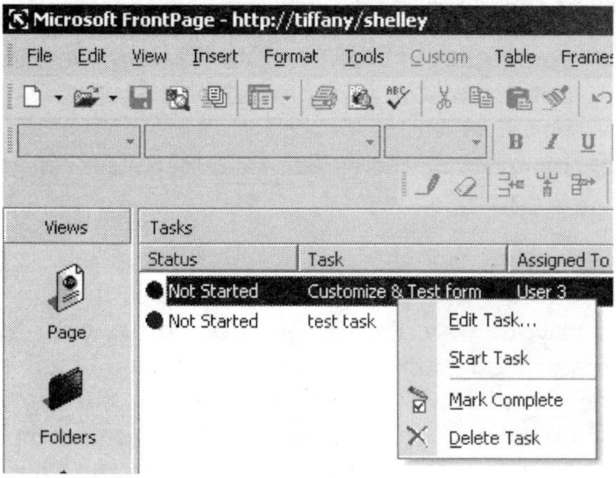

FIGURE 6–16 Task menu.

- Highlight a page in the Folder List and select Add Task from the Edit menu.
- Because you launched the Add Task dialog box with a page highlighted in the Folder List, the task is associated with this page (see Figure 6–17).

Notice that the task is Associated with the *feedback.htm* page.

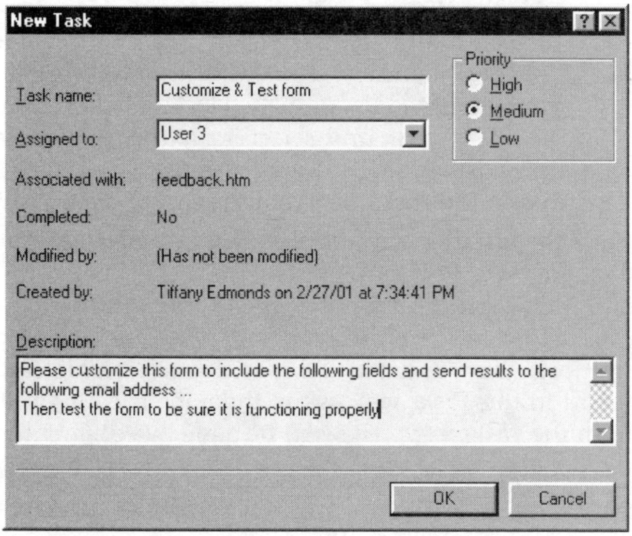

FIGURE 6–17 New Task—associated with a web page.

- When you click OK, this task will be added to the Tasks view.
- With the task associated to a Web page in the web, when you right-click the task in Tasks view, the menu gives the option to Start Task, which will launch the page from Tasks view (see Figure 6–16).

Review Status

Review statuses help in managing the progress of a team project from design to publish, when statuses are assigned to different files in your web. FrontPage 2002 comes with five default review statuses: Code Review, Content Review, Legal Review, Manager Review, and Denied. Adding your own custom review statuses is very simple and easy to do. We will go into more detail about custom statuses later in this section. Using the Reports view, you can also view pages in your web specifically by review status.

To add a review status to your files, use one of the following options:

1. With the page open in the FrontPage Editor, choose Properties from the File menu, then click the Workgroup tab in the Page Properties dialog box (see Figure 6–18).

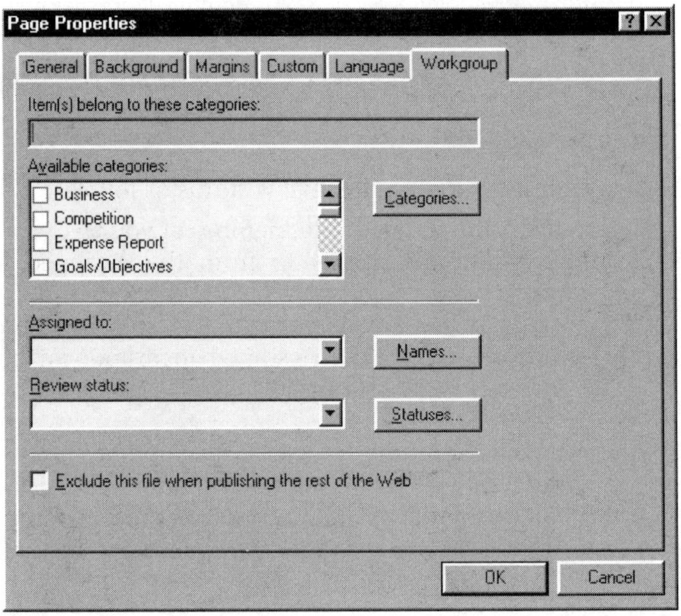

FIGURE 6–18 Page Properties dialog box—Workgroup tab.

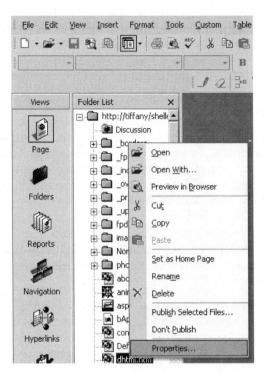

FIGURE 6–19 Adding a review status from the Properties menu.

2. Right-click the file in the Folder List and select Properties from the menu. Click the Workgroup tab (see Figures 6–19 and 6–20).

Continue adding the review status as follows:

• Select the name of the member of your team that you want to assign the review to from the Assigned to dropdown menu or

• Add a new member name to the list by clicking the Names button next to the Assigned to dropdown box. This will launch the Usernames Master List dialog box (see Figure 6–21).

• In the Usernames Master List dialog box, type the name of the new user you would like to add, then click the Add button. Repeat the addition of names for as many members as you would like to add to the master list, then click OK.

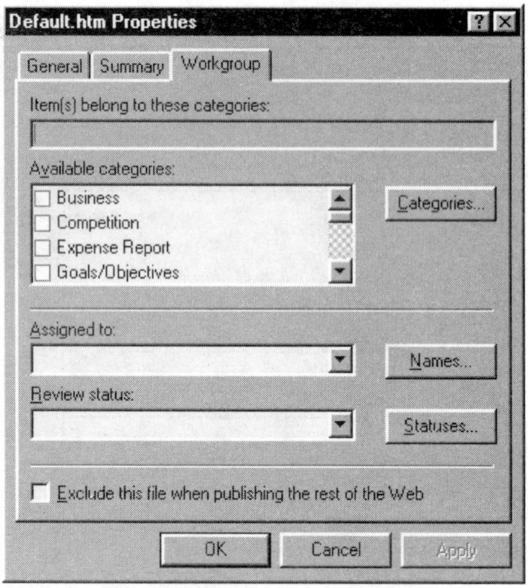

FIGURE 6–20 File Properties dialog box—Workgroup tab.

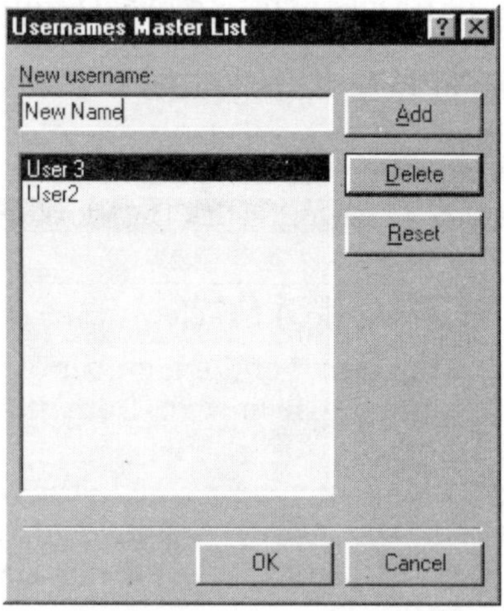

FIGURE 6–21 Usernames Master List dialog box.

- Next, select the review status to assign to the file from the dropdown menu under the Review status section (see Figure 6–22) or

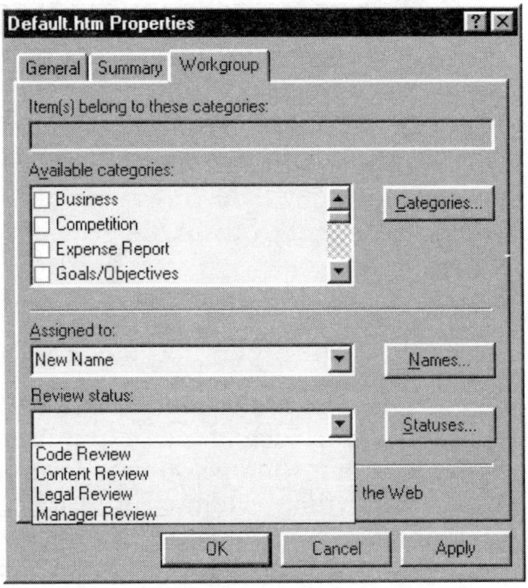

FIGURE 6–22 Adding a review status to a file.

- Add a new or custom review status by clicking the Statuses button next to the Review status dropdown box to launch the Review Status Master List dialog box (see Figure 6–23).

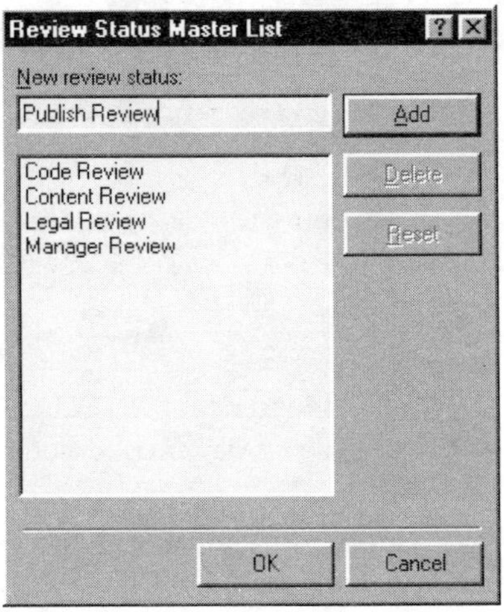

FIGURE 6–23 Review Status Master List dialog box.

- Type the name of the new or custom review status and click the Add button. Repeat the addition of any new review status names you would like to add to the master list, then click OK.
- Click OK in the File Properties dialog box. This completes the steps of adding a review status to a file in your web.

In FrontPage 2002, you can review the status of your Web pages and sort them by any of the headings in the Review view. To do this:

- Select Reports from the View menu, then choose Workflow. From the Workflow submenu, select Review Status (see Figure 6–24).
- To sort the files in this report, click on the appropriate column heading. Each of the column headings has an arrow next to it that will open a dropdown menu with the variables under that heading. For instance, in the Review Status dropdown menu, each review status is listed in the dropdown. Clicking any of those variables in the dropdown menu will sort the files and list only those that have the review status variable you selected (see Figure 6–25) Clicking on a name or title heading will sort the records alphabetically.

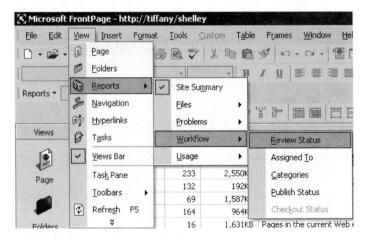

FIGURE 6–24 Review Status menu selection.

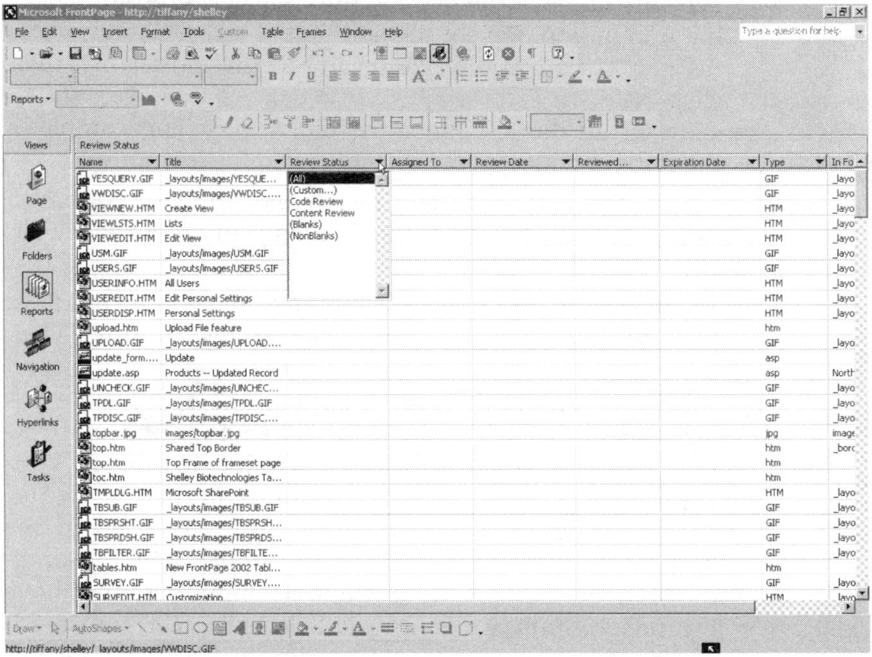

FIGURE 6–25 Review Status view.

- You may edit a review status or assigned to name by clicking in the appropriate cell for the file that you wish to edit. Clicking inside a cell will create a dropdown menu in that cell from which you may choose the name or review status (see Figure 6–26).

Categories

Categories can be used and applied to files that are associated with each other by a particular category to help manage the files in your web, especially large webs with lots of files. Any file in your web, such as image files and HTML files, can be grouped by category, even if they are stored in your web in different folders. Files can be viewed and sorted by category, as well. You can even build a site map by using categories. Customized category titles can be added to the master categories list, just like custom review statuses.

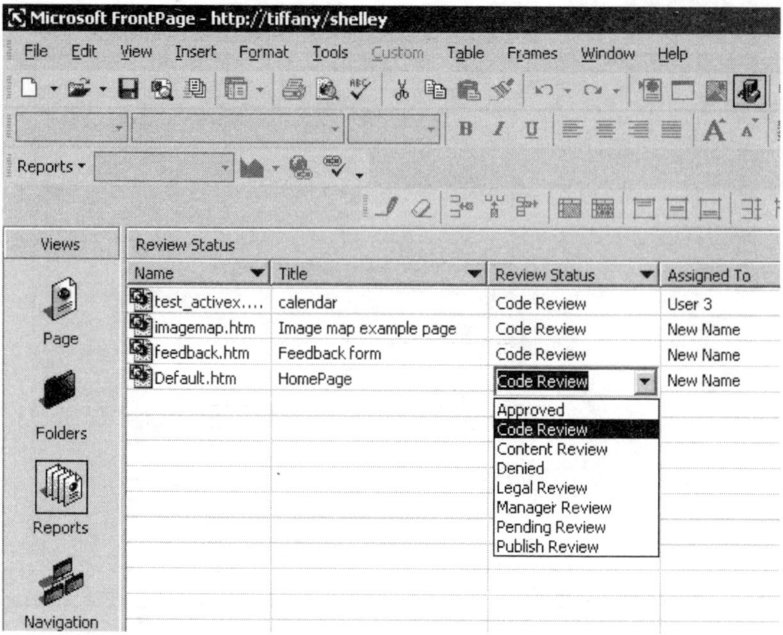

FIGURE 6–26 Review Status view.

To associate a file with a category:

- Right-click on the file in the Folder List or in any view other than the Tasks view, and select Properties from the menu.
- In the file Properties dialog box, click the Workgroup tab.
- In the Workgroup Properties dialog box, check the category with which you wish to associate your file. You may choose as many categories as applicable for the particular file (see Figure 6–27).

Create your own categories to add to the master categories list as follows:

- Click the Categories button next to the Available categories list.
- Type the name of the new category title you would like added to the master list in the Master Category List dialog box (see Figure 6–28).

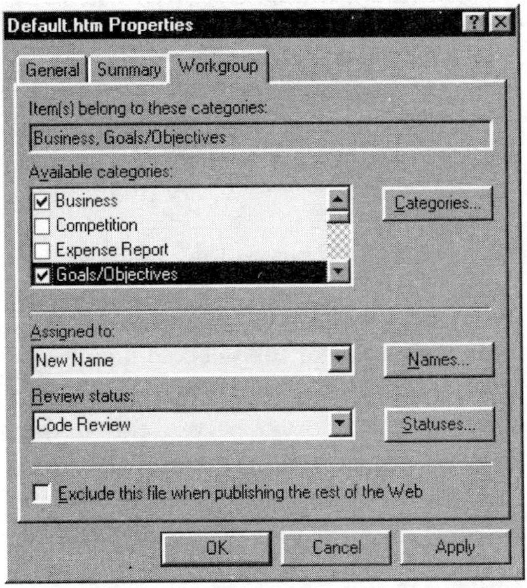

FIGURE 6–27 File Properties dialog box—Workgroup categories.

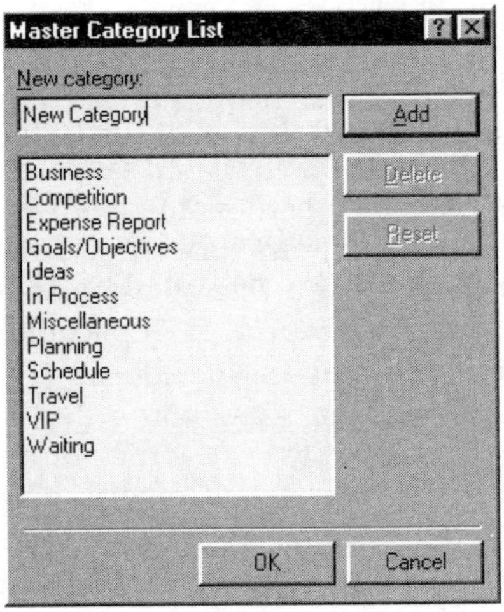

FIGURE 6–28 Master Category List dialog box.

- Click Add to add the new category title to the master category list.
- Repeat the steps of adding a new category title for each title that you want to add.
- Click OK to return to the Workgroup screen.
- Highlight any category title in the master category list and click Delete to remove any title that you do not want in the master list.
- Click Reset to restore the master category list to the default list.
- Click OK when you have checked the appropriate category or categories for the selected file.

You may associate multiple files at one time to a category, as well. To add a category to several files at one time:

- Select the Folders view from the Views list in FrontPage, or select Folders from the View menu.
- Select multiple files by holding the <Ctrl> key and clicking each file that you would like grouped by the same category in the Folders view (see Figure 6–29).
- Right-click any selected file and choose Properties from the menu.
- In the file's Properties dialog box, click the Workgroup tab.
- Select the category to which you would like to add the selected files in the master category list.

To view files by category in your web:

- Select Reports from the View menu. Choose Categories from the Workflow submenu (see Figure 6–30).
- Click the arrow next in the column heading *Category* to choose the category to sort the files by (see Figure 6–31).

When you choose a category from the Category list, FrontPage will then show you only the pages in the web that have been assigned to that particular category.

Another way to switch reporting views or categories within the selected reporting view is by using the Report toolbar that displays near the top of the screen when you are in the Reports view (see Figure 6–32).

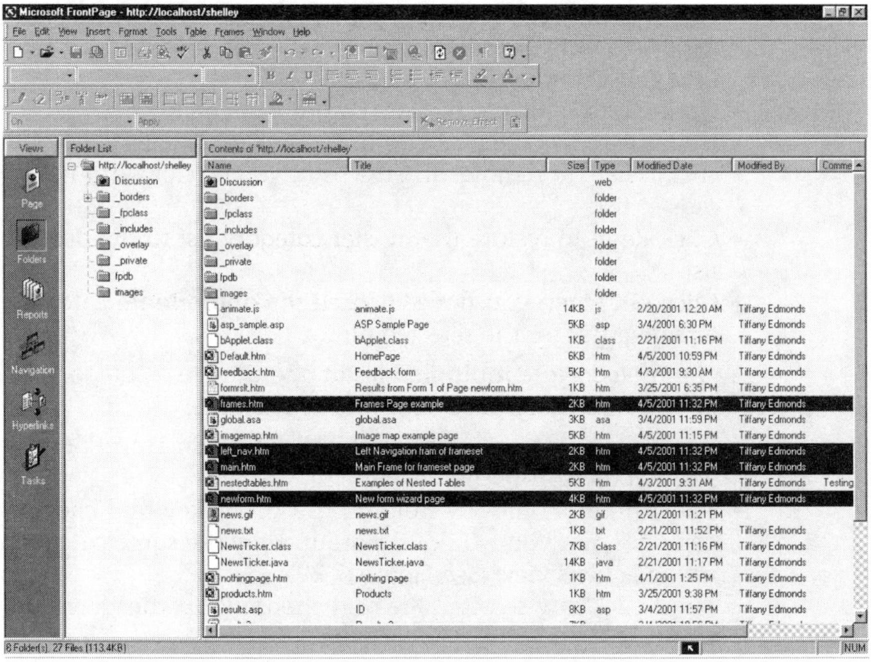

FIGURE 6–29 Folders view—selecting multiple files.

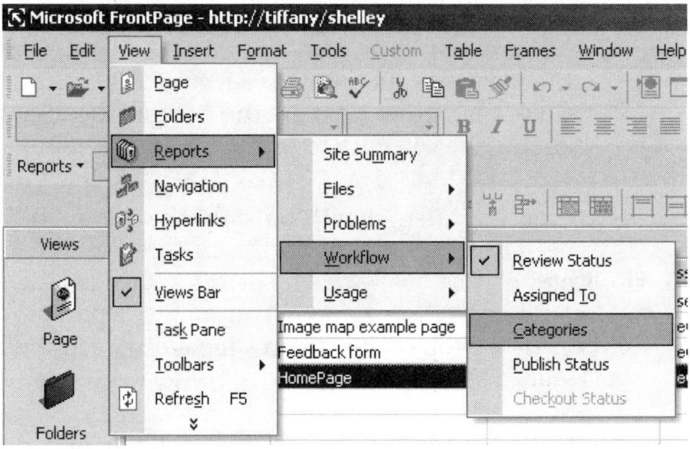

FIGURE 6–30 Categories selection from Report menu.

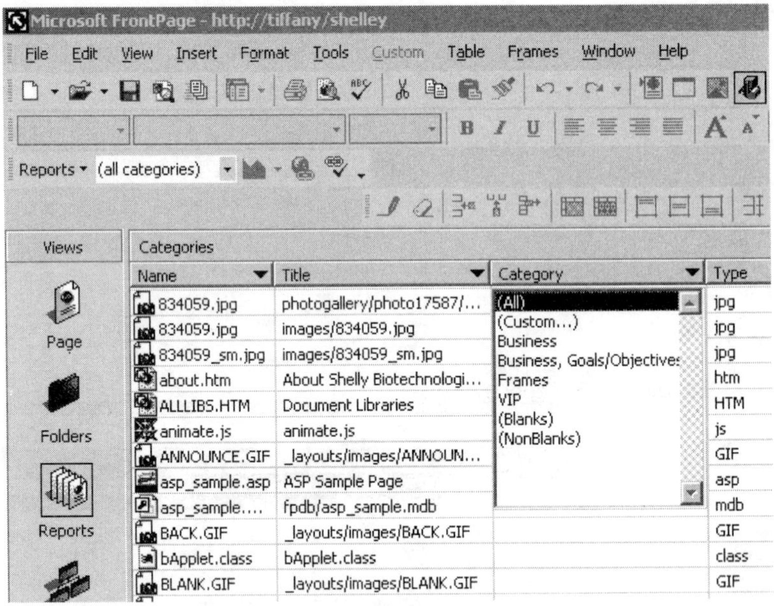

FIGURE 6–31 Reports—sort by category.

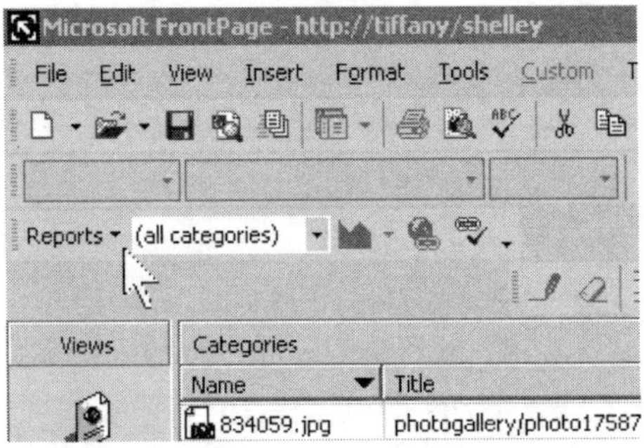

FIGURE 6–32 Reports toolbar.

- Select Categories in the dropdown menu of the Reporting toolbar by clicking the down arrow next to Reports (see Figure 6–33).
- Select Categories from the Workflow menu.
- In the dropdown menu next to the Reports view, select the category with which to associate the files (see Figure 6–34).

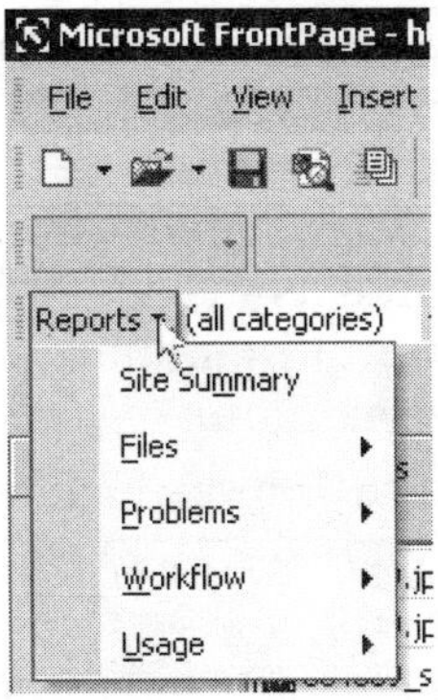

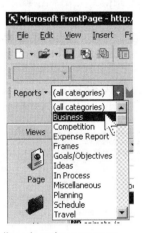

FIGURE 6–33 Reports views.

FIGURE 6–34 Report toolbar dropdown menus.

Create a Site Map by Category

A site map page can be very useful for your visitors to help aid in navigating the site or just to see all of the contents of a site on one page. The Table of Contents feature can be used to list all files in the web according to your navigation view in FrontPage. You may also create a site map that lists pages by their category and hyperlinks to the appropriate page listed.

To create a site map by category:

- Create a new page in your web or open the page in which you would like to list pages by category.

- Place your cursor on the page where you would like the list to begin. You may want to start with adding a heading that is the same name as the category and placing your cursor just under that heading
- Select Web Components from the Insert menu. Highlight Table of Contents in the left pane of the Web Components dialog box and highlight Based on Page Category in the right pane (see Figure 6–35).

Click the Finish button to launch the Categories Properties dialog box (see Figure 6–36), in which you will have the following options:

- Choose the category or categories that you would like listed by checking the appropriate category title in the master list.
- Choose a sort option from the dropdown menu to list files alphabetically by title or to list pages by the last modified date.
- Include the date the file was last modified.
- Include comments added to any file in the list.

In the FrontPage Normal view, the Category component will list the Page in Category link three times for each category added (see Figure 6–37); however, in Preview view or when viewing the

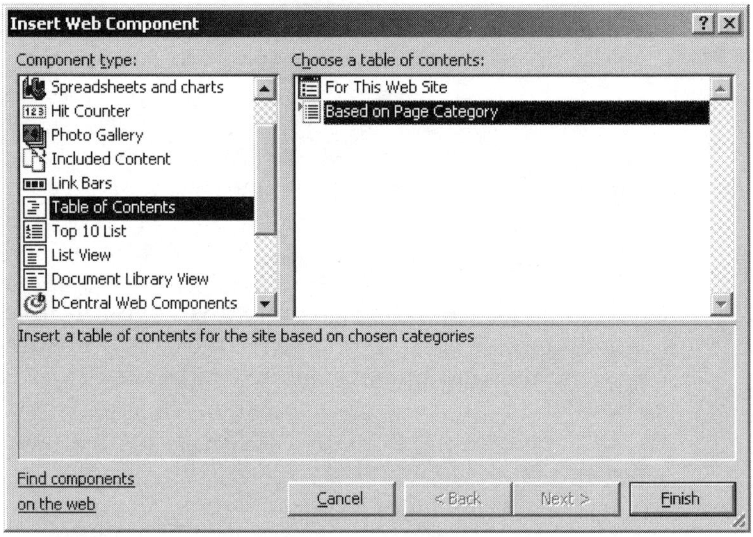

FIGURE 6–35 Insert Web Components dialog box—Table of Contents.

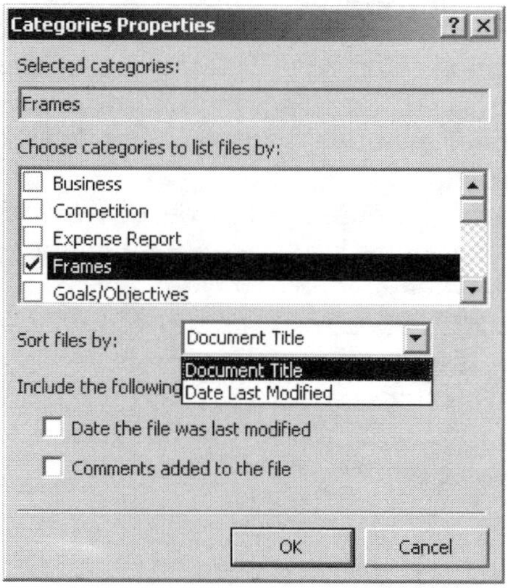

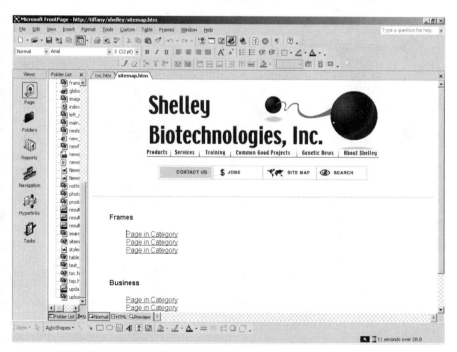

FIGURE 6–36 Categories Properties dialog box.

FIGURE 6–37 Normal view of site map by category.

page in a browser, the actual pages in the category will all be listed under the appropriate heading or where you inserted them on the page. FrontPage 2002 will also dynamically update the pages listed in the category, according to your modifications in the web; for example, additions and deletions of files from a particular category.

Move the mouse cursor over any category listing, and it will change to a hand holding an index card, which indicates that it is a FrontPage component. Right-clicking on a component will give you the option to choose Category Properties from the menu.

Now that you have the permissions set on the development web and an understanding of assigning tasks to users, review statuses, and categories, it is a good idea to examine FrontPage 2002's source control option.

◆ Source Control

Among the management tools introduced and improved upon in FrontPage 2002 is the source control feature. To use the source control feature, the remote server must have the FrontPage 2000 server extensions installed and functioning properly.

Source control is the feature that ensures that no two team members will overwrite each other's work on any particular page. Implementing the optional source control feature requires that each user "check in" and "check out" the files he or she is working on. If User 1 has the *feedback.htm* page checked out, User 2 cannot open that page for editing; User 2 will have access only to a read-only version of the page until User 1 checks the page back in. This is very useful for development webs or team projects where more than one person is collaborating on the same project, because it prevents two people from opening the same page at the same time.

To enable source control on a web:

- Select Web Settings from the Tools menu (see Figure 6–38). You must have Administrator rights to the web to enable source control.
- At the bottom of the window, check the Use document check-in and check-out option, then click OK.
- Next, you will be prompt to confirm or cancel this change to the web settings with a message that tells you that

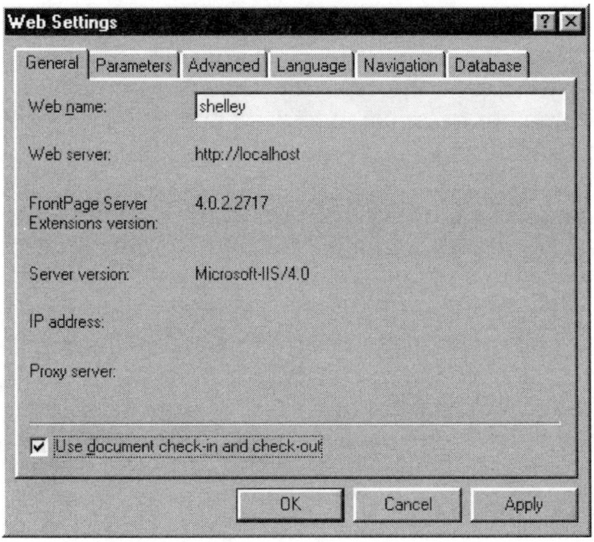

FIGURE 6–38 Web Settings dialog box.

FrontPage needs to recalculate the links in the web. Click the Yes button to proceed (see Figure 6–39).

- Click OK on the Web Settings dialog box.
- Notice that the files in Page view now have a green dot next to them, and double-clicking any file in the Folder List to open it will result in a prompt asking whether you want to check the page out (see Figure 6–40).
- Clicking Yes at this prompt will open the page by "checking it out" to you. Notice that a red checkmark is placed next to the file you have checked out in the Folder List, indicating that the file is checked out to you (see Figure 6–41).

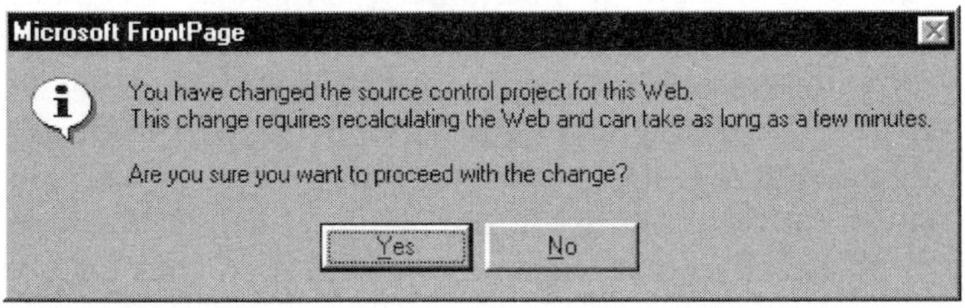

FIGURE 6–39 Recalculate message.

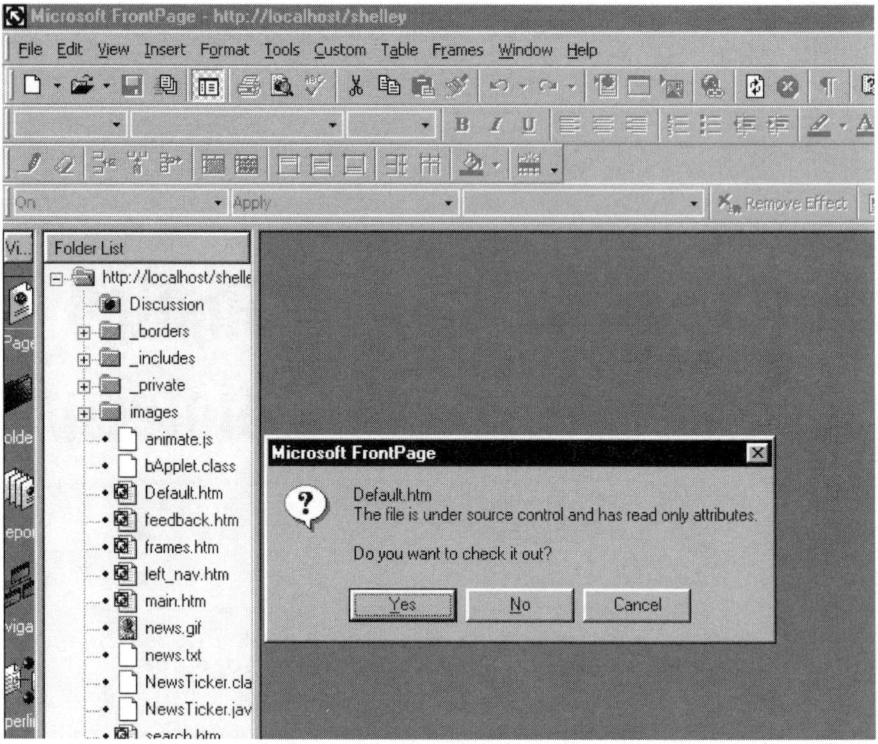

FIGURE 6–40 Page view with source control enabled.

The easiest thing to forget to do with source control enabled is to check files back in when you are done editing them. FrontPage offers no prompt to check a page back in when you close it. The file remains checked out until you right-click on the file in the Folder List and select Check in from the menu.

Files that are checked out to a user other than you are indicated with a tiny lock icon next to them. When you see this icon, you can double-click the file and a prompt will tell you to whom the file is checked out.

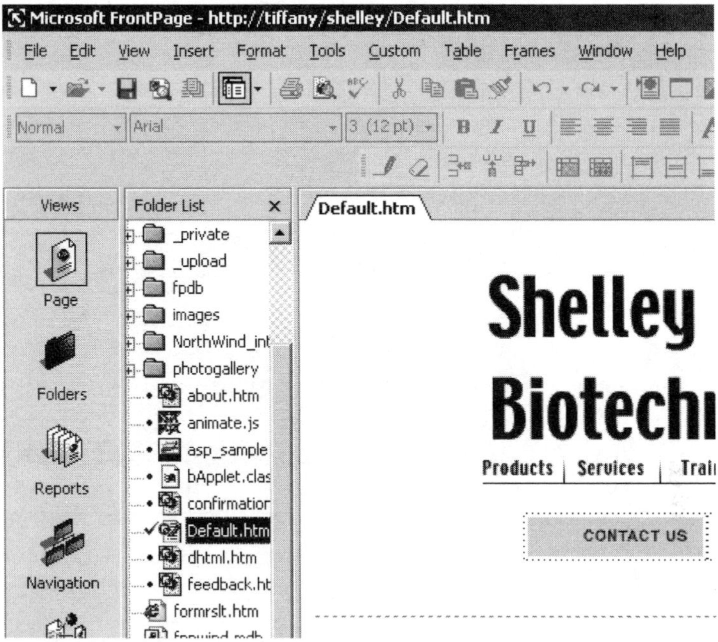

FIGURE 6–41 Page View under source control—checked-out page.

◆ Publishing Down from a Live Web

The process of publishing a web from a live or remote server down to a local hard drive is the same as publishing it from a local hard drive up to a remote server. We refer to the process of transferring files to a remote server, or Internet server, as *uploading* and the process of transferring files from a remote server, or Internet server, to your local hard drive as *downloading*. Publishing a FrontPage web from a remote server to your local hard drive is a process of publishing "down" to the hard drive.

Publishing down to a local hard drive that has the Personal Web Server (PWS) or Internet Information Server (IIS) installed is extremely easy, which is one of the advantages of using the PWS or IIS. We assume that you have a local copy of the *shelley* web already and that this web is stored on your hard drive at *http://localhost/shelley*. This being the case, we will publish the web down to this URL.

- Open the remote/live web in FrontPage 2002.
- When the web is fully loaded in FrontPage, choose Publish Web from the File menu.
- In the Publish Destination dialog box, enter the *http://local-host/shelley* URL in the Enter publish destination dropdown box (see Figure 6–42).
- Click the OK button, then FrontPage will open both the current web and the destination web in the Web Publish dialog box.
- Click Publish, and FrontPage will do the rest for you.

For those of you who do not have the PWS installed and do not work against a Web server, we will assume that you have a local copy of the *shelley* web stored on your hard drive at *C:\My Documents\My Webs\shelley*.

- Open the remote/live web in FrontPage 2002.
- When the web is fully loaded in FrontPage, choose Publish Web from the File menu.
- In the Publish Destination dialog box, enter the *C:\My Documents\My Webs\shelley* path in the Enter publish destination dropdown box (see Figure 6–43).
- Click the OK button, then FrontPage will open both the current web and the destination web in the Web Publish dialog box.
- Click Publish, and FrontPage will do the rest for you.

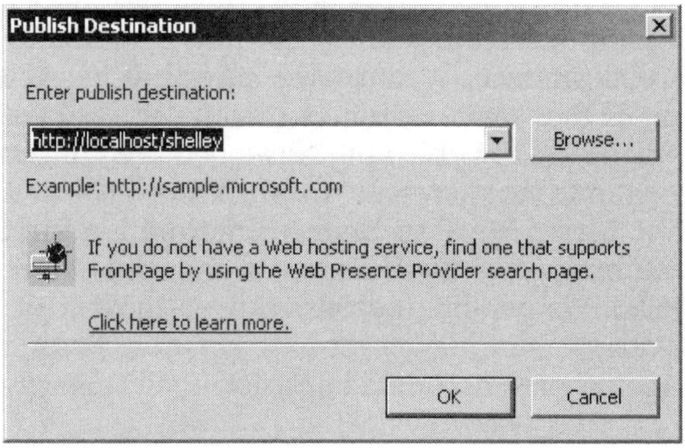

FIGURE 6–42 Publish Web dialog box.

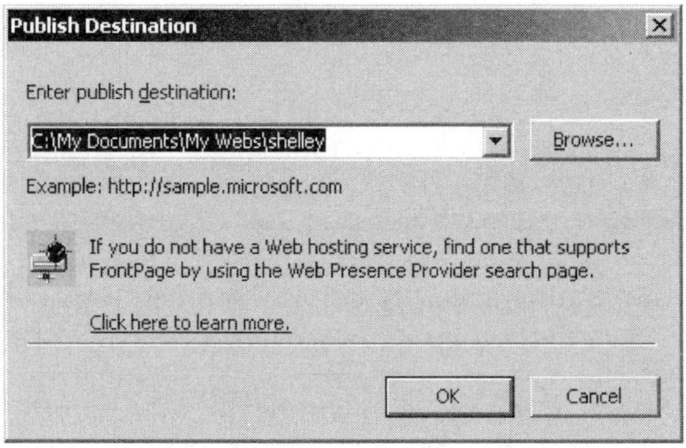

FIGURE 6–43 Publish Web dialog box.

Finally, the last option is to publish a remote web down to a local hard drive where no local copy of the web exists. Using either method of local storage, PWS/IIS or Disk-Based Web (DBW), simply add the path or *http://localhost/name* URL to where you want the local copy stored. This will enable FrontPage to create the files necessary on the local hard drive to publish the entire remote web down for you. Simply enter the path or URL to which you wish to publish in the Publish Web dialog box and click the Publish button. FrontPage will detect that there is no local copy already at this location and will simply publish the files down, without attempting to compare any local files to the remote files.

◆ SharePoint Team Services

Microsoft has introduced SPTS with its Office XP and FrontPage 2002 products. A SPTS Web site provides excellent management tools that team members can use to communicate, share documents, and work on projects together as a team. You can create a separate team Web site for each project.

Members of the team can work on the team project using nothing more then their web browser. Team members who use SPTS-compatible products, such as Office XP, can work seamlessly with the documents within the team web, saving documents, editing documents, and adding documents directly to the team web.

Built-in tools within a SPTS web, such as Document libraries, Surveys, Announcement lists, Task lists, Calendars, and more,

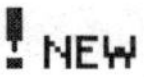

! NEW

FIGURE 6–44 New item graphic.

make managing the team project much easier and more organized. When members add new documents or items to the team web, those items are marked with a "new" graphic (see Figure 6–44) so that it is readily visible. Members may subscribe to the web to receive email notice when new items are added or edited in the web.

Lists of information can be displayed on the team web pages, so that team members can organize the information in many different ways, such as:

- By subject
- By due date
- By author

With the SPTS web, you can also:

- Sort the information to see only the information that applies to you.
- Hide information you're not interested in.
- Change the order that the information is listed.
- Set up customized views to make it easy for your team members to focus quickly on various and/or pertinent information.

In this section, we will create an SPTS web for the Shelley Biotechnologies Web site project. The SPTS must be installed on a Windows 2000 server or IIS. SPTS support is not available for older servers or on the PWS.

Let's create a SPTS web, using FrontPage 2002.

- In the Web Site Templates dialog box, highlight the Share-Point Team Web Site icon (see Figure 6–45).
- In the Specify the location of the new web box, enter the location where you wish to store your SPTS web and the name you want for it. In this example, we have set the path to *localhost* and the name to *shelleyteam* (*http://localhost/ shelleyteam*).
- FrontPage will create the web for you and will then load the web into your FrontPage Editor.

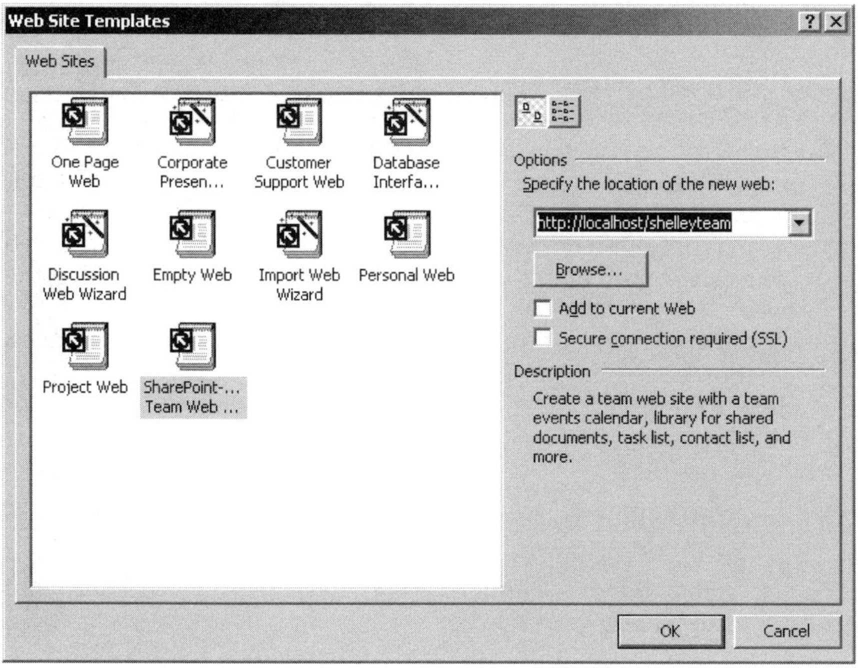

FIGURE 6–45 Web Site Templates dialog box.

Most changes, additions, and edits to documents in the web can be done through the browser, using the forms created in your team web (see Figure 6–46).

Click the Site Settings link at the top of the page to make changes to the team site, including (see Figure 6–47):

- Web site settings—Here, you set the name and description, and change the home page layout.
- Web Administration—Under this section, you are given links to make changes to change permissions, create a subweb, or go to the Web site administration screen.
- User Information—Here, you can change or view your user information.
- Modify Site Content—This section includes links to change the design of a list, document library, discussion board, or survey. Customize options include:
  - Customize Announcements
  - Customize Contacts

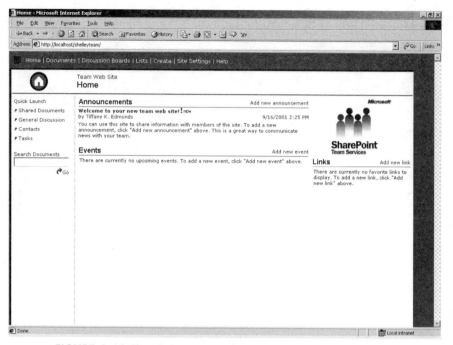

FIGURE 6–46 SharePoint team web.

- Customize Events
- Customize General Discussion
- Customize Links
- Customize Shared Documents
- Customize Tasks
- Create New Content

Making changes to the site permissions, such as adding new users and setting permissions for those users, is done through the link to Go to Site Administration. The process is the same as outlined and explained in this chapter under Setting permissions on an NT server running FrontPage 2002 extensions:

- After you click the link to Go to Site Administration, you will click the link to Change Subweb Permissions.
- Select the option to use unique permissions, then click the Submit button.
- When the page reloads, click the link at the top of the page to Administration.
- On the Administration page, you will see links to:

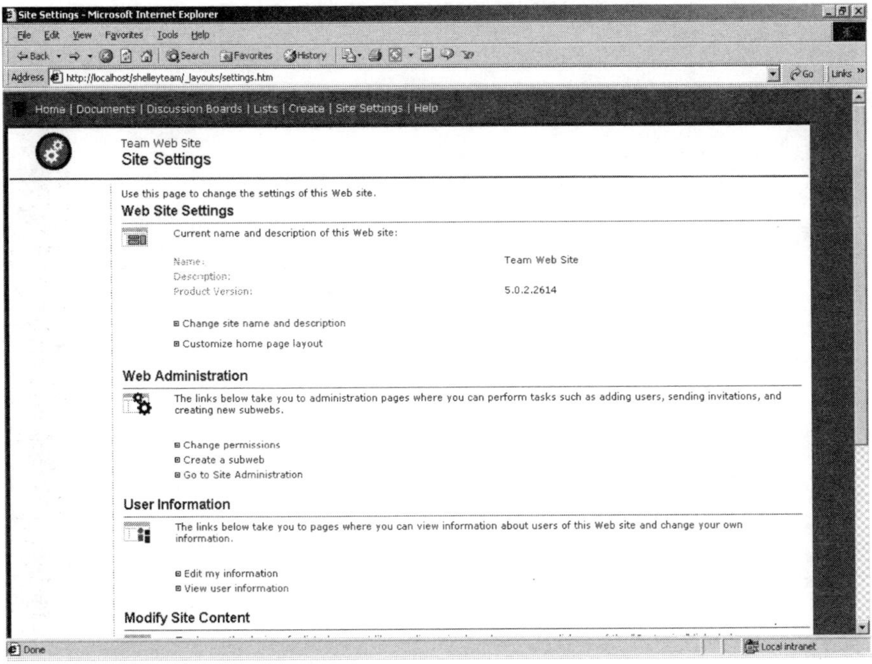

FIGURE 6-47 Team Web Site Settings screen.

- Manage Users
- Manage Roles
- Send an Invitation
- Click the Manage Users link to add or delete users and to set permissions for each of those users.

Through the Web Settings Administration (see Figure 6–47), you may make changes to the basic layout of the home page, using the Home Page Layout Administration screen (see Figure 6–48).

On this screen, you will see three columns. The right two columns in blue show the components currently on the home page. The left column in gray shows components that are not currently displayed on the home page. To move components on or off the home page display, click any component, drag it to the appropriate column, and click the Save button (see Figure 6–49)

When you submit the changes to the Home Page Layout Administrator the SharePoint team Web site will reload in your browser with the changes in effect.

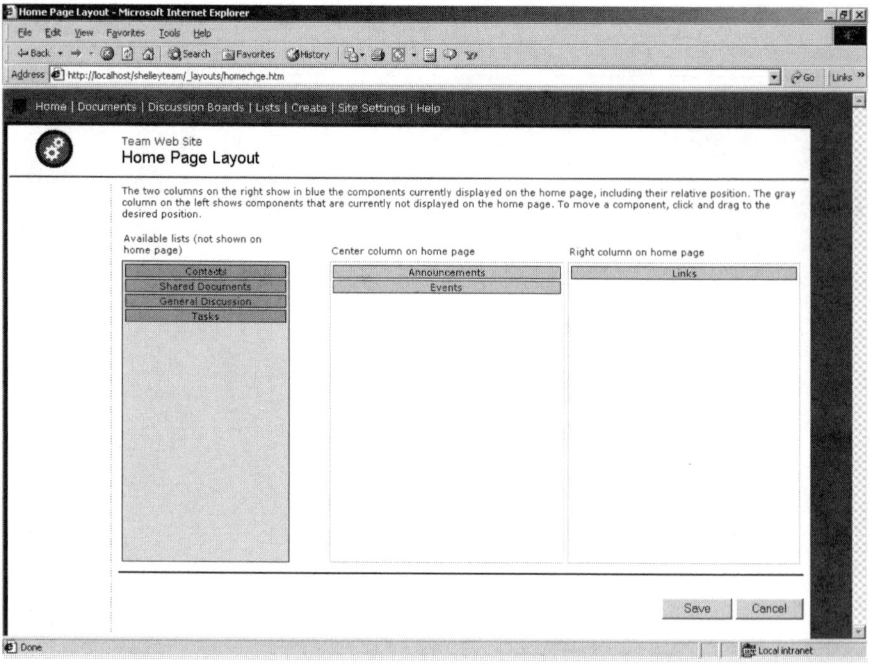

FIGURE 6–48 Home Page Layout Administration.

You may use FrontPage 2002 to make changes to the theme of the team site along with the graphics used on the team Web site, custom web pages added, and custom layout changes. For instance, we will change the logo graphic and some theme options for our Shelley Team web:

- Open the team Web site in FrontPage 2002
- Import custom images that you want to use on the team web into the images folder. (Shelley Biotechnologies logo and graphic examples for this book are available from *http://www.phptr.com/essential/frontpage2002*.)
- Open the home page for the team Web site in FrontPage— either *index.html* or *default.htm*.
- Highlight the SharePoint Team Services logo on the right of the page and replace it with your own logo graphic or the Shelley Biotechnologies logo (see Figure 6–50).
- Save the page, and you may preview the Web page in the browser or Preview view of FrontPage.

Team Web Site
Home Page Layout

The two columns on the right show in blue the components currently displayed on the home page, including their relative position. The gray column on the left shows components that are currently not displayed on the home page. To move a component, click and drag to the desired position.

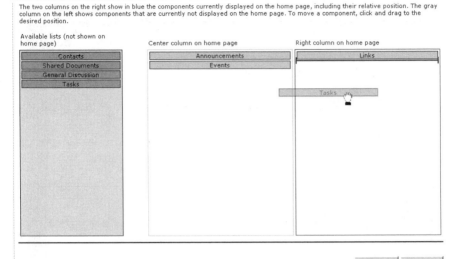

FIGURE 6–49 Home Page Layout Administration

FIGURE 6–50 Insert a custom logo graphic.

A theme of your choice, either preset or customized, can be applied to your team web as easily as with any other FrontPage web. To add a theme:

- Select Theme from the Format menu.
- In the Themes dialog box, select the option to set the theme for the current page (if you have a page open in the editor) or for all pages in this web.
- Select the theme you want to apply and click the OK button.
- FrontPage will apply the theme to the web or the page you selected (see Figure 6–51).

Another way to make changes to the appearance and colors in the team web is by making changes to the external style sheet. To do this:

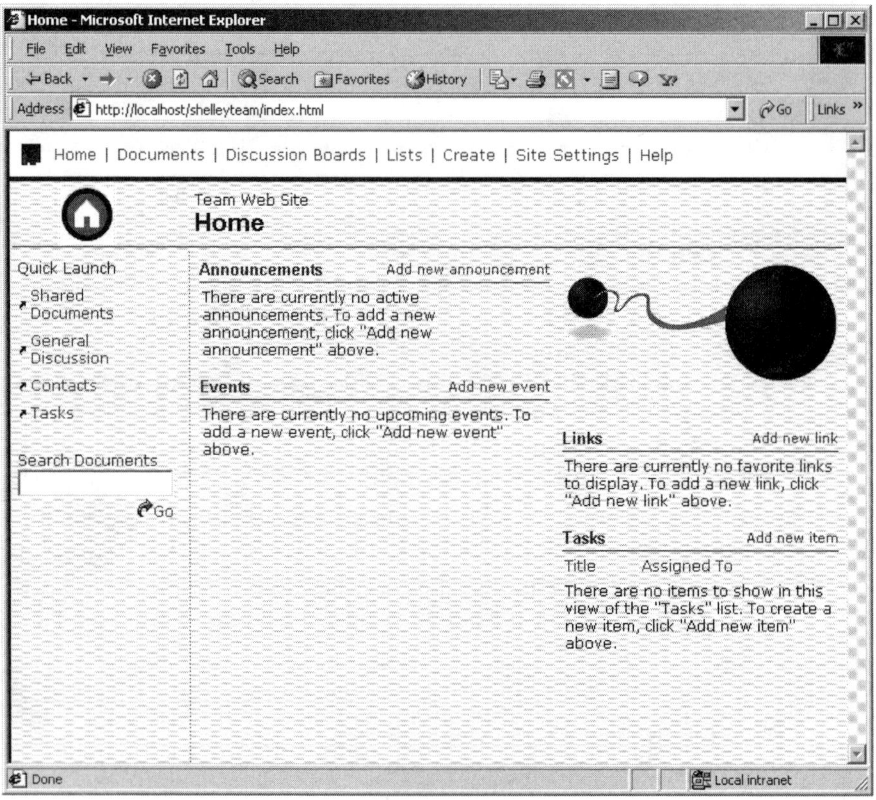

FIGURE 6–51 Team Web site with theme applied.

- From the Tools menu, select Web Settings.
- In the Web Settings dialog box, click the Advanced tab.
- Check the box to show hidden files and folders, and click the OK button.
- Once the web refreshes, you will see the folder called _Layouts.
- In the _Layouts/styles directory, open the file called *ows.css*. This is the file that contains the CSS for the default SharePoint Team web.

For this example, we will change the color of the right vertical border to match the blue color of the logo graphic.

- Open the *ows.css* file in FrontPage.
- Change the color hex code for the *.ms-main* and *.ms-banner-frame* under the background-color to #0059E7 and save the file.

When you view the home page in your browser, you will see that the color of the right vertical space and the color of the top margin space are a blue color that matches the logo graphic.

This is only one small example of how you can use the *ows.css* file to manipulate the look at feel of your team web.

You may change the properties of the links in the Quick Launch bar on the left of the team Web site home page. To do this:

- Open the home page in FrontPage.
- Right-click on the link bar component in the Quick Launch section of the page and select Link Bar Properties from the menu (see Figure 6–52).
- In the Link Bar Properties dialog box, you can add links, remove links, modify links, change the order in which the links appear, change link bars to feature, and select styles for the link bar (see Figure 6–53).

You can view the properties and customize layout options for the lists on the home page of the team web, as well. For example:

- Right-click over the section just below the Announcements heading and select View Properties from the menu (see Figure 6–54).
- In the List View Properties dialog box, you have the ability to change any of the default settings for the list displayed, fields shown, sort order, filter options (expires is the default filter set), or to change the style of the layout of the list (see Figure 6–55).

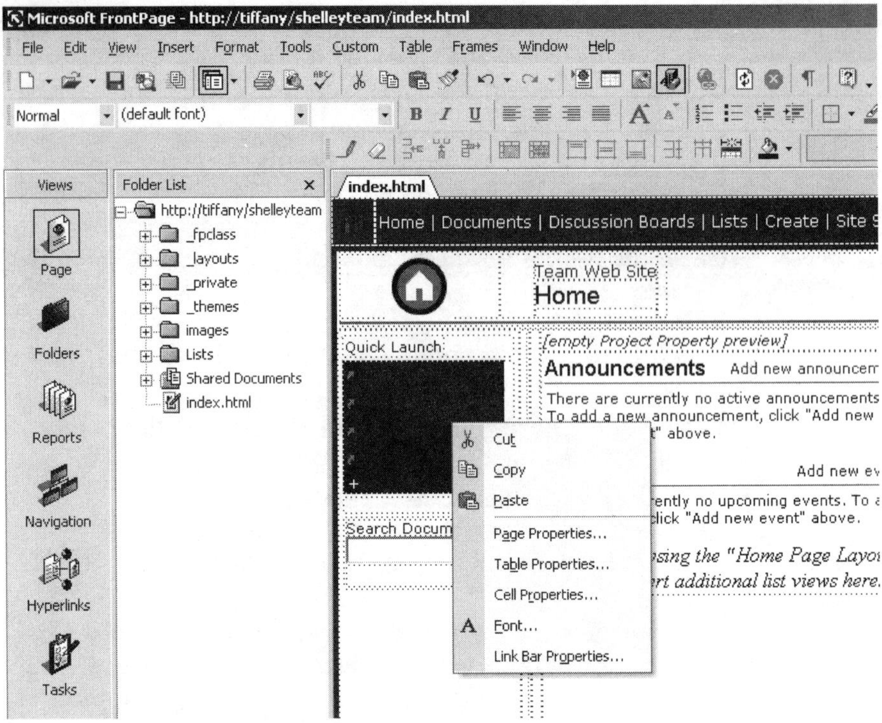

FIGURE 6–52 Selecting Link Bar Properties.

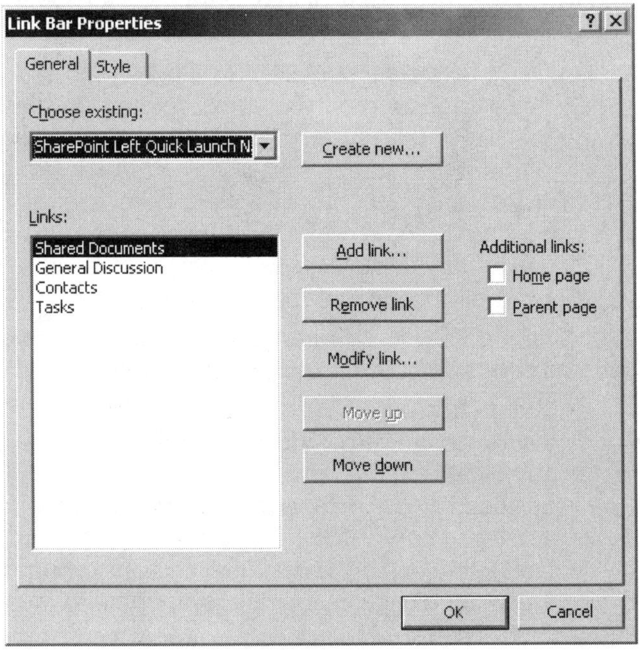

FIGURE 6–53 Link Bar Properties dialog box.

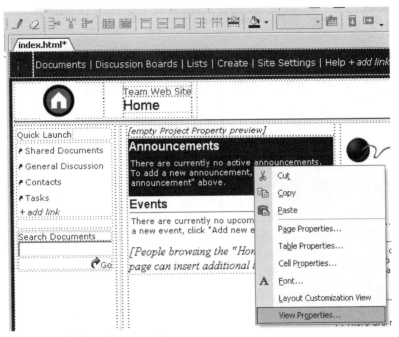

FIGURE 6–54 View List Properties menu.

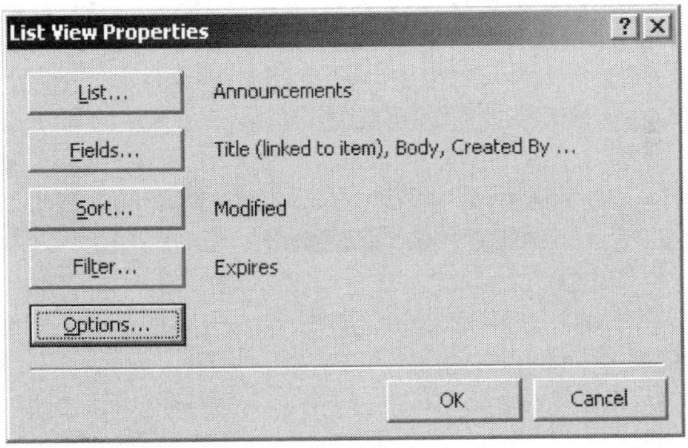

FIGURE 6–55 List View Properties dialog box.

- Click any of the buttons in the List View Properties box to make changes for the list displayed on the page.
- Clicking the Options button gives you options for how the list information and links are displayed on the page (see Figure 6–56).

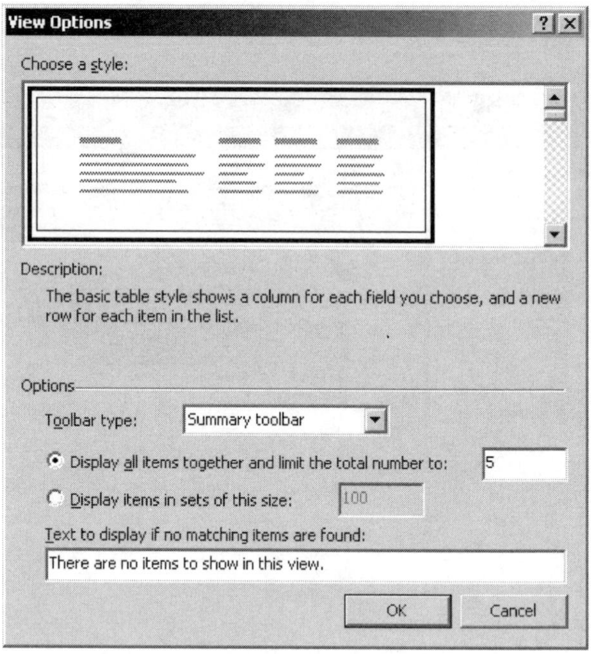

FIGURE 6–56 View Options dialog box.

- There are many styles in which to choose for the layout of information in your list. When you scroll through the different style options and highlight any of them, a description of that style is displayed just under the preview window.
- Further options for the layout include the toolbar type, the option to display all items together with the ability to set the limit on total number to display or to display items in sets of a size you specify, and the text to display if no items exist in the respective list.

By default, the home page in the team web shows the lists as Live Data view, but you can gain more individual customization options by switching the view of a list to Layout Customization view. To do this:

- Right-click your mouse over a list on the page and select Layout Customization View from the menu (see Figure 6–57).
- The way the list appears on the page in Normal view in FrontPage 2002 is much different then the default Live Data view (see Figure 6–58).

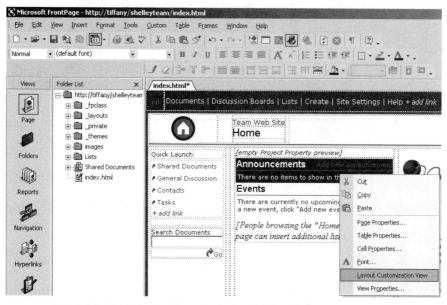

FIGURE 6–57 Selecting Layout Customization View menu.

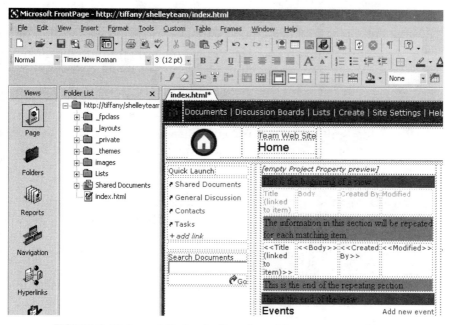

FIGURE 6–58 Layout Customization view of Announcement list.

- In this view, you have the ability to make changes to each individual List Field and to set the values of the List Field Properties, for example:
  - Right-click over one of the List Fields in the table and select List Field from the menu (see Figure 6–59).
  - In the List Field Properties dialog box, you can change the field name to display and choose to display the field name or the field value (see Figure 6–60).
  - Click the OK button when you have made your selection.

FIGURE 6–59 List Field menu.

FIGURE 6–60 List Field Properties dialog box.

Create Content Using the Web Browser

You can easily add and modify content using your Web browser on the SharePoint Team Web site. In this example, we will create a survey and link to it on the home page, using nothing more then the Web browser.

- Point your browser to your team Web site. For this example, we set the team Web site up at *http://localhost/shelleyteam*.
- Click the link to Create at the top of the Web page.
- On the Create Page, click the link for Survey (see Figure 6–61).
- The New survey page can be used to create a new survey simply by entering data into a form, such as the name of the survey, description, whether to add a link on the quick launch bar for the survey, and whether to include member names in the survey results display.
- Click the Next button to proceed.
- In the next screen, type the question for your survey and choose the type of answer to the question. Choose the settings for the survey, as well, such as:
  - Require a response
  - Display choices
  - Default answer
  - Type in the possible answers to the question
- When you are happy with the choices and entries, click the OK button (see Figure 6–62).

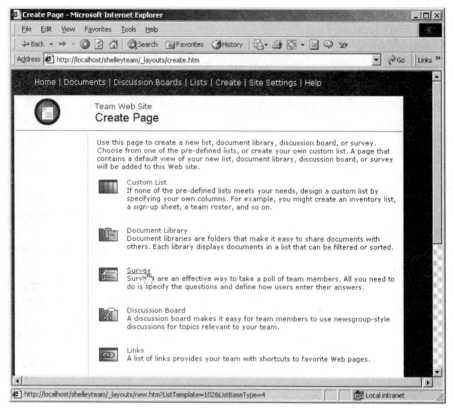

FIGURE 6–61 Create Page—Survey.

- When you click the OK button, you will be redirected to the Customize New Survey page, where you can add more questions to the survey, delete the survey, or modify the survey by clicking on the respective links from this page.
- Click the Home link to go back to the team Web site home page and see the new link to your new survey.

ADD AN ANNOUNCEMENT

You can add announcements to show up on your home page at the top of the page and alert team members of new items added or items of importance to the project. Simply click the link on the home page next to the Announcements heading to Add new announcement. This will launch the Announcement: New Item

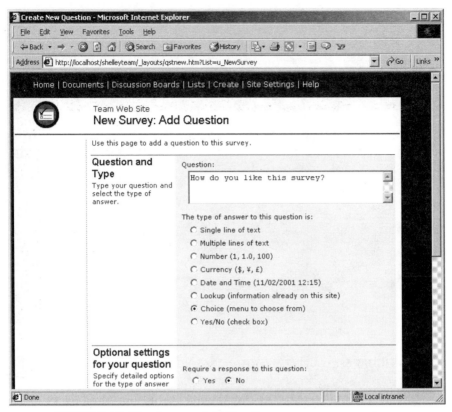

FIGURE 6–62 New Survey—Add Question screen.

screen where you can enter a title, description, and expiration date of the new item. (see Figure 6–63).

Next to the Expires box, you can type in a date or click the calendar icon to select a date from the calendar (see Figure 6–64).

Click the link to Save and Close when you are finished to post the Announcement to the home page (see Figure 6–65).

DOCUMENT LIBRARIES

The Document Libraries feature is a section of your team site where shared documents are stored for team members to share, edit, review, and add to. The default Document Library with the SharePoint team web is called *Shared Documents* and has a link to this library placed in the Quick Launch bar.

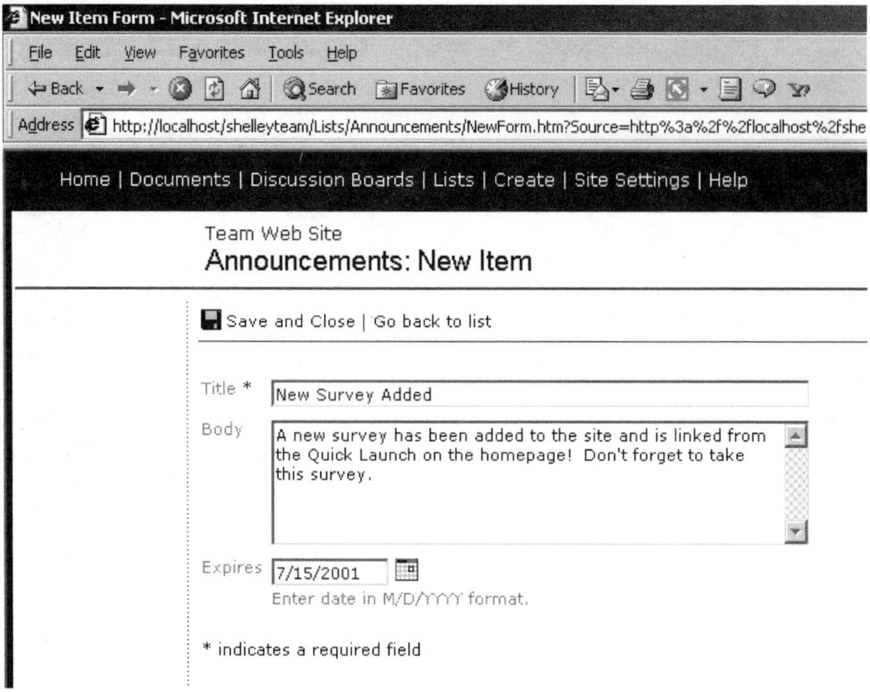

FIGURE 6–63 Add Announcement screen.

Files in the Shared Documents library are listed on the main page by title with properties information and hyperlinks to the file.

You can easily create new Document Libraries for your team web by clicking the Create link at the top of the pages of your team Web site. On the Create page, click the link to Document Library to open the New Document Library page (see Figure 6–66).

Simply enter the Name, Description, and document template type for your new Library and opt whether to link this library from the Quick Launch bar, then click the Create link to create your new Document Library.

You can specify a template for your documents in a Document Library to establish consistency among new documents created in your library. When the New Document link is clicked on the page that displays the Document Library, the template will open.

The template can be in several different formats, such as Word XP or HTML. The advantage to using a web-based file format is that the users or team members will not have to have the

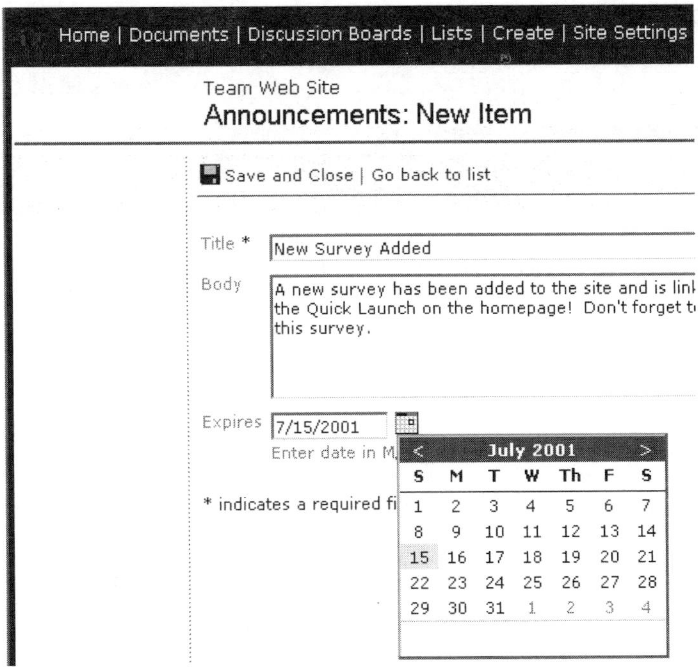

Home | Documents | Discussion Boards | Lists | Create | Site Settings

Team Web Site
Announcements: New Item

💾 Save and Close | Go back to list

Title * | New Survey Added

Body | A new survey has been added to the site and is link
the Quick Launch on the homepage! Don't forget t
this survey.

Expires | 7/15/2001
Enter date in M

* indicates a required fi

<	**July 2001**					>
S	M	T	W	Th	F	S
1	2	3	4	5	6	7
8	9	10	11	12	13	14
15	16	17	18	19	20	21
22	23	24	25	26	27	28
29	30	31	1	2	3	4

FIGURE 6–64 Select date from the calendar.

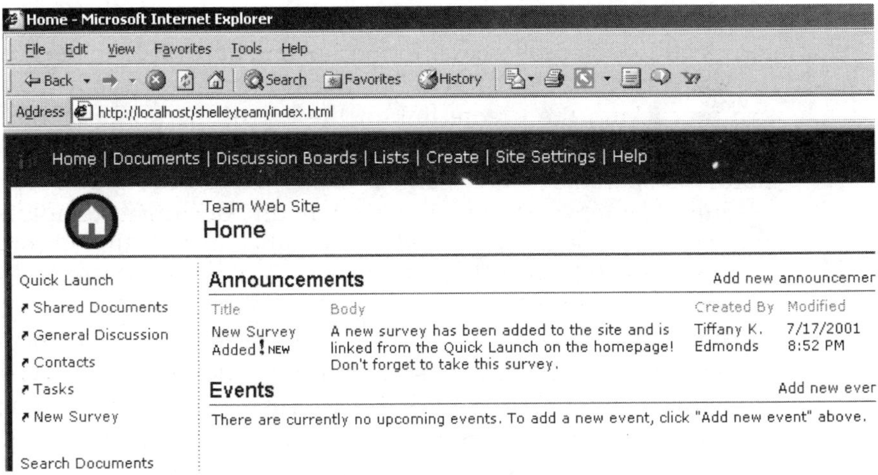

Home - Microsoft Internet Explorer

File Edit View Favorites Tools Help

← Back ▾ → ▾ ⊗ ⬚ ⌂ | ⬚ Search ⬚ Favorites ⬚ History | ⬚▾ ⬚ ⬚ ▾ ⬚ ⬚ ⬚

Address ⬚ http://localhost/shelleyteam/index.html

Home | Documents | Discussion Boards | Lists | Create | Site Settings | Help

Team Web Site
Home

Quick Launch

⬚ Shared Documents

⬚ General Discussion

⬚ Contacts

⬚ Tasks

⬚ New Survey

Search Documents

Announcements   Add new announcemer

Title	Body	Created By	Modified
New Survey Added **!NEW**	A new survey has been added to the site and is linked from the Quick Launch on the homepage! Don't forget to take this survey.	Tiffany K. Edmonds	7/17/2001 8:52 PM

Events   Add new ever

There are currently no upcoming events. To add a new event, click "Add new event" above.

FIGURE 6–65 New Announcement added on the home page.

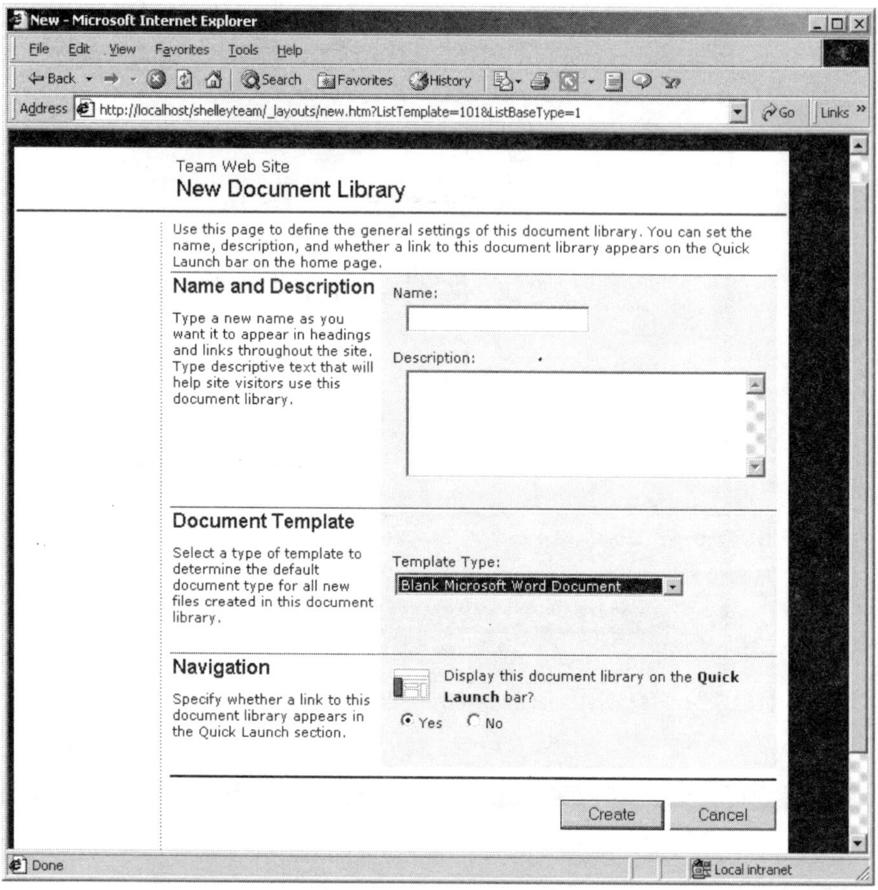

FIGURE 6–66 New Document Library screen.

appropriate program to read the file, they would simply need a Web browser.

To use a template for a Document Library you must have the template file stored in the SharePoint team web. To set up a Document Library to use a specified template:

- Right-click on the Document Library folder in the FrontPage 2002 Folder Fist and select Properties from the menu (see Figure 6–67).
- In the Properties dialog box, click the Settings tab.
- Check the box to Use a template for new documents (see Figure 6–68).

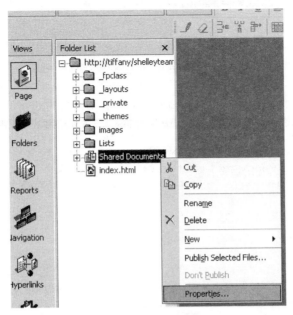

FIGURE 6–67 Document Library Properties menu.

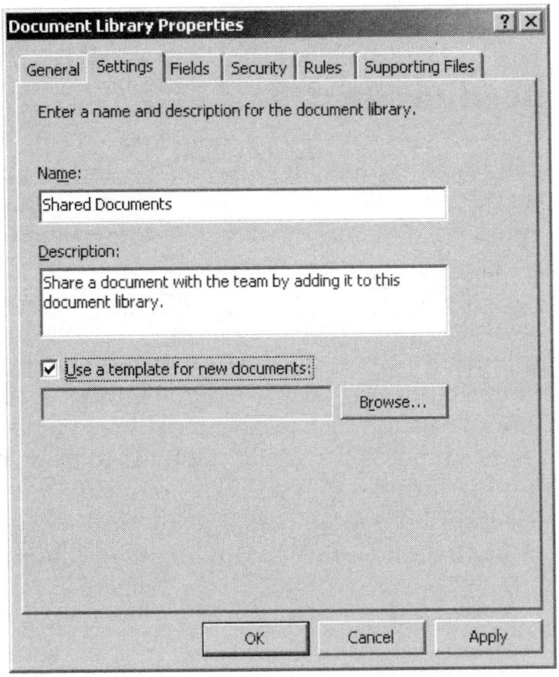

FIGURE 6–68 Document Library Properties dialog box.

- Click the Browse button and navigate in your web to the file you want to specify as the template for new documents created in that Document Library.

We have only begun to scratch the surface on the possibilities and the possible uses for the SPTS team web, but I hope that, with these basic introductions, you are comfortable diving in and creating your own team web for your project(s)! It is an exciting new technology that offers fantastic team project management tools in easy-to-create, -set-up, and -use forms via a Web browser.

◆ Recap

In this chapter, we discussed some of the basic and preliminary tools that FrontPage 2002 has implemented for better team management and remote site editing. These features open up many opportunities for collaboration on team projects with team members who may physically reside many miles and even countries apart!

◆ Advanced Projects

The advanced project for this chapter can be implemented and carried out for a web that is a team project or just for the individual who would like to learn to implement the tools discussed in this chapter.

Set a few goals for your web and open the remote, or live, web in FrontPage. Implement those goals for the web in the way of tasks, breaking the goals down into individual tasks to be completed by you or by possible team members. If this web is to be a collaborative effort, set permissions for your team members on the server and assign some of the tasks to those members. Lastly, publish the changes that you have made to the remote web down to your local hard drive. You may do this over your local copy of the *shelley* web or to a new location on your hard drive.

7 Personal Web Server

In This Chapter

- Installation and Location of Personal Web Server (PWS)
- Installing FrontPage 2000 Server Extensions
- Server Extension Maintenance and Advanced PWS Functions
- Recap
- Advanced Project

Many web developers prefer to test their Web pages before uploading them to the production Web server. For many standard HTML pages, this is easily done; however, many components and technologies expect special software to be running on a Web server in order to work correctly. If you want to test pages that use FrontPage components or Active Server Pages (ASP), for instance, you will need a separate Web server.

If you decide that you do need a separate Web server, you may first want to check with your ISP or IT department to see whether they have a Web server already set up for you to use for this purpose. If that is not an option for you, then you will need to configure your computer as a Web server.

- If you are running Windows 2000, the installation of Internet Information Server (IIS), FrontPage 2002 extensions, and SharePoint Team Services (SPTS) is explained in Chapter 1, "Getting Started."
- Windows 95 users cannot run any Office XP application, including FrontPage 2002.
- Windows ME does not support any Web server.
- Windows 98 SE can run the PWS but not the FrontPage 2002 extensions or SPTS. FrontPage 2000 extensions can be installed on the PWS, but some FrontPage 2002 features will not work on a Web server running only FrontPage 2000 extensions.

◆ Installation and Location of PWS

If you choose to install and run the PWS, it is helpful to understand how it works and how to install PWS. Once you have the PWS installed, you will need to know how to install the FrontPage server extensions on it as well.

About PWS

The PWS turns a Windows 95/98/98SE/NT-based PC into a small-scale Web server without having the cost of dedicating one PC to being the main Web server. It is ideal for developers, intranets, homes, schools, and small business workgroups. In corporations, any department or individual can post HTML documents and share information with anyone else in the company via the corporate intranet. Users of Windows 95/98/98SE/NT can now share Web content as easily as they share folders on a network, and developers can test their work on their local computers.

If you are running Windows 98, PWS version 4 is included on the CD. It can be found in the Add-ons folder, *D:\add-ons\pws\setup.exe*. If you are running Windows 95 or NT 4, download NT Option Pack 4, which is free to download and use at *http://www.microsoft.com/ntserver/nts/downloads/recommended/NT4OptPk/default.asp*. Win95 users will have the option to specify Win95 during the download process.

An installation using either of the above methods is completely painless, and the Installation wizard will walk you

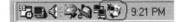

FIGURE 7–1 PWS icon in the system tray.

through the step-by-step process. The PWS will configure itself to start on the startup of Windows by default. You may notice after restarting your computer that a new icon resides in your system tray on the bottom right of your screen (see Figure 7–1).

Unless you specified differently during the installation, PWS version 4 will install in the *C:\WINDOWS\SYSTEM\inetsrv* directory. This is helpful to know in case you disable the Web server from startup by another program or by accident. Knowing the location in which it is installed will allow you to start it up again quickly and reset it to start on Windows startup. If you discover that the PWS is not located in *C:\WINDOWS\SYSTEM\inetsrv*, you can do a search on your computer for the *pws.exe* file to launch the PWS.

If you are running Windows 2000, the Web server is built into the operating system (see Chapter 1, "Getting Started," for installing IIS, FrontPage 2002 extensions, and SPTS).

The uses for PWS are many, but we will focus on its usefulness with regard to FrontPage in this book.

◆ Installing FrontPage 2000 Server Extensions

If you are upgrading from FrontPage 2000, the FrontPage 2000 server extensions are located on the CD. They are also available for download on the Microsoft Web site located at *http:// msdn.microsoft.com/library/default.asp?url=/library/en-us/dnservext/ html/Winfpse.asp.*

For those of you who installed FrontPage 2000 before the PWS and would like to install the server extensions now, we will describe the process in this section.

- First, make sure the PWS is running. The PWS will be in the system tray on the bottom right of your screen, near the system clock, if it is running (see Figure 7–1).
- Insert the FrontPage 2000 CD and run the *Servext.exe* file or double-click the *fpse2k_x86_ENG.exe* file that you downloaded from the Microsoft site.

- Click Install Now to let the Installation wizard install the extensions in the default directory. To select a custom directory, click the Customize button and select the directory.

Resource

- *http://officeupdate.microsoft.com/frontpage/wpp/serk/*

◆ Server Extension Maintenance and Advanced PWS Functions

This section describes some of the advanced maintenance and functions of the PWS and will help you understand how to troubleshoot problems that may occur with your PWS or FrontPage extensions. You will also gain a better understanding of how to change settings in your PWS that will affect your FrontPage Webs.

Advanced PWS Functions

For those of you upgrading the PWS from an older version, such as the FrontPage PWS, which shipped with FrontPage 98, or PWS version 2, which also shipped with FrontPage 98, you may note that PWS version 4 uses a different default directory. The default directory is the directory in which PWS will impose its extensions. This is the directory on your hard drive that will store all of the files that will be available through your Web server. By default, PWS version 2 uses *C:\WEBSHARE\WWWROOT* as the default directory. PWS version 4 uses *C:\Inetpub\wwwroot*. If you are upgrading and have established a number of files and directories in *C:\WEBSHARE\WWWROOT*, you can change the default directory in the PWS version 4 Advanced Properties window. To do this:

- Double-click the PWS icon in your system tray (see Figure 7–1). This will open the Personal Web Manager (see Figure 7–2).
- In the Personal Web Manager, you can stop the PWS from running by clicking the Stop button under the Publishing section. Once you stop services, the button will change to Start so that you can restart the Web server.
- Next, click the Advanced icon at the bottom left of the screen. This will open the Advanced Options window (see Figure 7–3).

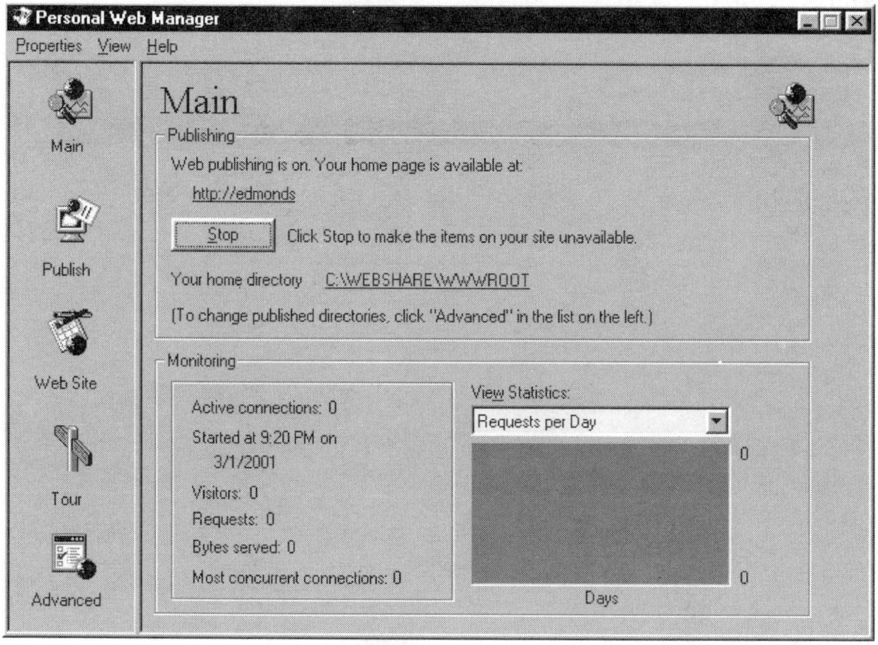

FIGURE 7–2 Personal Web Manager.

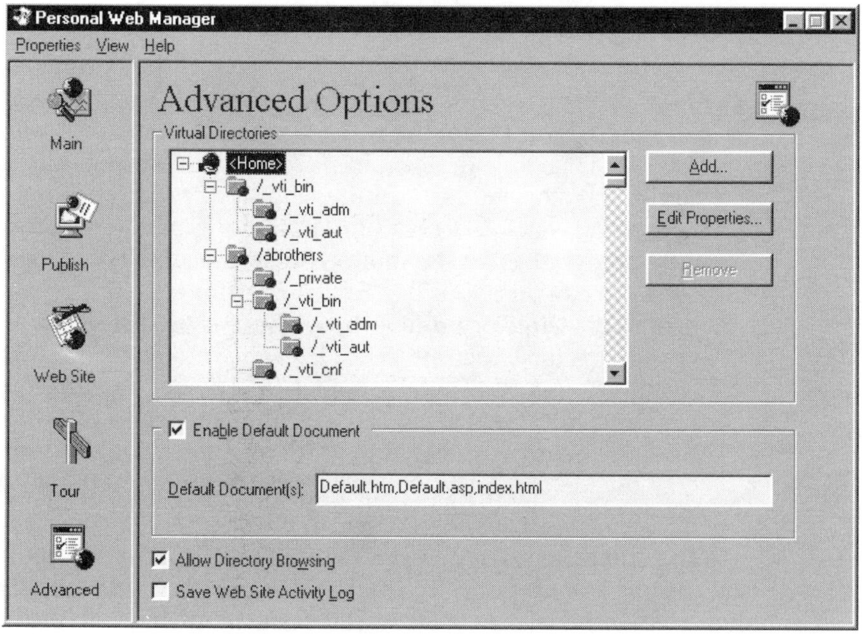

FIGURE 7–3 Advanced Options—Personal Web Manager.

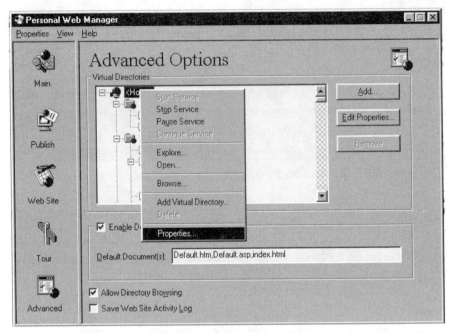

FIGURE 7–4 Properties menu selection.

- Right-click on <Home> at the top of the menu tree and choose Properties from the menu (see Figure 7–4).
- The Edit Directory dialog box is where you can specify a default directory other than the default directory that is set by the PWS version 4 installation. Either type the directory path or use the Browse button to locate and specify the exact directory on your hard drive (see Figure 7–5).
- In the Edit Directory dialog box, you may set permissions on the directory, such as Read, Execute, and Scripts Access. Execute access is usually applied to a folder or directory that must allow *.exe* files to be executed, as well as allow for the download of files within the directory from the local PWS. By default, new subwebs or directories in the PWS directory are not given Execute access.

In the Advanced Options window of the Personal Web Manager, you may also specify the Default Document. This tells the browser which page to look for as the home page in a web that is stored in the default directory when you use a URL without the

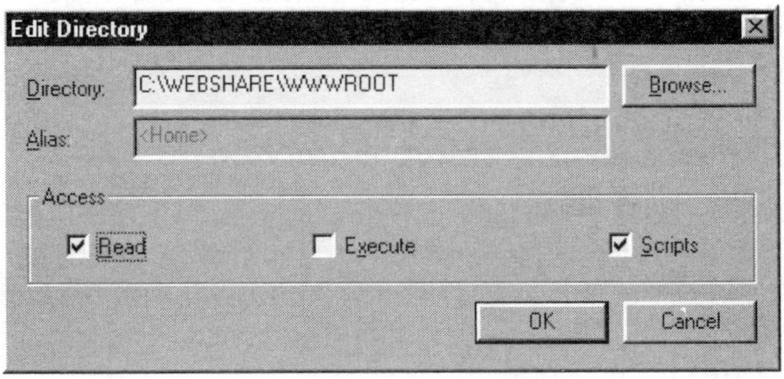

Edit Directory   ⊠

Directory: C:\WEBSHARE\WWWROOT   Browse...

Alias: <Home>

┌ Access ───┐
│   ☑ Read   ☐ Execute   ☑ Scripts   │
└───┘

                                        OK   Cancel

FIGURE 7–5 Edit Directory dialog box.

file name specified, such as *http://localhost/shelley,* rather than *http://localhost/shelley/index.htm.*

Specifying more than one file name in the Default Document box, such as *Default.htm, Default.asp, index.html* tells the browser to look first for *Default.htm;* if that is not found, then look for *Default.asp;* if that is not found, then look for *index.html.*

This setting also affects the FrontPage 2000 Navigation view with how it displays the home page. If you are using a home page named *index.htm* but *index.htm* is not specified as one of the default documents, then in the Navigation view, FrontPage 2000 will not show the house icon on the homepage (see Figure 7–6).

Without this house icon on the page you are using as the home page, FrontPage will not assign the HOME link properly to the navigation bar links on the page you want to use as the home page. Simply adding the *index.htm* file name in the Default Docu-

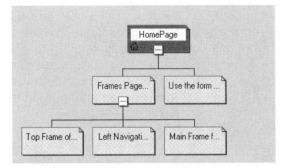

FIGURE 7–6 Navigation view.

ment box in the Advanced Options window of the Personal Web Manager will allow FrontPage to recognize the page as the home page.

Server Extension Maintenance

FrontPage 2000 server extensions administration tools are very different from previous server extensions administration tools. To access the Server Extensions Administrator, select Start then Programs then Microsoft Office Tools then Server Extensions Administrator (see Figure 7–7).

This will launch the Microsoft Management Console (MMC) (see Figure 7–8).

The MMC shows a list of all your FrontPage-extended webs in a file menu tree at the left of the screen. These are all of the webs that are stored in your default directory and do not include any of

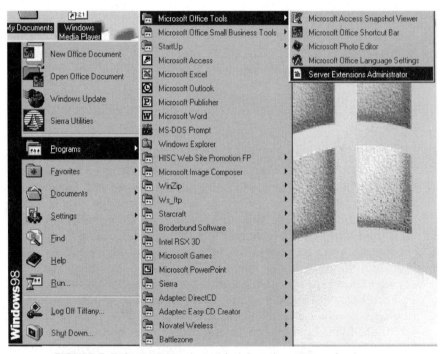

FIGURE 7–7 Server Extensions Administration menu selection.

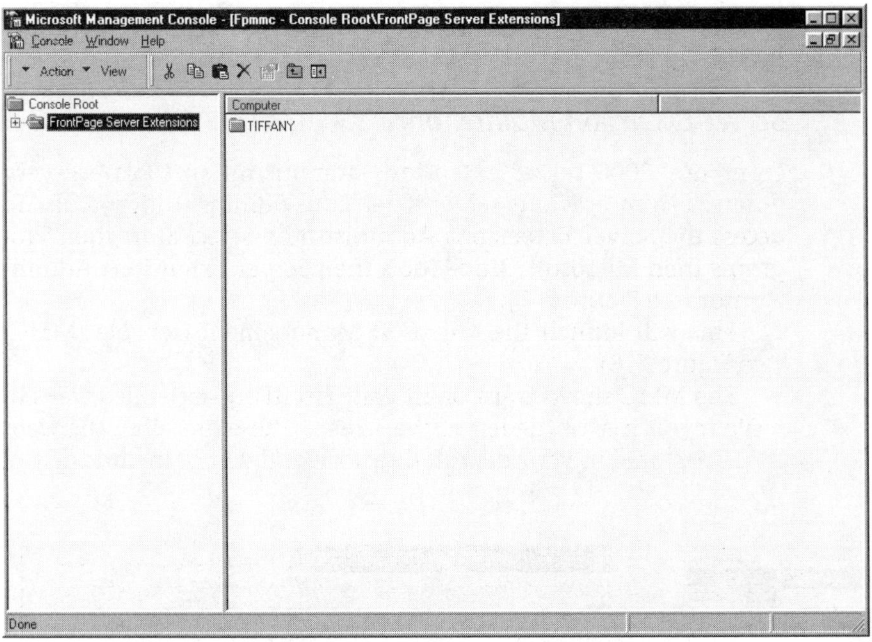

FIGURE 7–8 Microsoft Management Console dialog box.

your Disk-Based Webs (DBWs) (see Chapter 1, "Getting Started," for more on DBWs).

The MMC is where you administer the server extensions, setting certain rights to particular webs, reinstalling extensions on an individual web, and running check and fix options. In the MMC File menu, the typical structure is set up with the Console Root at the top. Under Console Root is FrontPage Server Extensions, and under this menu is Localhost, or most likely, Localhost is the name of your computer. See the following section on accessing your webs for more information on locating the name of your computer.

Expanding the menu under the name of your computer, or Localhost, will show you the port number, 80, which is where all of your webs are stored. You should see *shelley* listed under this menu if you have been working along with the tasks and examples in this book. Select this option from the left menu list. Notice that it is listed with *(subweb)* next to the name. Right-click on this menu option to see the administrative options you have at your disposal in the MMC (see Figures 7–9 and 7–10).

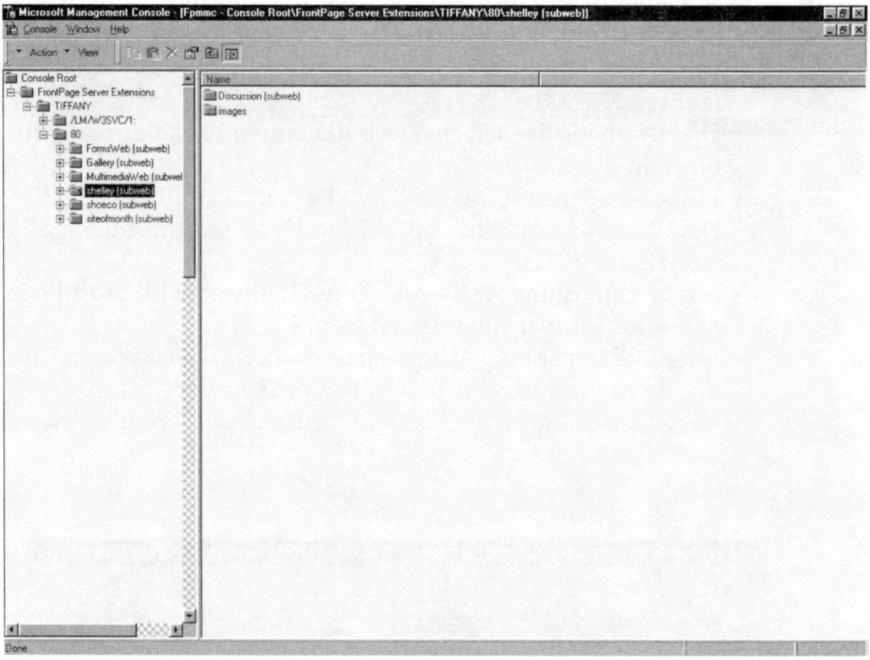

FIGURE 7–9 Microsoft Management Console.

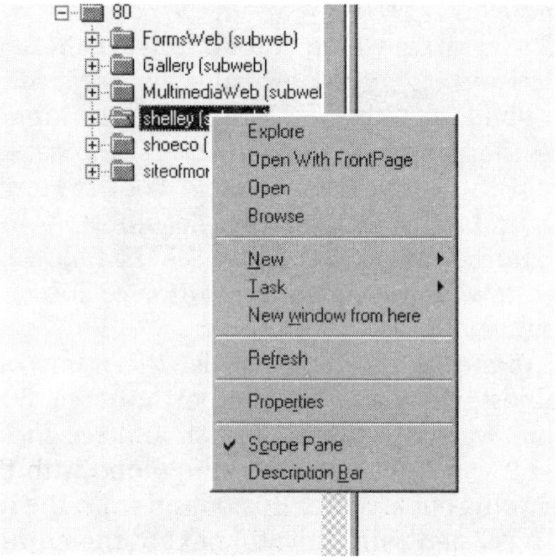

FIGURE 7–10 Administrative tools menu.

In this menu, you may choose from the following:

- Explore—launches the selected web in Windows Explorer.
- Open with FrontPage—launches the selected web in FrontPage 2000.
- Open—opens the selected web like any other folder on your hard drive.
- Browse—opens the selected web in your default browser.
- New Menu—from this option, you will see another menu (see Figure 7–11).
- Server Extensions Web—adds a new subweb with FrontPage extensions under the selected web.
- Server Extensions Administrator—adds permissions for another administrator to administer the server extensions.
- Task Menu—from this option, you will see another menu (see Figure 7–12).

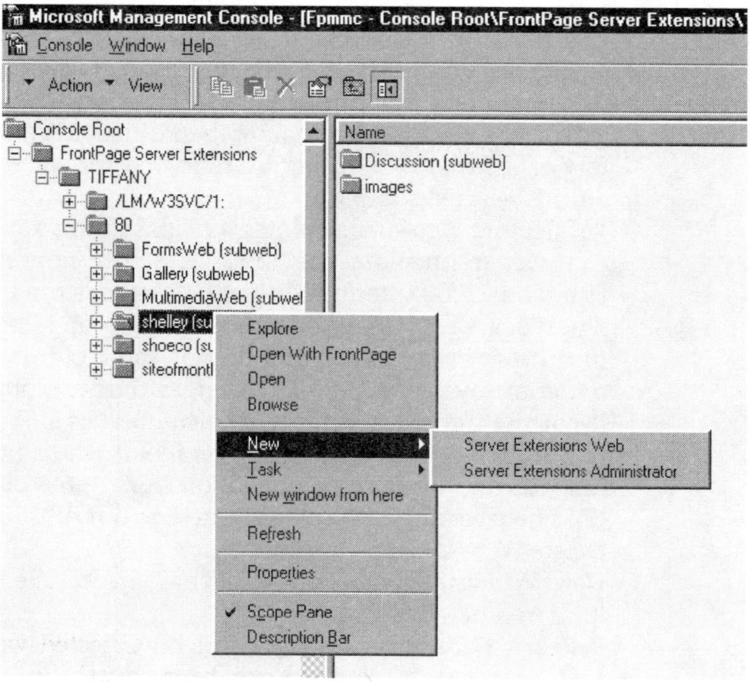

FIGURE 7–11 New submenu.

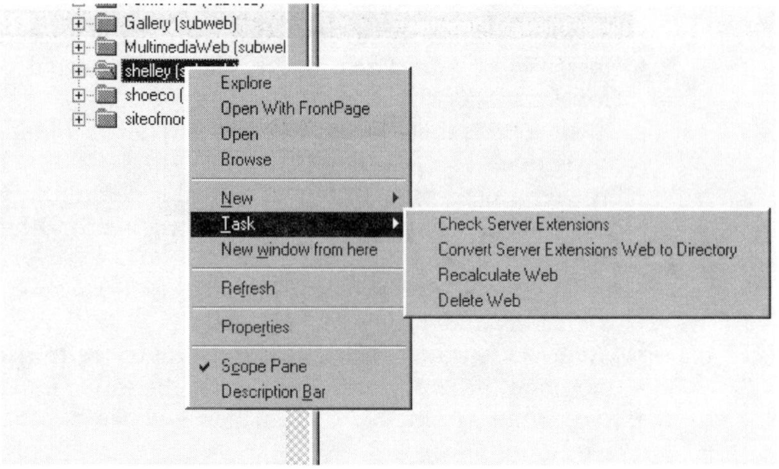

FIGURE 7–12 Task submenu.

- Check Server Extensions—checks the integrity of the server extensions on the selected web and shows you a report.
- Convert Server Extensions Web to Directory—removes the extensions on this specific subweb and converts it to a directory of the root web, rather than having specific extensions on this selected subweb.
- Recalculate Web—recalculates the links in this subweb. You can also recalculate the links within a subweb in the FrontPage 2000 interface. When you remove a page from a FrontPage web, it may be necessary to recalculate webs so that these link components do not show old or outdated material and provide links to pages that no longer exist. Recalculating a web simply recalculates the link information stored in FrontPage extension files, such as navigation links on the FrontPage navigation bars, table of contents links generated by FrontPage, and search results links.
- Delete Web—deletes web entirely.
- New Window from Here—launches the selected web by itself in a new MMC window.
- Refresh—refreshes the content of the selected web in the MMC, in case changes have been made since initially launching the MMC.
- Properties—shows the properties of the FrontPage 2000 server extensions for the selected web (see Figure 7–13).

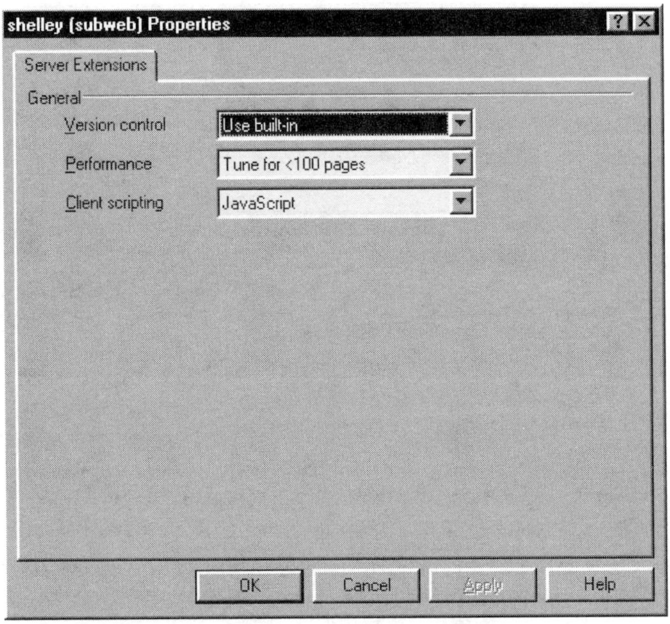

FIGURE 7-13 Server Extensions Properties dialog box.

Some of the menu items we reviewed in this section can also be selected in the FrontPage 2000 interface, such as:

- Recalculating a web
- Adding or removing subwebs
- Converting a directory to a FrontPage extended subweb
- Converting a FrontPage extended subweb to a directory of the parent web

FrontPage 2002 Server Extension and SPTS Maintenance

Maintenance and administration of the server extensions has never been easier than it is now with FrontPage 2002 and SPTS. The Administrator is easily accessible, and administration can be done using nothing more than a Web browser.

To open the server extension and SPTS administrator, double-click the icon for Administrative Tools in the Control Panel (see Figure 7-14).

FIGURE 7-14 Control Panel.

In the Control Panel, double-click the shortcut icon for Microsoft SharePoint Administrator. This will launch the Server Administration in your Web browser (see Figure 7–15).

repoint/fpadmdll.dll

osoft SharePoint
rver Administration

links below take you to administration pages where you can specify the rights available for roles, set installation defaults, such as her Web document discussions are turned on or off, and reset user passwords.

- Set list of available rights
- Set installation defaults
- Reset user password
- Reset MSDE Database password

ual Servers

following virtual servers are available on this machine. To perform site administration tasks for a virtual server, click the virtual server e. To specify configuration settings for a virtual server, click **Administration**. To Extend Microsoft SharePoint to a virtual server, click nd. To upgrade to the latest version of Microsoft SharePoint, click **Upgrade**.

Name	URL	Version	
Default Web Site	http://localhost	5.0.2.2623	Administration

FIGURE 7-15 Server Administration.

In this screen, you may:

- Set a list of available rights
- Set installation defaults
- Reset user password
- Reset MSDE database password

You will also see the section for Virtual Servers with a list of Virtual server names under it. The Default Web Site has the URL next to it set to *http://localhost,* with a link to Administration. When you click the link to Administration, the Virtual Server Administration opens in your browser (see Figure 7–16).

Under the Administration section on this page, you are able to link to the following:

- Uninstall Microsoft SharePoint—Use this link to uninstall Microsoft SharePoint from the virtual server and all

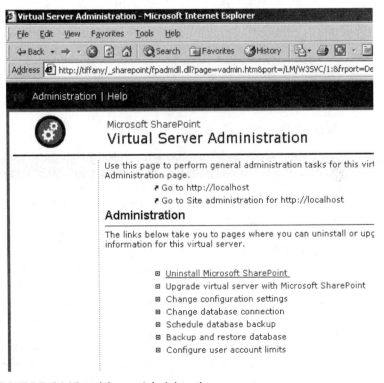

FIGURE 7–16 Virtual Server Administration.

subwebs under it. You can do a full uninstall or opt not to do a full uninstall.

- Upgrade Virtual Server with Microsoft SharePoint—Upgrade the server on this page and set the Administrator username, specify database settings, and choose the type of upgrade from the following options:
  - SharePoint-based Web site
  - SharePoint-based Web site—This preserves a home page if one exists.
  - SharePoint-enabled blank Web site—This enables features such as Document Libraries and lists.
- Change configuration settings—Use this page to set general configuration settings, such as enable authoring, configure the SMTP server for email transport for forms and subscriptions, performance settings, and security settings.
- Change database backup—This page can be used to view and change your database settings.
- Backup and restore database—Backup and restore your database by specifying a path and file name to backup the database to. To restore a database, simply specify the backup file to restore from.
- Configure user account limits—Specify the number of unique user accounts that can be set for this server.

Accessing Webs through the PWS

Browsing Web pages through your default Web browser when the PWS is in use is very simple. The first thing that you need to understand is the relationship between the Localhost and the computer hosting the PWS. On the computer hosting the PWS, the Localhost and computer access the same default directory.

Localhost is commonly used, particularly if on a PC and not an intranet. The reason for this is that it does not matter what the PC name is or what it may change to with regard to viewing Web pages in the browser because Localhost and "computername" look in the same directory for the files being called. This translates simply to the URL that is used in the address bar to locate and browse the FrontPage-extended web.

If the computer name is *tiffany*, then *http://localhost/shelley* and *http://tiffany/shelley* will pull up the same exact web on the PC hosting the PWS.

If you are working on an intranet and the PWS is hosted on another computer, you would need to use the name of the host computer to pull up the *shelley* web; for instance, the URL you would need to enter into the address bar in your default Web browser would be *http://tiffany/shelley* because using the *http://localhost* URL would force the browser to look for a local PWS, rather than the intranet PWS.

To determine the name of your computer and/or change the name of your computer:

- Select Start then Settings then Control Panel.
- In the Control Panel, double-click the Network icon and click the Identification tab at the top of the Network dialog box (see Figure 7–17).
- The Computer name is listed in the top text box.
- The Workgroup is listed after the Computer name.
- Change the Computer name in this dialog box if you want.

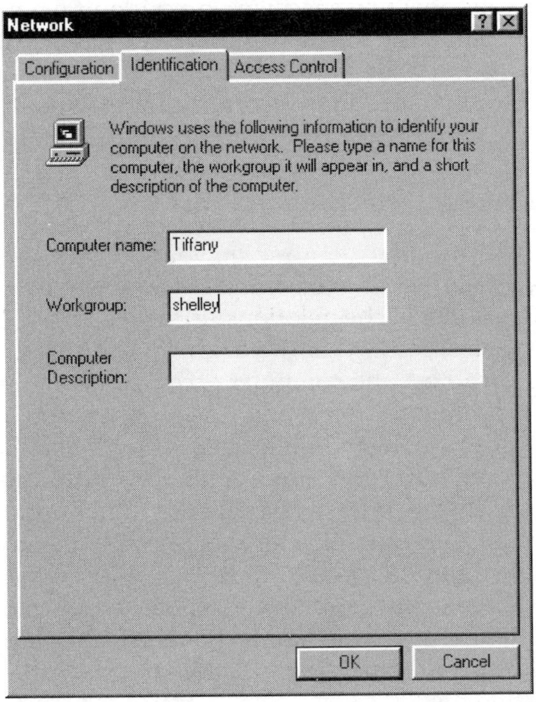

FIGURE 7–17 Network dialog box—Identification tab.

◆ Recap

This chapter discussed some of the basics of PWS, Personal Web Manager, and FrontPage 2000 extensions installation. Learning the basics of the Personal Web Manager will help you manage your PWS. With the basic tools we have reviewed on the MMC, you will also be able to administer your FrontPage 2000 server extensions on your PWS and troubleshoot some problems that you may encounter while working with your FrontPage-extended webs.

◆ Advanced Project

Determine whether you have the PWS installed and the name of your computer. Install the PWS if no PWS is installed already on the computer. Install the FrontPage 2000 server extensions on the PWS and browse the MMC to get a feel for the administrative tools available for the FrontPage 2000 server extensions.

8 Database Connections in FrontPage

IN THIS CHAPTER

- Getting Started
- Database Results Wizard
- Importing a Database into FrontPage
- Verifying Your Database Connection
- Database Interface Wizard
- Recap
- Advanced Projects

FrontPage 2002 offers greater functionality with built-in database features. Some of the things you can do with FrontPage 2002 and an Access database are:

- Create a database with a form
- Set up a database connection using Open Database Connectivity (ODBC)
- Set up a database connection using ActiveX Data Objects (ADO)
- Use a form to post information to a database
- Use a form to retrieve information from a database
- Use a hyperlink with parameters to retrieve information from a database
- Create an active hyperlink using a field in a database
- Display images using data from a database

- Allow specified or all users to modify and delete records from the database via a browser, using online forms

To use Active Server Pages (ASP) features, you must have an ASP-enabled server, such as:

- Microsoft Internet Information Server (IIS) version 3.0, Microsoft Internet Information Server (IIS) version 4.0 for Microsoft Windows NT Server, or Microsoft Internet Information Server (IIS) version 5.0 for Microsoft Windows 2000.
- Microsoft Peer Web Services for Microsoft Windows NT Workstation with the ASP engine added.
- Microsoft Personal Web Server (PWS) for Microsoft Windows 95 with the ASP engine added.
- Microsoft PWS 4.0.

If you intend to make extensive use of complex Access database and ASP work, you may need to learn ASP programming. The Database Interface wizard is a great way to get started and learn some of the functionality available with database connections and ASP.

◆ Getting Started

Let's start by creating a database and a form for adding data into that database.

- Create a new page in your *shelley* web and save the page as *aspexample.asp*. To save the page with the *.asp* extension, you can either manually type the full filename, including the *.asp* extension, or you can choose the Active Server Pages option from the Save File as Type dropdown menu in the Save As dialog box.
- On the *aspexample.asp* page, insert a one-line text box using the Insert/Form menu.
- Place the cursor on the page between the text box and the Submit button and press <Enter> twice.
- Next, copy and paste the text box three times under the first one.
- In the Form Fields Properties dialog box for each form field, name the form fields *Firstname, Lastname, Phone,* and *email.* Then place your cursor in front of each form field and add the descriptive text for each field with a colon in front of it (see Figure 8–1).

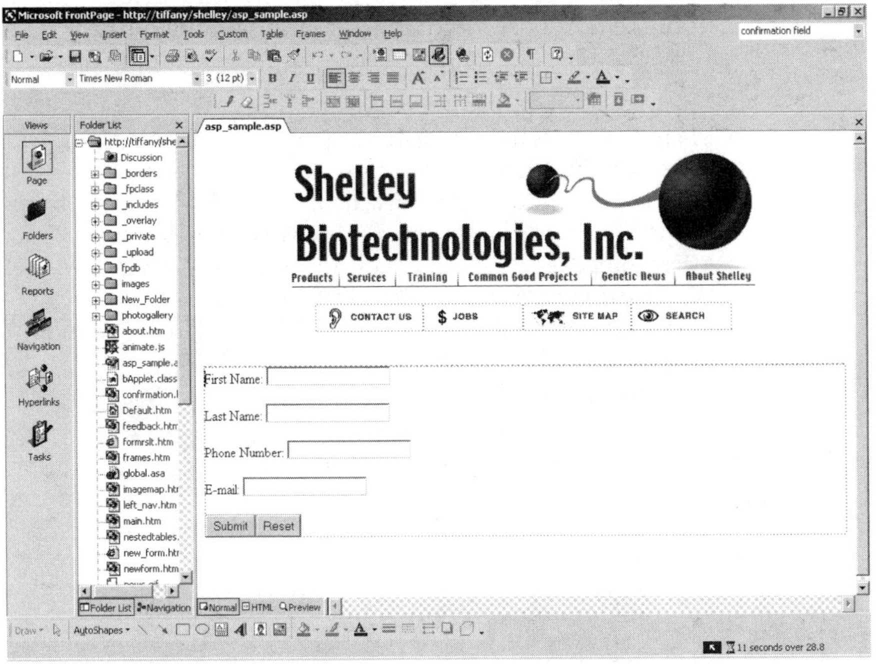

FIGURE 8–1 Creating an ASP form to send results to a database.

- Right-click inside the form and select Form Properties.
- Choose the Send to database option, then click the Options button (see Figure 8–2).
- In the Options for Saving Results to Database dialog box, click Create Database (see Figure 8–3).
- FrontPage 2002 will create a database for your form results. Once FrontPage has completed the creation of the new database in the Options for Saving Results to Database dialog box, click OK, then click OK in the Form Properties dialog box to save the page.

View the *aspexample.asp* page in your browser and submit the form a few times with a few examples or test results to begin adding records to your newly created database. If you try to view the page and encounter a page not found error instead of your *aspexample.asp* page with the form on it, it may be necessary to reboot your computer for your new database connection to take effect. Some systems require a reboot before the page will display properly.

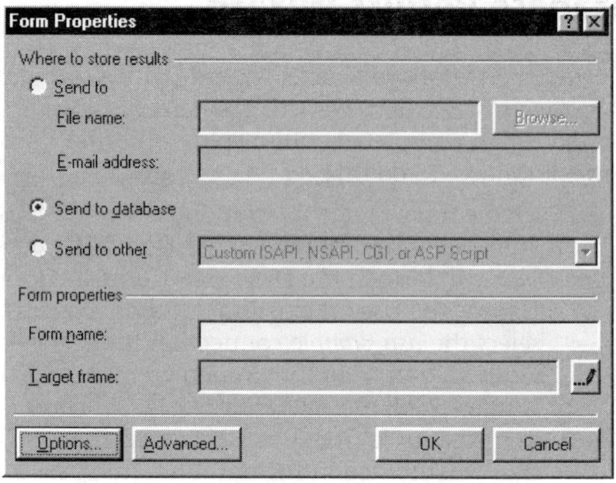

FIGURE 8–2 Form Properties dialog box.

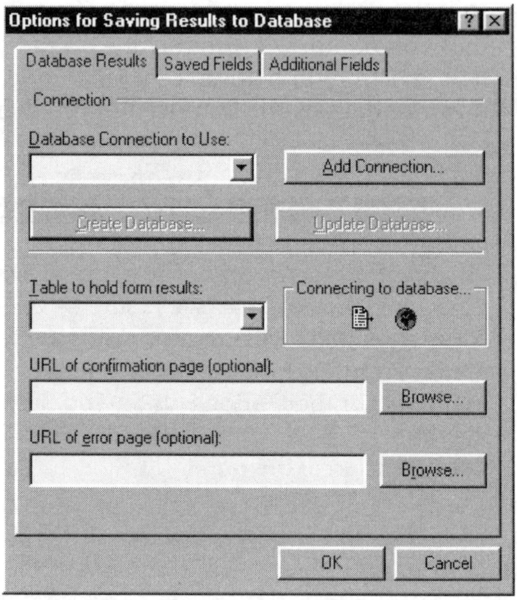

FIGURE 8–3 Options for Saving Results to Database dialog box.

◆ Database Results Wizard

Using the Database Results wizard (DRW) and database connection we just created, we will create a display records page. This page, when completed, will display all of the records that are in the database. To do this:

- Create a new page in FrontPage.
- From the Insert menu, choose Database, then select Results. This will launch the DRW (see Figure 8–4).
- Choose the Use an existing database connection option and select the *asp_sample* connection that we created in the previous section from the dropdown menu. Click Next.
- In Step 2 of the DRW (Figure 8–5), choose Results as the Record Source from the dropdown menu. This is the table that was created in the database from the previous section.
- In the next step, click the Edit List button to edit the list of database fields to display on the page (see Figures 8–6 and 8–7).
- Highlight each Displayed fields option in the right pane that you do not want to include on the display page. I suggest selecting all fields except Firstname, Lastname, Phone, and email. Click the Remove button, then click OK.

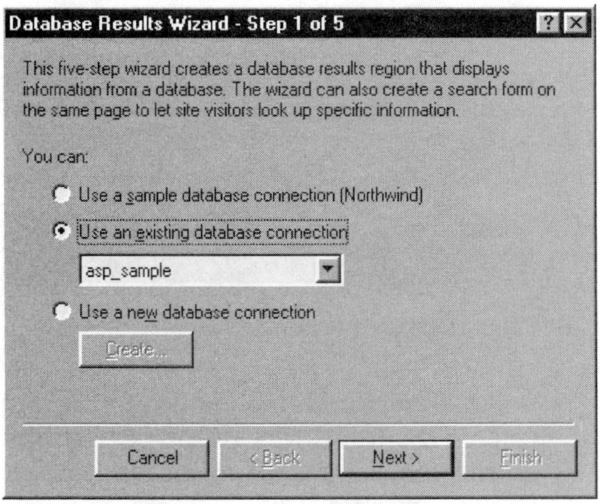

FIGURE 8–4 Database Results wizard—Step 1.

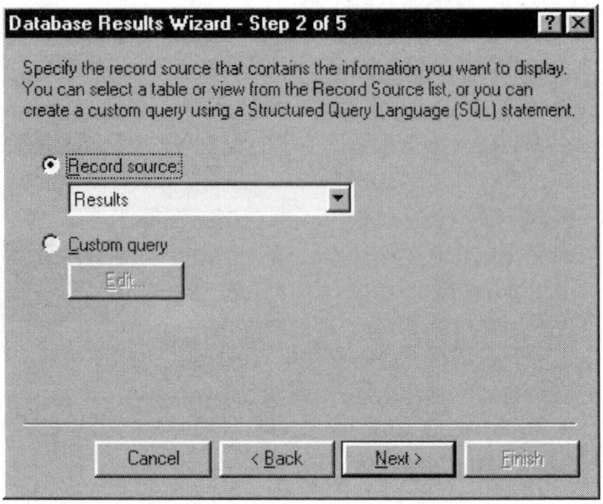

FIGURE 8–5 Database Results wizard—Step 2.

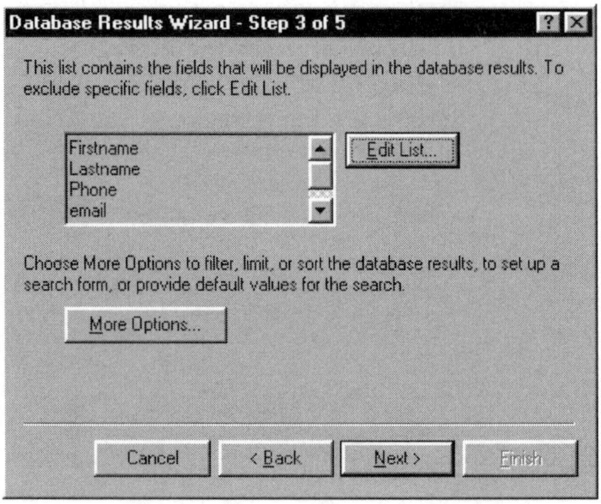

FIGURE 8–6 Database Results wizard—Step 3.

- Select some formatting options for the display records page. Choose the Table—one record per row option from the drop-down menu under the formatting choices (see Figure 8–8). Choose whether to have a border on your table. Check the final two options for:
  - Expand table to width of page
  - Include header row with column labels

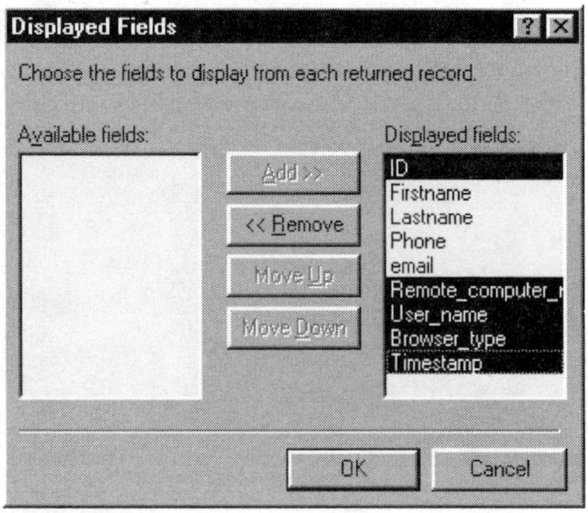

FIGURE 8-7 Displayed Fields dialog box.

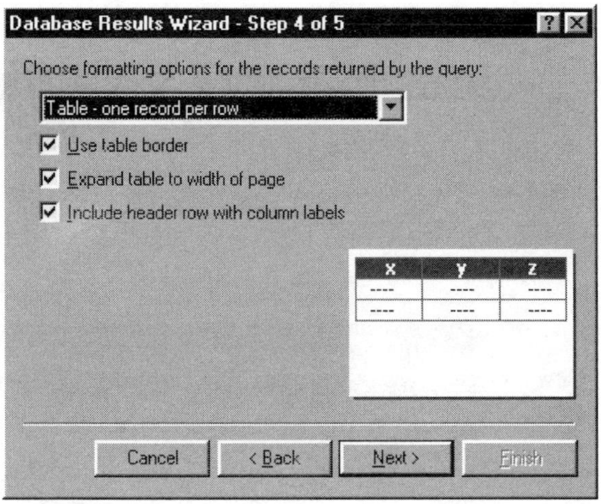

FIGURE 8-8 Database Results wizard—Step 4.

- In the last step of the wizard, choose the Split records into groups option and enter 5 in the text box next to records per group. Click Finish (see Figure 8–9).
- Save the page as *results.asp* and view the page in the browser.

In FrontPage, the table has code in the cells, and some rows may be highlighted in yellow and blue (see Figure 8–10).

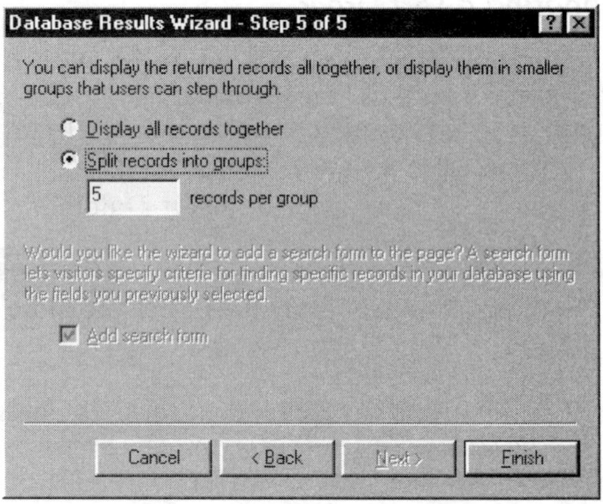

FIGURE 8–9 Database Results wizard—final step.

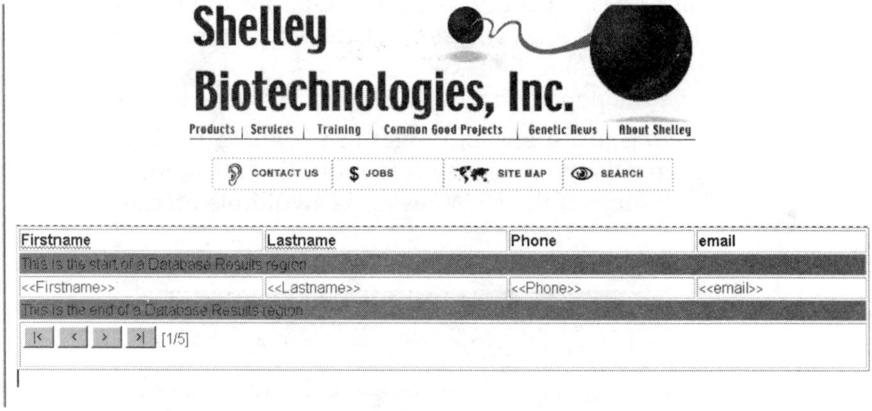

FIGURE 8–10 Database table.

In the browser, the page will display nicely with each record you added to the database displayed in the table, one record per row. You can edit the table properties in the FrontPage Editor like you would any other table. You may also right-click inside the table and choose Database Results Properties from the menu to make changes in the display.

Choosing a Sort Order

Another option that you can set in the DRW is the sort order of your records display. This can be very useful if you have large numbers of records in your database. To select the sort order:

- Right-click in the database results table on the *results.asp* page you just created. Select Database Results Properties from the menu.
- Click Next on the first two steps of the DRW. In the Step 3 dialog box (see Figure 8–6), click the More Options button.
- In the More Options dialog box, click the Ordering button (see Figure 8–11).
- In the Ordering dialog box, select the fields you wish to be the sort order. For this example, choose Lastname and click the Add >> button. Then choose Firstname and click the Add >> button. This will sort the records to display by the Lastname in alphabetical order, and the secondary sort order will be Firstname (see Figure 8–12).
- Click OK in this and the More Options dialog boxes. Click Next in the next two steps of the DRW, then click Finish in the last step of the DRW.
- Save the page and view the *results.asp* page in the browser.

These are just a few examples of what can be done with the DRW in FrontPage 2002. See Appendix C, "Miscellaneous References," for some of the DRW resources available on the Internet.

FIGURE 8–11 More Options dialog box.

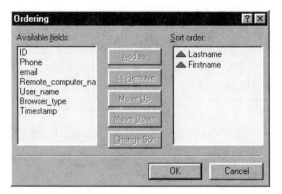

FIGURE 8–12 Ordering dialog box.

◆ Importing a Database into FrontPage

If you have an Access database that you would like to work with in FrontPage 2002, you can import that database into your FrontPage web. Because the file has an *.mdb* file extension, FrontPage 2002 will automatically create the ODBC connection for you when you import the database into your web.

To import the database into your web:

- Select Import from the File menu. In the Import dialog box, click the Add File button.
- Navigate to the file on your hard drive that you want to import into the web and click Open.
- In the Import dialog box, you will see the file that you just selected in the import list. Click OK to begin the import process (see Figure 8–13).
- FrontPage will give you a prompt to choose a name for the ODBC connection. Enter a short, descriptive name for this connection and click Yes (see Figure 8–14).
- FrontPage will then prompt you to store your web in the *fpdb* folder. Click Yes (see Figure 8–15).

Your database has now been successfully imported into the FrontPage web, the ODBC connection has been established for you, and you are ready to work with the records in this web with the DRW.

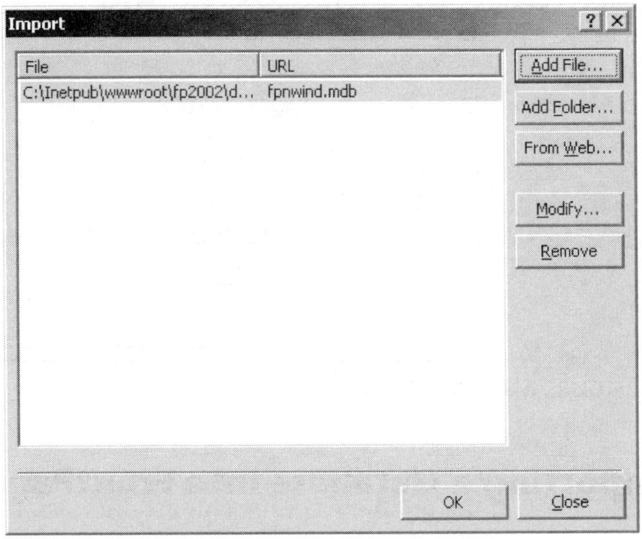

FIGURE 8–13 Import dialog box.

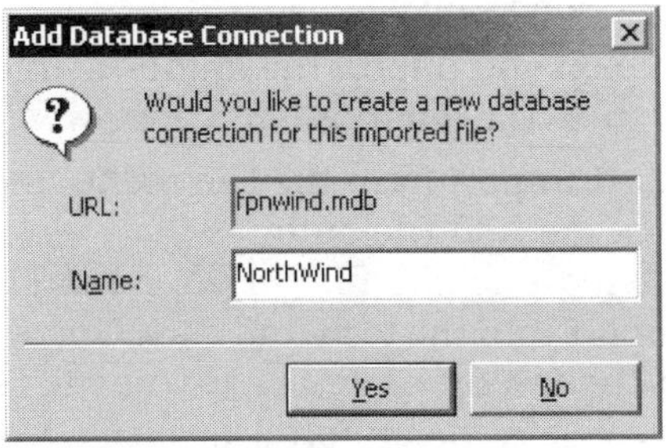

FIGURE 8–14 Add Database Connection dialog box.

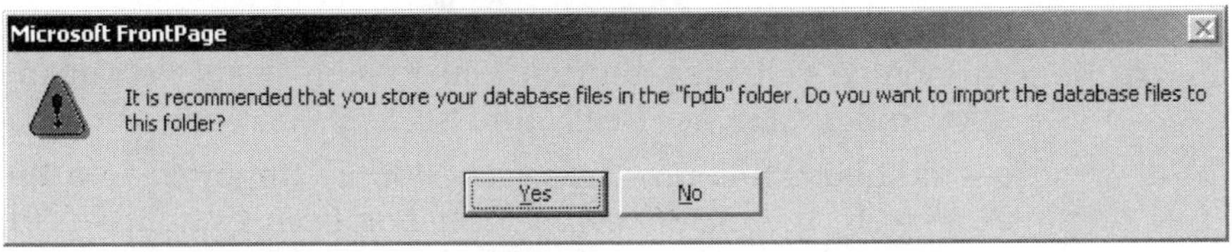

FIGURE 8–15 Import database alert box.

◆ Verifying Your Database Connection

To verify your database connection in FrontPage 2002:

- Select Web Settings from the Tools menu.
- In the Web Settings dialog box (see Figure 8–16), click the Database tab. Unverified database connections will appear with a question mark.
- Click once on a database connection that you would like to verify in the connection list, then click the Verify button. The verified database connection will now show a checkmark instead of a question mark next to it (see Figure 8–17).
- If a database connection does not validate, click the Modify button to adjust the database connection settings.

To modify the database connection:

- Highlight the database connection you would like to modify in the database connection list and click the Modify button (see Figure 8–17).
- In the Database Connection Properties dialog box, select the Type of connection from the list (see Figure 8–18):

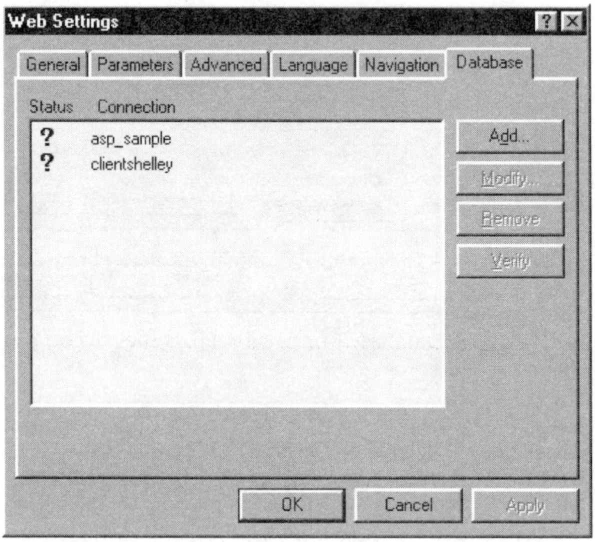

FIGURE 8–16 Web Settings dialog box—Database tab.

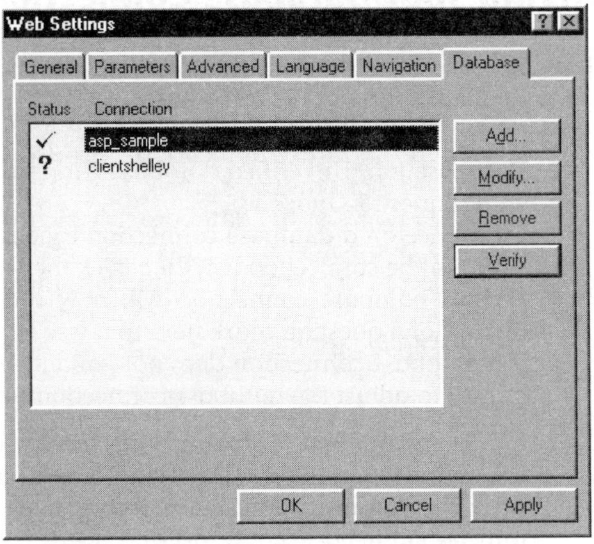

FIGURE 8–17 Web Settings dialog box—verified database connection.

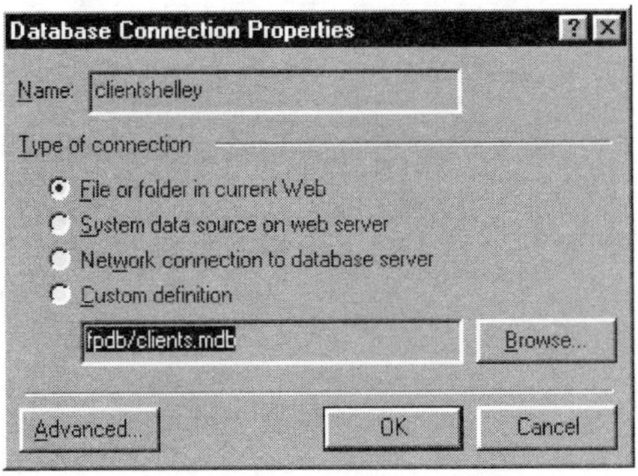

FIGURE 8–18 Database Connection Properties dialog box.

- File or Folder in current Web
- System data source on web server
- Network connection to database server
- Custom definition

• For a file- or folder-type connection, use the Browse button to navigate to the database for which you wish to modify the database connection.

- For a System data source on web server-type of connection or Data Source Name (DSN)-type connection, use the Browse button to select the system DSN for the database to which you want to connect.
- To create or modify a Network connection to database server-type of connection, click the Browse button and specify the Type of database driver, the Server name, and the Database name of the database to which you want to connect (see Figure 8–19).
- To connect to or create a Custom definition type of connection, click the Browse button. Select a file or Universal Data Link (UDL) file in the web.

or:

- Type a custom connection string in the Database Connection Properties dialog box and click the Advanced button at the bottom of the dialog box (see Figure 8–20).
- Type the Authorization information (username and password) and the custom Connection string, then click OK.
- In the Database Connection Properties dialog box, click OK.
- Now you may verify your new or modified connection in the Web Settings dialog box if a question mark appears next to it. Otherwise, you may simply click OK again.

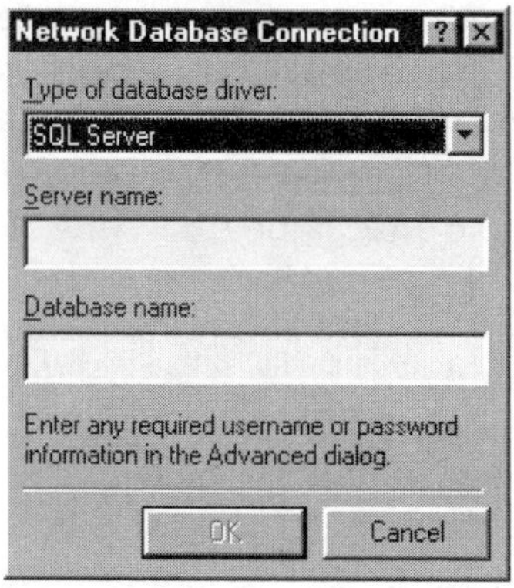

FIGURE 8–19 Network Database Connection dialog box.

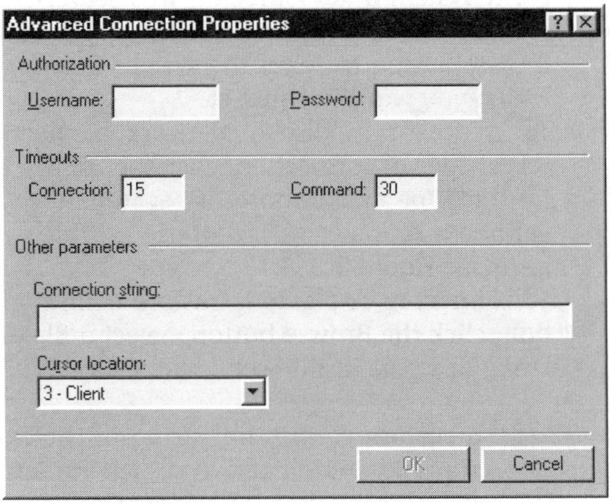

FIGURE 8–20 Advanced Connection Properties dialog box.

◆ Database Interface Wizard

FrontPage 2002 has added a new feature to the program called the Database Interface Wizard (DIW). With this wizard, you can create a set of front-end administration pages for adding, modifying, and deleting records in your database through the browser using forms. In this section, we will add a Database Interface using the wizard for our Shelly Biotechnologies Web site.

- From the File menu, select New then Page or Web.
- From the Task pane under the New from templates section, choose Page Templates.
- In the Web Site Templates dialog box, highlight the DIW icon and check the box to Add to current web (see Figure 8–21).
- Click the OK button to begin the DIW.
- In the first step of the DIW, you are given three options to choose from. For this example, we will use an existing database connection to the Northwind database. If you do not already have a database connection to the Northwind data-

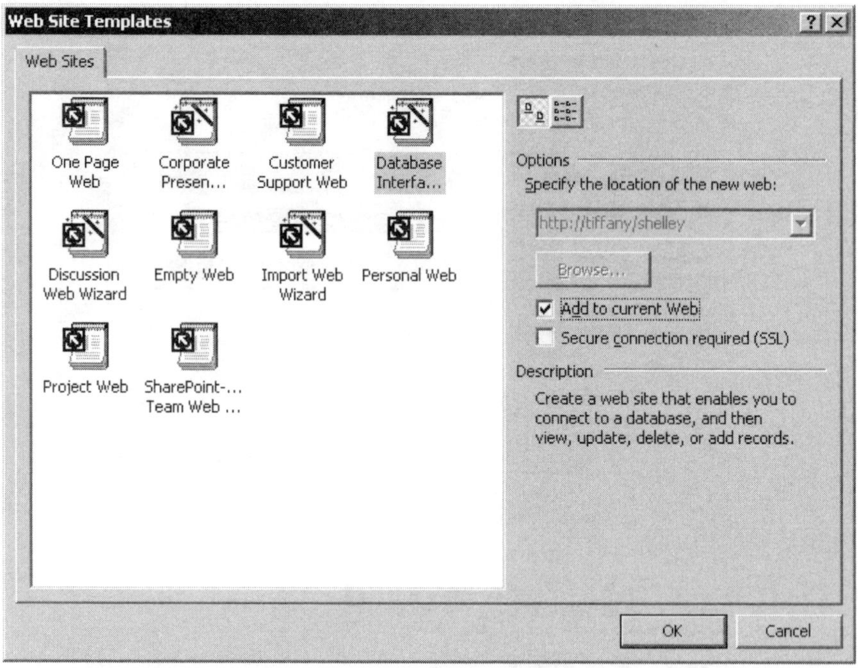

FIGURE 8–21 Web Site Templates dialog box—Database Interface wizard.

base setup, you may choose to Create a new Access database within your web and set up the Northwind database, choose to use another existing database, or choose to use a sample database connection (Northwind; see Figure 8–22) Click the Next button after you have made your selection.

- In the next screen, choose the table or view from the database that you want to use with this connection. For this example, we will set up a products database interface, so choose Products from dropdown menu (see Figure 8–23). Click the Next button to continue to the next step.

- The next step is to configure the form field list for the fields in your database. If you would like to modify the form fields used for the fields in this list, highlight the field in the list and click the Modify button. Once you are satisfied with the form field list, click the Next button (see Figure 8–24).

- Next, choose the pages you would like the wizard to create for your database. The options are:

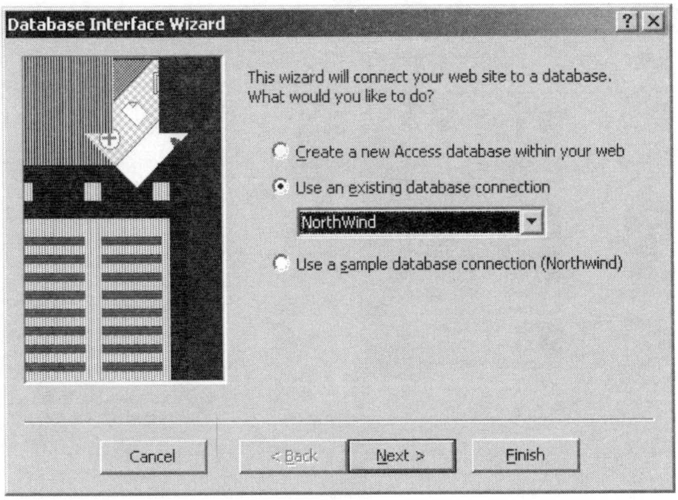

FIGURE 8-22 Database Interface wizard—Step 1.

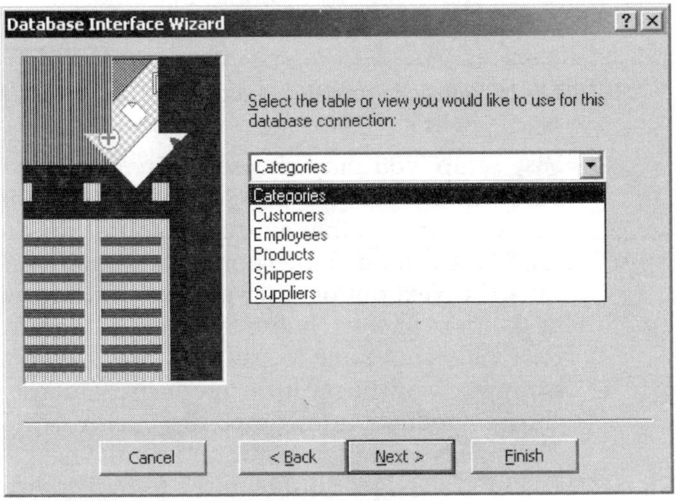

FIGURE 8-23 Database Interface wizard—Step 2.

- Results Page—this is the page that is used to display the records in your database.
- Submission Form—a form used to submit new records to the database.

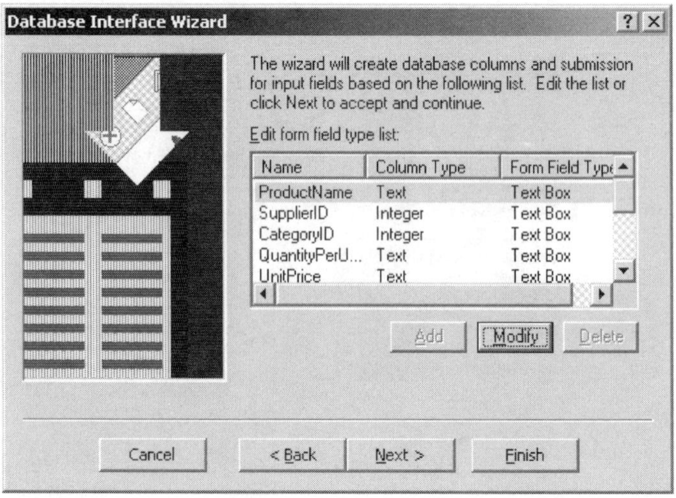

FIGURE 8–24 Database Interface wizard—Edit form field type list.

- Database Editor—a set of pages that are used to add, modify, and delete records from the database.
- Place check marks next to each of these selections for this example (see Figure 8–25). Click the Next button to continue.
- In the next step, you need to choose whether to password-protect the administration pages generated by the wizard. If

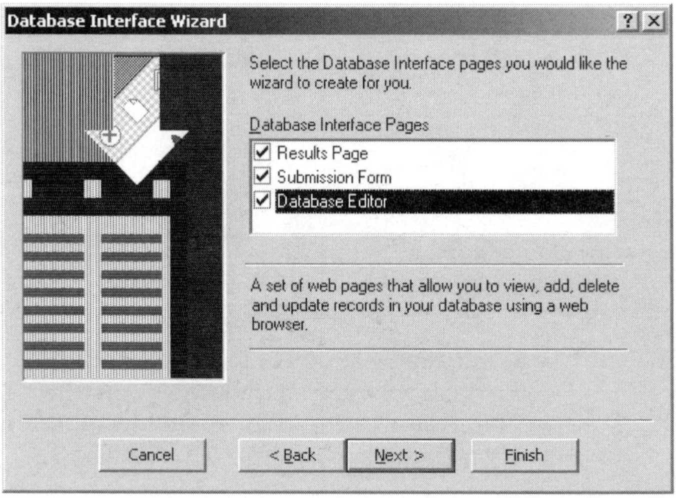

FIGURE 8–25 Database Interface wizard—Database Interface pages.

you want only one administrator or only registered users to have access to the Database Administration pages, enter a username and password in this box. Otherwise, you can choose not to protect your database by password (see Figure 8–26). Click the Next button to proceed.

- In the final screen, the DIW will show you a summary of the pages that it will generate for your database interface and the location in which it will store the files it generates. Click the Finish button to complete the wizard (see Figure 8–27).

The DIW will create the pages for your database interface and open each of them in the FrontPage editor for you to review and customize to the look at feel of your site (see Figure 8–28).

For example, let's customize the look and feel of the *results_page.asp*

On the *results_page.asp*, add a top shared border to the page. Right-click on the page and select Page Properties from the menu, then select a white background for the page. Right-click over the Data Results Component on the page and select Database Results Properties. In the DRW, change the formatting options for the results to List—one field per item in step 4 of the wizard.

You can change the font properties of the text on the page, then save the page. View the page in the browser to see the new page (see Figures 8–29 and 8–30).

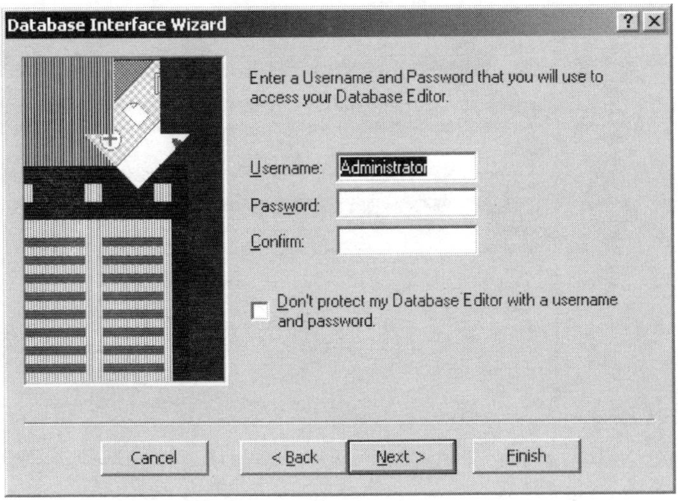

FIGURE 8–26 Database Interface wizard—username and password screen.

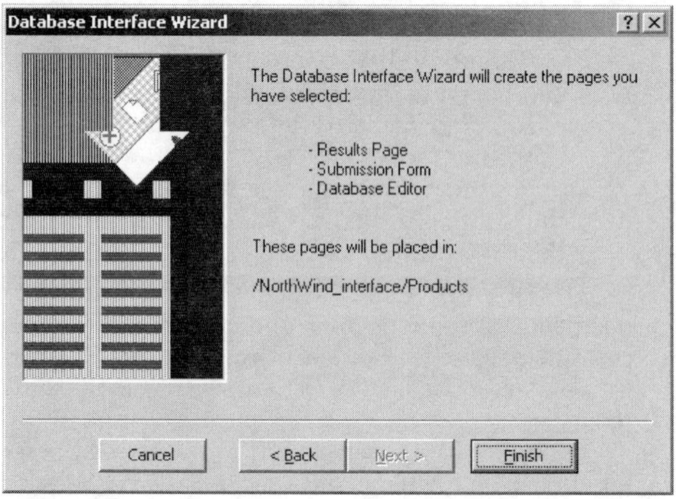

FIGURE 8–27 Database Interface wizard—summary of pages creating.

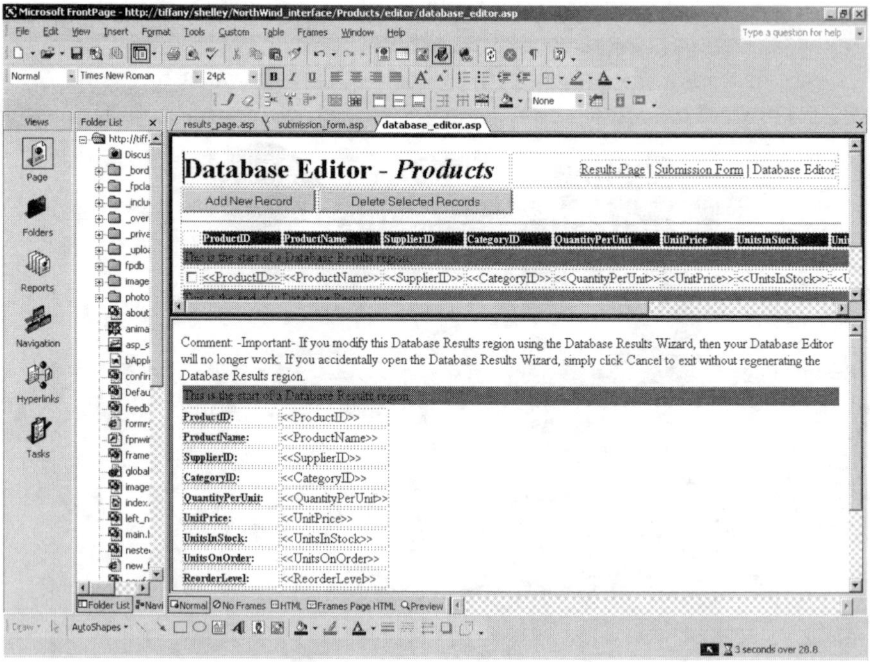

FIGURE 8–28 Database Interface pages completed.

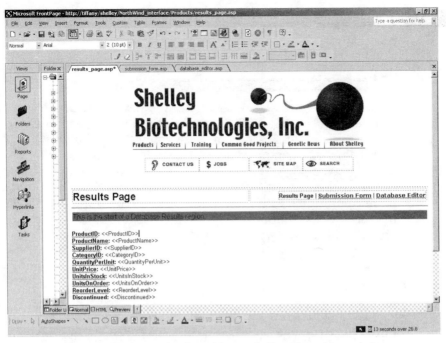

FIGURE 8–29 Customized *results_page* in FrontPage Normal view.

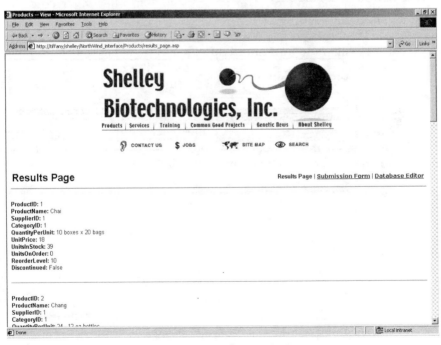

FIGURE 8–30 Customized *results_page* in the browser.

◆ Recap

In this chapter, we reviewed some of the basics and preliminary features that FrontPage 2002 offers with its built-in database connectivity capabilities. The database connectivity features, DRW and DIW, allow nonprogrammers to create interactive and dynamic Web pages that previously were possible only for those with programming skills. For advanced users and those who are more comfortable with programming and ASP, FrontPage allows the ability to enhance these database connectivity features greatly and create very powerful database-driven Web sites.

◆ Advanced Projects

Create a database using FrontPage 2002 and set up an add records form. If you have a database stored in another location on your hard drive or would like to create one in Access, import that database into your FrontPage web and create an add records form, in addition to the one created for you when you created the database in FrontPage.

Practice creating several display records pages in FrontPage, using different formatting specifications, including setting specific table properties in the FrontPage Editor after using the DRW.

Create a database interface using the new FrontPage 2002 DIW.

Visit some of the sites listed in Appendix C under the "Database Results Wizard and Connectivity Resources" section and learn some more about FrontPage 2002's capabilities with regard to database connectivity and interactive pages.

A FrontPage Image Tools

FrontPage 2002, like any program in the Microsoft Office 2000 suite, has a wide array of toolbars. Any toolbar can be dragged from the toolbars at the top or the bottom of the screen to become a floating toolbar or can be changed from being a floating toolbar to a permanent part of the default toolbars at the top or bottom of your Editor window. In this section, we will elaborate on the Image toolbar and what each icon is for.

◆ Image Formatting

As a floating toolbar, the Image Formatting toolbar appears in FrontPage 2002 as shown in Figure A–1.

FIGURE A–1 Floating Image Formatting toolbar.

As a fixed toolbar and by default, the Image Formatting toolbar appears on the bottom of the FrontPage 2002 Editor when an image has been selected (see Figure A–2).

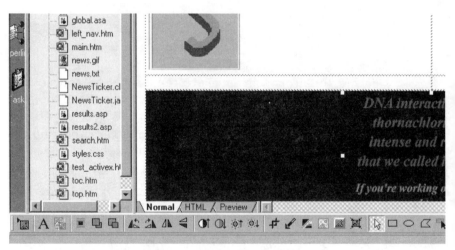

FIGURE A–2 Fixed Image Formatting toolbar.

Image Formatting Tools

FIGURE A–3 Insert Picture from File icon.

This icon will launch the Insert Image dialog box. This saves several steps in the process of inserting an image on the page.

FIGURE A–4 Text Tool icon.

With an image selected in the FrontPage Editor, clicking this tool will open a text box on the selected image and allow you to add text over the image. The image must be a *.gif*-formatted image to use the text tool on the image.

If you attempt to apply the Text tool to a *.jpg*-formatted image, you will be prompted with an alert box, notifying you that FrontPage will convert the image to a *.gif*-formatted image. This process will reduce the number of colors in the image and could deteriorate the quality of the image greatly (see Figure A–5).

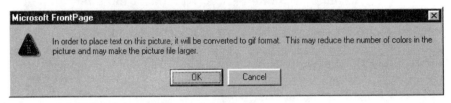

FIGURE A–5 Image Text tool alert box.

FIGURE A–6 Auto Thumbnail icon.

Clicking this icon will make a thumbnail-sized copy of the selected image. The thumbnail properties can be set in the Page Options dialog box under the Tools menu.

The Auto Thumbnail feature is also available by holding the <Ctrl> key and pressing the <T> key on the keyboard.

Positioning Tools

FIGURE A–7 Position Absolutely icon.

Clicking this icon will use absolute positioning with the selected image. Once you click the absolute positioning tool, you will be able to move the image freely to any place on the page without restrictions. Positioning allows images and text to be placed anywhere on the page; however, it relies on the user having a browser that supports CSS 2.0.

You should experiment with this tool in several browsers to ensure that you do not end up with an undesired effect in older browsers.

FIGURE A–8 Bring Forward icon.

This tool is an absolute positioning tool that will bring the selected image to the top "layer" of the page content. It will allow the image to be placed over the top of other images and/ or text.

FIGURE A–9 Send Backward icon.

This tool is an absolute positioning tool that will force an image to the bottom "layer" and allow other text and images to be placed over the image. This is a similar effect to using an image as a background, but it uses CSS. Therefore, not all browsers support absolute positioning. It does allow for more precise placement of an image on the page than does a standard Hypertext Markup Language (HTML)-coded background image.

Image Placement Tools

FIGURE A–10 Rotate Left icon.

This tool rotates selected image to the left.

FIGURE A–11 Rotate Right icon.

This tool rotates selected image to the right.

FIGURE A–12 Flip Horizontal icon.

This tool flips a selected image horizontally.

FIGURE A–13 Flip Vertical icon.

This tool flips a selected image vertically.

Image Appearance Tools

FIGURE A–14 More Contrast icon.

This tool adds more contrast to the selected image.

FIGURE A–15 Less Contrast icon.

This tool reduces the contrast of the selected image.

FIGURE A–16 More Brightness icon.
This tool increases the brightness of the selected image.

FIGURE A–17 Less Brightness icon.
This tool reduces the brightness of the selected image.
Miscellaneous Image Editing Tools

Miscellaneous Image Editing Tools

FIGURE A–18 Crop Image icon.
This tool allows you to crop the selected image, which you have already inserted on your page. To use the tool:

• Select the image you want to crop.
• Select the Crop Image tool. This will place a mask over the image, with "nodes" on it (see Figure A–19).

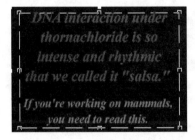

FIGURE A–19 Crop image.
Use your cursor to grab one of the nodes and shape the dashed line around the area of the image that you want to retain; anything outside the dashed lines will be cropped out. Once you have the area that you want to keep within the dashed lines, double-click on the page. Everything outside the dashed line will be removed. FrontPage 2002 will prompt you to save the image when you close the page.

FIGURE A–20 Set Transparency Color icon.
This tool can be used only on a .gif image. Simply select an image, click this tool, move the tool over the image on the color that you want to become transparent, and click with your mouse on the color you have chosen to be transparent.

FIGURE A–21 Black and White icon.
This tool converts an image to black and white.

FIGURE A–22 Washout icon.
This tool creates a washed-out or semitransparent effect on the selected image.

FIGURE A–23 Bevel icon.
This tool adds a beveled edge to the selected image.

FIGURE A–24 Resample icon.
After making changes to an image, either in size or in effect, using any of the image tools, you can "resample" an image, which saves the changes you made to the image. This will over-write the original image you have stored in the web.

FIGURE A–25 Select icon.
This tool is chosen by default when an image has been selected.

Hotspot/Image Mapping Tools

FIGURE A–26 Rectangular Hotspot icon.
This tool creates a rectangle-shaped hotspot on the selected image. To use this tool, click the Rectangular Hotspot tool, then left-click at the top left corner of the area you would like to be the beginning of the rectangular hotspot, and drag the dashed line to the bottom right corner of the area you want selected as the rectangular hotspot.

FIGURE A–27 Circular Hotspot icon.
This tool creates a circular-shaped hotspot on the selected image. To use this tool, click the Circular Hotspot tool, then left-click at the top left corner of the area you would like to be the beginning of the circular hotspot, and drag the dashed line to the bottom right corner of the area you want selected as the circular hotspot.

FIGURE A–28 Polygonal Hotspot icon.

This tool creates a polygonal-shaped hotspot. This tool is great for oddly shaped areas of an image on which you would like to place a hotspot. To use this tool:

• Click the Polygonal Hotspot tool.

• Left-click on the starting point of the area you want to make a hotspot.

• Move your cursor to another outer edge of the area to create a dashed line from the starting point to the next spot. Using your mouse, create a sort of dot-to-dot outline around the area on which you want to create this hotspot.

• When the endpoint meets the beginning point, the hotspot is complete, and you will be prompted for the page or URL to link to from this hotspot.

FIGURE A–29 Highlight Hotspot icon.

This tool highlights the hotspots on an image to aid in manipulating their locations by using drag-and-drop or by editing the hyperlink properties of a hotspot.

FIGURE A–30 Restore icon.

This tool restores an image to its original status or the last saved version of the image. Once an image has been resampled and saved, it cannot be restored. The image can be restored as long as the image has not been saved or resampled.

B Troubleshooting FrontPage 2002 and Server Extensions

Understanding some of the more common problems that come up when using FrontPage 2002 and how to troubleshoot errors when necessary are extremely valuable for any production activity, including Web design with FrontPage 2002.

◆ Publishing Errors and Warning Messages

Publishing errors and warning messages occur when you attempt to publish your FrontPage Web. Some of the more common errors and warning messages are described in this section.

Publishing Error Message

It seems a fairly common problem with FrontPage 2002, when trying to open a remote server or publish to a remote server that you previously opened or published to in earlier versions, to get the following error: *The file you are trying to reach is not accessible, is password protected or has a "/" or "\".*

To work around this problem and open your remote web, you can:

- Open the web in question in Microsoft Internet Explorer (IE).
- Click the Edit button on the toolbar in IE (see Figure B–1).
- Enter your username and password when prompted for them.
- You should now be able to publish the changes you made to the remote server to your local hard drive.
- If the publish option is grayed out when you try to publish the web to your local hard drive:
  - Go to Start > Find > Files and Folders.
  - Do a search for all .web files by entering **.web* in the Search for box.
  - Also delete all FrontPage and Windows Temp files.
  - Now try to open and publish your web with FrontPage.
- Be sure that you include the *http://* in the URL that you enter for publishing or opening of a remote web

FIGURE B–1 Edit button in IE.

Publishing Web Structure Message

FrontPage has detected that changes you have made to the navigation structure conflict with changes that another author has made to the web to which you are publishing (see Figure B–2).

If you receive this message and do not know why or are not sure which option to choose, select the option to replace the navigational structure of the destination web.

This message usually occurs when the name of a web that you have previously published to changes. FrontPage detects that the same files exist on both webs—the one you are publishing and the one you are publishing to—but the different name of the destination web is what causes this error or prompt to appear.

Could not find a Web server at 'www.xxxx.com' on port 80

This error indicates that the server to which you are publishing does not have the FrontPage server extensions installed. Contact the server administrator or technical support for the remote host when you receive this error.

Web busy or cannot open _vti_pvt\service.lck

If you receive this error when publishing your web to a remote server, contact the server administrator or technical support. The server may need to be restarted.

FIGURE B–2 Publishing Web Structure message box.

NTLM error while publishing to an NT server

If you are publishing to an NT server, you may receive the following error during a publish:

The server couldn't log you on because its only authentication scheme is NTLM and you are connecting to it via a proxy server. Try adding the servers to the exceptions box in the Tools/ Options/Proxy Settings/Advanced dialog or request the server administrator to enable another authentication scheme.

Call your server administrator and have "basic" authentication enabled on your web.

◆ Miscellaneous Errors

Several common miscellaneous errors often occur with FrontPage. Some of the most common errors are described in this section.

[FrontPage Save Results Component] shows on page

This indicates that the server extensions have become corrupt. To correct this, the server administrator will need to run a check to fix the server extensions and possibly reinstall them.

Hover buttons do not show on the page

Be sure that the *fphover.class* and *fphoverx.class* files are uploaded with the rest of the web. These files should be stored in a folder called *_fpclass*.

Hover buttons do not play the sound file added

The sound file associated with a Hover button effect must be in the .au format to work with the Hover buttons.

Permissions in the Tools > Server menu are grayed out

Some Web hosting companies restrict the level of FrontPage extensions allowed on their clients' accounts. Usually, a company that restricts the extensions will also not allow permissions to be set on a subweb using FrontPage. If your web is fully loaded in FrontPage and you are still getting the grayed-out permissions, contact your Web host provider.

Zero margins work in IE, but not in NN

If you have set your page properties in FrontPage to zero top and left margins, you will find that this does not work in NN. Setting the page margins in FrontPage adds two attributes to the <BODY> tag in the HTML code:

- topmargin="0"
- leftmargin="0"

Only IE browsers recognize these attributes. To set page margins in NN, click the HTML View tab and add the following two attributes in the <BODY> tag:

- marginheight="0"
- marginwidth="0"

Background sound does not play in NN browsers

NN does not support the <bgsound> tag that FrontPage uses to insert a background sound on a page.

There is a workaround for this, however: You can add the following code to allow music to be played in either IE or NN version 4 browsers:

- Hidden background sound:

```
<embed src="whatever.mid" loop="true" autostart="true"
hidden="true">
<noembed>
<bgsound src="whatever.mid" loop="true" autostart="true"
hidden="true">
</noembed>
```

Change whatever.mid to the filename of your sound file.

- Sound on a page that works with on/off controls:

```
<embed src="whatever.mid" loop="true" autostart="true"
height="25" width="100" controls="smallconsole">
<noembed>
<bgsound src="whatever.mid" loop="true" autostart="true"
height="25" width="100" controls="smallconsole">
</noembed>
```

Place your cursor on the page in Normal view, where you would like the sound controls to appear, then click the HTML View tab and paste or type the code. Replace whatever.mid with the filename of your sound file.

This page contains elements that may need to be saved or published to display properly

You may receive this message when you preview a page in FrontPage 2002's Preview view and the page has FrontPage components. The reason for this is most likely that you have a Disk-Based Web (DBW). Browser time features or FrontPage components that require the FrontPage extensions must be working on an HTTP server on which the FrontPage server extensions are installed. If you are publishing this page or web to a server that has the FrontPage extensions but you are creating the page on a DBW, you will not be able to test the page or component until it is published to the extended server.

Pasting text from Microsoft Word adds a lot of extra proprietary code

A known occurrence with pasting text from MS Word to FrontPage is that the paste adds a lot of Office-specific code to the HTML of the Web page. The code does not usually affect the way the browser displays the Web page, but it can make the load time slower because it adds a lot of extra HTML code. It can also make it difficult to troubleshoot a problem on the page in the HTML code. The reasoning behind this Office-specific code being retained is that it saves Office document settings that can be used when the page is opened in Office. To prevent this from happening, you can try either of the following suggestions:

- Copy the text from MS Word, then choose Paste Special from the FrontPage Edit menu. Select the option that you want, such as normal paragraphs or normal paragraphs with line breaks, to prevent all of the Office-specific code from being copied into your HTML.
- Download the Office HTML filter from the Microsoft site at *http://officeupdate.microsoft.com/2000/articles/oRemove-Markup.htm.*

C Miscellaneous References

◆ Resources

In addition to this book and the manual included in your FrontPage 2002, there are many available resources on the Internet for FrontPage. Some of these resources on the Internet are help email lists, newsletters, newsgroups, and message forums that offer quick answers to questions you may have as you use FrontPage. Other resources include Web sites that offer add-ins for FrontPage to extend your product and macros that you can download and install to work with FrontPage.

Mailing List

- FPlist:
  http://groups.yahoo.com/group/FPlist/
  This is the largest and most active discussion list for
  FrontPage users with various experience levels. Members of
  this list help one another with questions and answers that
  arise daily while using this software package.

NewsGroups

- Microsoft FrontPage:
  microsoft.public.frontpage.client
- Microsoft SharePoint Team Services:
  microsoft.public.sharepoint.teamservices
  These are the official FrontPage newsgroups hosted by
  Microsoft.

Discussion Forums

- AnyFrontPage:
  http://www.anyfrontpage.com
  Discussion board forums for all versions of FrontPage and
  SharePoint Team Services
- SharePoint Tips:
  http://www.sharepointtips.com
  Discussion board forums for SharePoint Team Services. This
  forum is an extension of the Microsoft SharePoint Team Services Newsgroup

Ezine Newsletter

- AnyFrontPage Bytes:
  http://www.anyfrontpage.com/bytes

FrontPage Web Sites

- Microsoft FrontPage 2002:
  http://www.microsoft.com/frontpage
- at-frontpage.com:
  http://www.at-frontpage.com
- AccessFP:
  http://www.accessfp.net

DHTML References

- *http://webopedia.internet.com/TERM/d/dynamic_HTML.html*
- *http://www.dhtmlzone.com/*
- *http://www.dynamicdrive.com*

CSS References

- *http://html.tucows.com/designer/intertut/csstut2.html*
- *http://wdvl.com/Authoring/Languages/XSL/Example/css.html*
- *http://builder.cnet.com/Authoring/CSS/*

ASP Resources

- *http://www.asp101.com/*
- *http://asp-dev.aspin.com/*
- *http://www.web-savant.com/users/kathi/asp/*

Java and JavaScript References

- *http://www.javascripts.com*
- *http://javascript.internet.com/*
- *http://www.gamelan.com*
- *http://javaboutique.internet.com/*
- *http://www.javashareware.com/CFScripts/Japplets.cfm*
- *http://www.online-magazine.com/java2_s.htm*

Server Extensions Resource

- *http://officeupdate.microsoft.com/frontpage/wpp/serk/*

Database Results Wizard and Connectivity Resources

- Microsoft 2000 Database Resource Center:
  http://support.microsoft.com/support/frontpage/fp2000/rc/datarc.asp
- ZDNet:
  http://www.zdnet.com/zdhelp/stories/main/0,5594,2400752-1,00.html
- Spooky's Databases:
  http://www.outfront.net/spooky/index.htm

Book References

- *Essential CSS and DHTML for Web Professionals*, Second Edition by Dan Livingston and Micah Brown
- *Essential CSS and DHTML for Web Professionals*, First Edition by Dan Livingston and Micah Brown
- *Essential JavaScript for Web Professionals* by Dan Barrett, Dan Livingston, and Micah Brown

Miscellaneous References

- Microsoft—Extend FrontPage 2000 with Visual Basic for Applications:
  http://officeupdate.microsoft.com/2000/articles/fpvba.htm
- Microsoft Web Presence Provider Search:
  http://www.microsoftwpp.com/wppsearch
- at-frontpage.com Frames Tips and References:
  http://www.at-frontpage.com/framestips.htm
- Microsoft—Remove MS Word Code:
  http://officeupdate.microsoft.com/2000/articles/oRemoveMarkup.htm

Index